BROWNING'S TRUMPETER

ROBERT BROWNING
(In a photograph distributed by the London Browning Society in 1881.)

BROWNING'S TRUMPETER

THE CORRESPONDENCE OF ROBERT BROWNING
AND FREDERICK J. FURNIVALL
1872–1889

EDITED BY
WILLIAM S. PETERSON

"His peculiarities and defects are obvious—and some of his proceedings by no means to my taste: but there can be no doubt of his exceeding desire to be of use to my poetry, and I must attribute a very great part indeed of the increase of care about it to his energetic trumpet-blowing."   ROBERT BROWNING

WASHINGTON, D.C.
DECATUR HOUSE PRESS
1979

Designed by William S. Peterson
Typeset by the Cottage Press, Greenbelt, Maryland
Printed by Universal Lithographers, Inc., Lutherville-Timonium, Maryland

LIBRARY OF CONGRESS CATALOGING IN PUBLICATION DATA

Browning, Robert, 1812-1889.
    Browning's trumpeter.

    Includes index.

    1. Browning, Robert, 1812-1889—Correspondence. 2. Furnivall, Frederick James, 1825-1910. 3. Poets, English—19th century—Correspondence. 4. Literary Historians—England—Correspondence. I. Furnivall, Frederick James, 1825-1910. II. Peterson, William S. III. Title.
PR4231.A348 1979   821'.8 [B]   79-1253
ISBN 0-916276-05-8

Decatur House Press, Ltd.
2122 Decatur Place, NW
Washington, D.C. 20008

Contents

Illustrations

Preface

This volume consists of the correspondence—so far as it can now be located and reassembled—of Robert Browning and Frederick James Furnivall, the energetic founder of Victorian literary societies (including the original London Browning Society) and one of Browning's most frequent correspondents during the later 1870s and 1880s. Of the 168 letters in the main sequence, 148 are from Browning to Furnivall and fourteen from Furnivall to Browning. (The sequence also includes one letter from Furnivall to the *Academy*, one from him to Professor Hiram Corson, one from Mrs. Katherine Bronson to Furnivall, two from Sarianna Browning to him, and one from Robert Wiedeman Barrett ["Pen"] Browning to him.) The very small proportion of surviving letters from Furnivall should not surprise us, for we know that Browning systematically destroyed most of his personal papers near the end of his life.

For twenty of the letters I have had to rely upon printed texts and facsimiles, and for two I have used contemporary transcriptions; most of the remainder I have transcribed from the holographs (though a few were transcribed from photocopies). Of those letters which I print in their entirety, 107 are either previously unpublished or have been published only in part. The largest group of letters, nearly all previously unpublished, is in the Huntington Library (eighty letters, of which seventy-seven were written by Browning). The other major repositories are the Armstrong Browning Library (sixteen letters), the Folger Shakespeare Library (twelve), the Houghton Library (eleven), and the British Library (nine). Several other libraries hold from one to three letters each. (In Appendix A the holographs of the sixteenth, seventeenth, nineteenth, and twentieth letters were recently discovered to be missing in the Folger Library, and I have therefore transcribed these from a microfilm made earlier for another scholar.)

In the Huntington Library are two envelopes (postmarked 22 January 1876 and 26 February 1883) addressed by Browning to Furnivall for which I have not found accompanying letters. I have not included in this edition a printed announcement of an exhibition of Pen Browning's pictures, addressed by Browning to Furnivall and postmarked 22 March 1880 (Huntington), nor have I printed some correspondence between Pen Browning and Furnivall after Robert Browning's death (though I have included three letters from Browning's sister and son to Furnivall written during the poet's lifetime).

In addition, Appendix A offers a narrative account, in the form of twenty-three letters (thirteen of which are previously unpublished) and a broadside, of a quarrel within Furnivall's New Shakspere Society in which Browning became deeply, albeit reluctantly, involved. Appendix B reprints two articles in the *Pall Mall Gazette*, written by Furnivall shortly after Browning's death, in which he recalled his association with the poet.

The provenance of the Browning-Furnivall correspondence is complex and at times obscure, since Furnivall began disposing of his Browning letters once it became clear in the 1890s that he would be unable to publish them himself. The chief obstacle to their publication was Pen Browning, who was distinctly unhappy about Furnivall's genealogical inquiries. "Young Browning is *very* savage with me for proving that he is descended from a footman, & has no right to the Arms that he flaunts on his gondoliers' blouses [in Venice]," Furnivall wrote on 20 May 1895 to Walter B. Slater (Texas). Pen, he added, "wd. never consent to my printing his father's letters. When Wise or any one else does it privately, he never hears of it, I suppose; & if he does, doesn't care to take action against a stranger."

In another note from Furnivall to Slater, written on 17 May 1895 (King's), we catch a glimpse of Furnivall rather carelessly selling some of the letters:

As to Brs. letters: I put the 3 & 4 page ones at £1 each; the shorter ones at 10/-. On this scale the enclosed 11 are £10; but if you think this is too much,

send me what you think the letters worth. Lately, Wise chose 20 to copy &
print: some of these enclosed he has had: perhaps all: I took no note of them.
If you like uncopied ones—or an additional lot—you can have em. I've given
up the idea of printing them, as I shall never have money for it.

At the sale of Slater's library on 22-23 February 1945 (Hodgson),
twenty-four letters from Browning to Furnivall were grouped together in Lot 285. Another early purchaser was Harry Buxton Forman, who may have bought some letters directly from Furnivall
or perhaps acquired them from Slater or Wise; in any event, ten
letters from Browning to Furnivall, which are included in the present volume, appeared in the sale of Forman's library (Anderson
Galleries, 15 March 1920, Lot 129).

The large group of letters retained by Furnivall was sold by his
daughter-in-law, Mrs. Olive Mary Furnivall, through Maggs (December 1952 and July 1953) as part of a general collection of his papers; these were purchased by the Huntington Library. One letter
which she kept at the time has recently been given by Furnivall's
granddaughters to the reconstituted Browning Society of London.
The single Browning letter owned by the Library of King's College,
London, was found in one of Furnivall's books when the College
acquired his library. As for the other letters from Browning to Furnivall that are scattered about in so many libraries, I cannot trace
the provenance of most of them with any certainty, though it
should be mentioned that five of the Armstrong Browning Library's letters were purchased from a New York autograph dealer,
Walter R. Benjamin.

In 1895 Thomas J. Wise issued a circular to former members of
the Committee of the defunct London Browning Society, asking
for contributions to sponsor several publications once contem-
plated by the Society; of the five projects listed, only the *Letters
from Robert Browning to Various Correspondents* was carried
through to completion. The first volume of it appeared in that
year—"privately printed," in Wise's usual fashion—with an announcement on its cover that it was "Printed for Members of the
[Browning] Society only." A second volume followed in 1896,
and two volumes of a second series appeared in 1907 and 1908. Altogether the four volumes printed forty-three letters from Browning to Furnivall. These were all reprinted in 1933 in a volume en-

titled *Letters of Robert Browning Collected by Thomas J. Wise* and edited by Thurman L. Hood, Dean of Trinity College, Hartford, Conn. (published in the U.S.A. by Yale University Press and in Britain by John Murray).

Several of Wise's annotations (also reprinted by Hood) were based on memoranda and notes by Furnivall, some of which are preserved in the British Library; naturally I have quoted these in the notes of the present edition. Hood may also have had access to Furnivall's personal copy of *Letters to Various Correspondents* (now in the King's College Library), since Furnivall's marginalia in those volumes occasionally reappear, without attribution, in Hood's notes in *Letters of Robert Browning*. Wise's transcriptions of the letters to Furnivall, I might add, are reasonably accurate, though he extensively altered Browning's punctuation and occasionally deleted or rearranged paragraphs.

In 1902 Wise's American client, John Henry Wrenn, wrote to him: "I saw recently in New York at a Booksellers Shop the 2 volume edition of Browning's letters which you issued a few years ago—accompanying these 2 volumes were all of the original letters with Envelopes, all addressed to Mr. Furnivall. The price asked I think was about $225." To this surprising report Wise replied: "I think these could only have been about a dozen or so of the letters. I possess several, which I bought from Furnivall and other men, and received from Browning myself. Most of them I know could not be bought. The price would be a great bargain indeed if the two volumes contained all the letters." (*Letters of Thomas J. Wise to John Henry Wrenn*, ed. Fannie E. Ratchford [New York, 1944], p. 290.) It seems likely that the letters which Wrenn saw were the eleven letters now in the Harry E. Widener Collection of the Houghton Library: the Library's records show that these were originally inserted in a copy of *Letters to Various Correspondents*, First Series, which was once in the libraries of D. F. Appleton and Henry W. Poor.

In transcribing the Browning-Furnivall correspondence, I have attempted to reproduce the letters as faithfully as possible. This means in particular that I have not altered the peculiar orthography of Furnivall, who, in addition to all his other causes, was a passionate advocate of spelling reform. (However, I have lowered all raised characters.) Fortunately Browning's handwriting is extremely legible, and Furnivall's only slightly less so. My nemesis was A. B. Grosart, five of whose letters I print in Appendix A. His handwriting is the worst I have encountered in many years of reading nineteenth-century correspondence and literary manuscripts: John Nichol, in a letter to Swinburne of 11 March 1881 (see Appendix A), speaks of it as "the most exasperating characters ever laid before me." Hence several words in his letters have eluded me in the end and are rendered merely as "illegible."

In the textual note which appears at the beginning of the notes for each letter, I have recorded the address and postmarks on the front and back of every surviving envelope. In addition, I have transcribed Furnivall's frequent notations and marginalia on both envelopes and letters. On the few occasions when I have labeled his written comments on the envelopes "notes" rather than "note," this indicates that they were written in more than one shade of ink or pencil lead (and thus were presumably composed on separate occasions). If a marginal comment by Furnivall seemed to refer to the entire letter, I placed it in the textual note, but if it was associated with a particular sentence or passage in the letter, I inserted it in a subsequent note.

I have made no effort to record every prior publication of each of the letters; instead I have noted only one or two of the most important or accessible texts. When my transcription is based on a previously printed text, that fact is signaled by the appearance of the word "text" at the beginning of the textual note.

I have made only three significant alterations in the letters. In all of Furnivall's letters to Browning, I have deleted the phrase "From F. J. Furnivall" which is printed on his letterhead stationery. I have placed all postscripts at the end of letters, even when they appear elsewhere in the holographs. And in transcriptions based on printed texts, I have changed the address and date to Browning's normal style; I have not tampered with such texts in any other way, though I often strongly suspected that Browning's usual spelling and punctuation had been altered by a previous editor.

My work on this book has extended over a number of years, and during that time I have had the pleasure of visiting many libraries in England and America, and have been the recipient of much courtesy and generosity from both individuals and institutions. I am happy to be able to record here my indebtedness to them.

First, it must be emphasized that I could not have completed the book without the research and travel grants which were awarded by the American Philosophical Society, the Henry E. Huntington Library and Art Gallery, the University of Maryland Faculty Research Board, and the National Endowment for the Humanities.

Among the many individuals who helped this book on its way, I should mention especially John Murray, Esq., the owner of the Browning copyright, who has given me permission to publish the Robert Browning letters in this volume and has allowed me to read and quote the unpublished correspondence between Browning and George Murray Smith; Mrs. Jean Gordon and Mrs. Ruth Davies, F. J. Furnivall's granddaughters, who have permitted me to read his early diaries and have provided much useful information about the Furnivall family; and Mr. Philip Kelley, who, with his matchless knowledge of the Browning correspondence, has rendered assistance in ways too numerous to describe. Others include Mrs. Elaine Baly (Browning Society of London), Mrs. Brenda Colloms (Working Men's College, London), Mrs. Betty Coley (Armstrong Browning Library), Professor Frank DiFederico, Kenneth Garside, Esq. (King's College Library, London), Professor David Greenwood (University of Maryland), Professor Michael Hancher (University of Minnesota), Mr. Mihai H. Handrea (Carl H. Pforzheimer Library), H. A. Harvey, Esq. (King's College Library), Dr. Jack W. Herring (Armstrong Browning Library), Dr. Julia Markus, Edward R. Moulton-Barrett, Esq., Miss K. M. Elisabeth Murray, David Muspratt, Esq. (Working Men's College), Dr. Eleanor L. Nicholes (Wellesley College Library), Miss Ann Phillips (Newnham College Library), D. S. Porter, Esq. (Bodleian Library), and Dr. Lola Szladits (Berg Collection).

The following libraries and society have given me permission to quote unpublished letters and other manuscript materials in their possession: the Armstrong Browning Library, Baylor University; the Beinecke Library, Yale University; the Henry W. and Albert A. Berg Collection, the New York Public Library (Astor, Lenox, and

Tilden Foundations); the Bodleian Library, Oxford University; the British Library, Department of Manuscripts; the Brotherton Library, University of Leeds; the Browning Society of London; the University of Edinburgh Library; the Folger Shakespeare Library, Washington, D.C.; the Houghton Library, Harvard University; the Humanities Research Center, University of Texas; the Henry E. Huntington Library and Art Gallery, San Marino, Calif.; the King's College Library, London; the Newnham College Library, Cambridge University; the John M. Olin Library, Cornell University; the Carl H. Profzheimer Library; the Princeton University Library; the University of Reading Library; the Rutgers University Library; the Scripps College Library; the Smith College Library; the University of Virginia Library; and the Wellesley College Library.

Most of the research for this book was done in the Library of Congress, the Folger Shakespeare Library, and the Huntington Library. I have been able to complete it at the Bodleian Library, under pleasant circumstances, while on sabbatical leave from the University of Maryland.

Oxford   W.S.P.
January 1978

Abbreviations and Cue Titles

ABL	The Armstrong Browning Library, Baylor University, Waco, Tex.
Alma Murray	*Ten Letters of Robert Browning Concerning Miss Alma Murray* (Edinburgh, 1929).
Berg	The Henry W. and Albert A. Berg Collection, the New York Public Library (Astor, Lenox, and Tilden Foundations).
Bibliography	Frederick J. Furnivall, *A Bibliography of Robert Browning from 1833 to 1881*, issued separately in 1881 and also in *BSP*, I, 21-170.
BL	The British Library, Department of Manuscripts.
BNP	Leslie N. Broughton, Clark S. Northup, and Robert Pearsall, *Robert Browning: A Bibliography, 1830-1950* (Ithaca, N.Y., 1953).
Bodleian	The Bodleian Library, Oxford University.
Browning Collections	Sotheby, Wilkinson, and Hodge sale catalogue of the estate of Robert W. B. ("Pen") Browning (April and May 1913).
"Browning in Venice"	Katherine Bronson, "Browning in Venice," *Cornhill Magazine*, 85 (February 1902), 145-71.
BSP	*The Browning Society's Papers* (1881-91).
Collins	Thomas J. Collins, ed., assisted by Walter J. Pickering, "Letters from Robert Browning to the Rev J. D. Williams, 1874-1889," *Browning Institute Studies*, 4 (1976), 1-56.
DAB	*The Dictionary of American Biography.*
DeVane	William C. DeVane, *A Browning Handbook*, 2nd ed. (New York, 1955).
DI	*Dearest Isa: Robert Browning's Letters to Isabella Blagden*, ed. Edward C. McAleer (Austin, Tex., 1951).
DNB	*The Dictionary of National Biography.*
Domett	*The Diary of Alfred Domett, 1872-1885*, ed. E. A. Horsman (1953).

ABBREVIATIONS

Folger	The Folger Shakespeare Library, Washington, D.C.
Furnivall	*Frederick James Furnivall: A Volume of Personal Record* (1911).
Greer	Louise Greer, *Browning and America* (Chapel Hill, N.C., 1952).
HEH	The Henry E. Huntington Library and Art Gallery, San Marino, Calif.
HL	The Houghton Library, Harvard University.
IG	*Intimate Glimpses from Browning's Letter File*, ed. A. J. Armstrong (Waco, Tex., 1934).
King's	King's College, London, Library.
LL	*Learned Lady: Letters from Robert Browning to Mrs. Thomas FitzGerald, 1876-1889*, ed. Edward C. McAleer (Cambridge, Mass., 1966).
LRB	*Letters of Robert Browning*, ed. Thurman L. Hood (New Haven, Conn., 1933).
LVC	*Letters from Robert Browning to Various Correspondents*, ed. Thomas J. Wise. 1st Ser., 2 vols. (privately printed, 1895-96). 2nd Ser., 2 vols. (privately printed, 1907-08).
MEB	Frederic Boase, *Modern English Biography*, 6 vols. (Truro, 1892-1921).
Murray	The archives of John Murray (Publishers) Ltd., London.
NL	*New Letters of Robert Browning*, ed. William C. DeVane and Kenneth L. Knickerbocker (New Haven, Conn., 1950).
NSST	*New Shakspere Society Transactions* (1874-89).
Oracle	William S. Peterson, *Interrogating the Oracle: A History of the London Browning Society* (Athens, Ohio, 1969).
Orr	Mrs. Sutherland Orr, *Life and Letters of Robert Browning*, rev. by Frederic G. Kenyon (1908).
Swinburne Letters	*The Swinburne Letters*, ed. Cecil Y. Lang, 6 vols. (New Haven, Conn., 1959-62).
Texas	The Humanities Research Center, University of Texas, Austin.
WW	*Who Was Who.*
WWA	*Who Was Who in America.*
Yale	The Beinecke Library, Yale University.

Place of publication for all books is London unless otherwise noted.

ABBREVIATIONS

⟨ ... ⟩   Passage which is illegible or physically damaged, or has been deleted in printed text. (Square brackets are used, however, to indicate illegible passages in postmarks and envelope addresses.)

⟨   ⟩   Conjectural restoration.

[   ]   Editorial interpolation.

[...]   Editorial deletion.

*   Embossed or printed letterhead address.

Introduction

I

"His peculiarities and defects are obvious," Robert Browning said of Frederick James Furnivall, "—and some of his proceedings by no means to my taste: but there can be no doubt of his exceeding desire to be of use to my poetry, and I must attribute a very great part indeed of the increase of care about it to his energetic trumpet-blowing."[1] Browning's evaluation is essentially correct, for the founding by Furnivall (with the assistance of Miss Emily Hickey) of the London Browning Society in 1881 was probably the decisive factor in creating the wave of "Browning madness" which swept across Britain and America during the last decade of the poet's life.

If Furnivall had done nothing more than foster the late Victorian Browning cult, he would deserve at least a prominent footnote in English literary history.[2] But the Browning Society, a significant episode in itself, was merely one chapter in a long career characterized by inexhaustible enthusiasm and vigor. Furnivall was for several decades an influential teacher and administrator at the London Working Men's College, was mainly responsible for the genesis of the *Oxford English Dictionary*, was the founder of seven important literary and philological societies, and was himself the editor of hundreds of historical and literary documents. Throughout his life, with a fierce intensity which staggers the imagination, he found time also to scull and cycle, to cultivate friendships with many of the leading writers and scholars of the day, and to quarrel eventually with most of them.

A man of titanic energy, he inevitably evoked contradictory responses among those who knew him. To Swinburne he was an "incomparable blackguard," and to A. B. Grosart a "contemptible creature" (see Appendix A, below); to Edith Rickert he was a person of "almost complete selflessness,"[3] and to Bernard Shaw, Furnivall "was a good sort; but his quarrels were outrageous. . . . He could not behave himself in a controversy, always making such a fool of himself that it was impossible to feel angry with him."[4] Alois Brandl, an admirer, remarked that "he was not a philologist of thorough linguistic training: I should not even care to assert too positively that he could conjugate an Anglo-Saxon verb."[5] Furnivall himself was aware of this paradox and, with characteristic good humor, gloried in it: in 1910, at the end of a lifetime of strenuous philological endeavors, he acknowledged that "I have never cared a bit for philology; my chief aim has been throughout to illustrate the social condition of the English people in the past."[6] As a philologist, literary critic, and controversialist, he was deeply flawed, yet it is not an exaggeration to describe him as the father of English studies. He is, moreover, one of the most colorful literary personalities of the Victorian age.

Furnivall was born on 4 February 1825 in Egham, Surrey, the eldest of nine children of George Frederick Furnivall (1781-1865), a prosperous surgeon and owner of the Great Foster House Lunatic Asylum.[7] George Frederick was a stern man of more common sense than imagination; he strongly disapproved when his son, during the 1850s, gradually abandoned law in favor of literary scholarship, yet the relationship between son and father must have remained friendly to the end, for he was named one of the executors of George Frederick's will drawn up in 1857. In F. J. Furnivall's earliest surviving diaries, we catch glimpses of a conventionally pious adolescent (sitting through two or three services each Sunday, and faithful in his attendance at family prayers) who is remarkable only in his physical and intellectual restlessness: when he is not taking long walks or playing leapfrog, he is reading Dickens, "Tales of Chivalry," and Robin Hood. From another source we know that Furnivall's lifelong interest in older literatures was kindled in 1842, when he was seventeen, by reading Tennyson's "Morte d'Arthur."[8]

After attending schools at Englefield Green, Turnham Green, and Hanwell, Furnivall studied briefly at University College, Lon-

FREDERICK J. FURNIVALL
(In a photograph taken in 1876.)

FURNIVALL FAMILY TREE

(Based on entries in the Furnivall family Bible owned by the Library of King's College, London.)

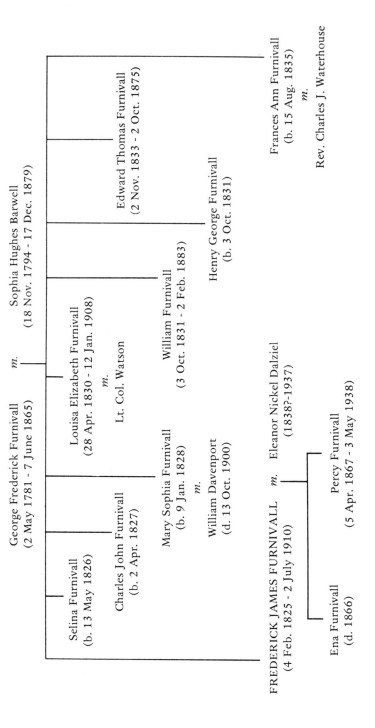

don, and in October 1842 enrolled at Trinity Hall, Cambridge, where (according to his own later testimony and the even more convincing evidence of his diaries) he read little and spent most of his time on the river. But at Cambridge he met Daniel Macmillan, the bookseller and publisher, who opened his "boating mind" by stimulating his literary interests; Furnivall, always impulsive, begged his father for "a few thousand pounds to go into partnership with the Macmillans instead of to the Bar," and of course the elder Furnivall refused.[9] Furnivall entered Lincoln's Inn in January 1846 and was called to the bar at Gray's Inn in January 1849. He practiced law as a conveyancer, with always great infrequency and reluctance, from 1850 until 1872.

The diaries record graphically the ferment of his mind during the early years in London. Though still a faithful churchgoer, Furnivall was discussing Biblical criticism with Arthur P. Stanley and *Vestiges of Creation* with the Rev. Hugh R. Haweis, another celebrated Broad Churchman. He became a devotee of Jenny Lind's concerts. He joined the Whittington Club, which had been founded on Radical principles in 1846 and admitted women on equal footing with men as members.[10] Above all, while studying law in the chambers of Bellenden Ker, he became acquainted with John Malcolm Ludlow, F. D. Maurice, Charles Kingsley, Thomas Hughes, and others who were intent upon putting Biblical principles into practice by overcoming class barriers. By 1851 Furnivall's reading was oscillating wildly between the traditional theology in which he had been raised and the heady new ideas he was encountering in London: on 22 January, for instance, he devoted the evening to "Mill's Political Economy, & the Biblical Cyclopaedia," and on 2 June he stayed up till 1:30 in the morning perusing the Bible ("as usual"), Mill, and Tennyson. He was also reading Kingsley, Carlyle (whose address appears in his 1848 diary), Mrs Gaskell (whom he met in 1851), Shakespeare, Shelley, Keats, and especially Ruskin.

Furnivall made Ruskin's acquaintance probably in the late 1840s, and Ruskin remained, both in person and in his writings, the greatest influence upon Furnivall's life.[11] "Ruskin was one of the most generous and honourable of men, with the most pretty manners and delightful ways," he declared in old age, "and I retain of him recollections more pleasant than of any other man."[12]

Furnivall was soon a regular caller at Denmark Hill ("Ruskin showed me his Turners, about 20 of them . . . lunch, looked at the pictures again," he recorded in his diary on 18 February 1851), and in March of that year he had very little sleep for several nights while he made his way through *The Stones of Venice*. He was profoundly impressed by Ruskin's arguments for the dignity of labor and the necessity of art—that is to say, craftsmanship—in the lives of workmen.

When, therefore, in 1854 Furnivall and his Christian Socialist companions established the Working Men's College (which grew out of an earlier educational experiment at Little Ormond Yard), he arranged to reprint and distribute Ruskin's chapter on "The Nature of Gothic" at the first meeting of the College. Ruskin himself, to Furnivall's surprise, volunteered to teach an art class, which apparently produced as many moments of high comedy as Ruskin's later attempt at road-building near Hinksey. One student, for example, announced stubbornly that he wished to learn to draw cartwheels and nothing else[13]—an encounter which perhaps inspired the following Ruskinian memorandum to the authorities of the College:

> The teacher of landscape drawing wishes it be to generally understood by all his pupils, that the instruction given in his class is not intended either to fit them for becoming artists, or in any direct manner to advance their skill in the occupations they at present follow. They are taught drawing, primarily in order to direct their attention accurately to the beauty of God's work in the material universe; and secondarily that they may be enabled to record with some degree of truth, the forms and colours of objects when such record is likely to be useful.[14]

Furnivall threw himself into the activities of the Working Men's College with characteristic abandon. Like his later societies, the College drew out the best in him because it stood for both socialist principles and an egalitarian form of scholarship. He taught classes in English grammar and literature, served on the College Council, and was unofficially in charge of College social life. Furnivall later summed up the experiences there, which were among his happiest, in these words: "We studied and took exercise together, we were comrades and friends, and helpt one another to live higher, happier, and healthier lives, free from all stupid and narrow class humbug."[15]

However, between Furnivall and Maurice theological differences were developing, as evidenced by this entry (for 3 March 1859) in the diary of A. J. Munby:

My Latin class [at the W.M.C.] in the evening. Went to [Alexander] Macmillan's afterwards, & found him with [R. B.] Litchfield, Furnivall & Vernon Lushington, discusssing one of those College jars which *will* occur: how Furnivall wants to read Mill on Liberty with his class, & Maurice objects to it as a contemporary book on an unsettled question. F. will kick, but Maurice will conquer: for all submit to him, not because he is *Principal* but because he is *Maurice*. Inevitable, & quite right too. Then the talk grew towards Genesis & Geology: Macmillan holding that Maurice had fully explained Chap. I—Litchfield & Furnivall laughing to scorn (though with full recognition of Maurice's greatness) his, or any, reconcilement—Vernon mediating in his clear earnest way—I as usual, watching.[16]

Furnivall also challenged Maurice's moral authority by sponsoring dances (which were officially condemned by the College Council in January 1861) and Sunday excursions into the country. The excursions produced an earnest pamphlet from Maurice entitled *The Sabbath-Day: An Address to the Members of the Working Men's College* (1856), and young Octavia Hill (whose life had been changed when Furnivall introduced her to Ruskin's writings in 1852) reluctantly abandoned the practice after Maurice persuaded her that it was spiritually better to spend Sunday in church than on one of Furnivall's geological expeditions.[17] Furnivall maintained his connection with the College for many years and never abandoned most of the ideals of Christian Socialism, but by the following decade he saw himself as an agnostic.

Meanwhile Furnivall had joined the Philological Society in 1847 and became an Honorary Secretary in 1853, in which capacity he helped to lay the groundwork of what was to become the greatest of all works of lexical scholarship, the *Oxford English Dictionary*. Eventually he was supplanted by Dr. Murray as editor, but Murray himself admitted that the conception of a completely new dictionary, the initial organization, and much of the preliminary research had all emanated from Furnivall.[18] What this early philological experience revealed to Furnivall was that no history of the English language could yet be written because so much of the early literature was available in manuscript form only.

Furnivall's response to this discovery was to establish a series of societies, all of which—with the notable exception of the Browning Society—had as their primary function the publication, by means of subscription, of manuscripts and rare books: the Early English Text Society (1864), the Chaucer Society (1868), the Ballad Society (1868), the New Shakspere Society (1873), the Browning Society (1881), the Wyclif Society (1882), and the Shelley Society (1885). There is no denying that much of the textual work of these societies was amateurish and slipshod; Furnivall and his co-workers often displayed more energy than expertise, and modern scholars are still busily re-editing their books. But when one takes into account the pioneering character of their labor and the sheer bulk of their publications, Furnivall's achievement is impressive indeed. More than any other man or woman in the nineteenth century, he laid the essential foundations for the modern study of English language and literature.

Furnivall's societies were conducted on the same principles of joyous spontaneity and haphazard organization which had characterized his earlier activities at the Working Men's College. Furnivall himself did much of the editing, introducing his books with curious, idiosyncratic "Forewords" (a word he popularized because he wanted an Anglo-Saxon alternative to "Preface"),[19] in which he gave vent to an extraordinary range of opinions and prejudices. In one published in 1866 he offered this pragmatic (but surely defective) philosophy of editing:

... the time that it takes to ascertain whether a poem has been printed or not, which is the best MS. of it, in what points the versions differ, &c., &c., is so great, that after some experience I find the shortest way for a man much engaged in other work, but wishing to give some time to the Society, is to make himself a foolometer and book-possessor-ometer for the majority of his fellow members, and print whatever he either does not know, or cannot get at easily, leaving others with more leisure to print the best texts. He wants some text, and that at once.[20]

Whatever one may think of Furnivall as editor, the candor of that passage is impressive—and typical. As he explained in print the following year, since nearly all the copies of his books went to members of the Early English Text Society, "I conceive myself entitled to write Prefaces as to a circle of my Friends; for such I look on Subscribers as being."[21]

Furnivall's societies, even as they kept the presses rolling, generated some of the most vitriolic literary controversies of the Victorian period. "As to objectors, all I require of 'em is evidence of work, insight, and thought," Furnivall wrote in 1887. "When I see imposters like . . . Swinburne, [and] Fleay, who know as much early English as my dog, & who fancy they can settle Chaucer difficulties as they blow their noses, then I ridicule or kick them. But earnest students I treat with respect, & am only too glad to learn from them."[22] To younger scholars especially and to the few writers whom he really liked (such as Ruskin and Browning), Furnivall was unfailingly generous and helpful, but towards his numerous enemies he behaved like a man possessed. And yet even when he was publicly exchanging invectives with an antagonist, he was capable of making private gestures of reconciliation. "I am very glad you write to me, as, if we are to fight, we'd better shake hands first, & also when we're finisht," he declared to one such opponent in 1903.[23] The implied pugilistic metaphor is significant: Furnivall (a "muscular agnostic," in Bernard Shaw's witty phrase) naively imagined his quarrels to be an adult equivalent of the schoolground fight, and he always supposed that afterwards the participants would slap each other on the back and receive compliments from the spectators on their prowess as boxers. Not surprisingly, most of the recipients of Furnivall's verbal abuse did not share his enthusiasm for this improbable sporting metaphor.

Fiery and vindictive as Furnivall might be in public controversy, he was nevertheless an idealist who had devoted his life to literary study with a magnificent disregard for his own welfare. After the loss of his inheritance (which had been unwisely invested in Overend and Guerney's bank) in 1867, he was compelled to live very frugally, for his writing and editing brought in little money. "I go on as before," he commented wryly to a friend in 1876: "Chaucer & Early English—always busy, always earning nothing."[24] There were unsuccessful applications for the Secretaryship of the Royal Academy (1873), the Principalship of University College, Bristol (1877), and several librarianships; but in later years he had to support himself primarily with the modest income that accrued to him as a trustee of one of the family estates and with the Civil List Pension that was awarded in 1884.

In 1862 Furnivall married Eleanor Nickel Dalziel (1838?-1937), sister of W. A. Dalziel, one of Furnivall's students at the Working Men's College and afterwards Honorary Secretary of the Chaucer Society and the Early English Text Society. Turning to Munby's diary again, we find an amusing picture of the pair in the year of their marriage:

> After dinner, I went to Ely Place by appointment to see Furnivall. Found him in a strange dingy room upstairs; the walls & floor and chairs strewn with books, papers, proofs, clothes, everything—in wondrous confusion; the table spread with a meal of chaotic and incongruous dishes of which he was partaking, along with 'Lizzy' Dalzell [sic], the pretty lady's maid whom he has educated into such strange relations with himself, and for whose sake he has behaved so madly to Litchfield & others of his best friends; & her brother, a student of our College. F., who was pleasant & kindly to me as ever, was enjoying a vegetarian banquet of roast potatoes, asparagus, & coffee! ... 'Missy', as F. calls the girl, is his amanuensis and transcribes: takes long walks too with him and others, of ten and twenty miles a day; which is creditable to her: and indeed she seems a quiet unassuming creature.[25]

Precisely what Eleanor Dalziel's social background was is not clear: Munby, in describing her as a "pretty lady's maid," may well have been projecting one of his habitual fantasies about working-class women. But that she was youthful and very pretty is undoubtedly true. A photograph of the Furnivalls[26] from this period shows her seated in the conventional Victorian fashion, looking appropriately demure and attractive, while Furnivall (in an unconscious parody of the standard pose of the *paterfamilias*) stands next to her and leers in an irrepressibly mischievous way.

The Furnivalls had two children—one of whom died in infancy and the other became a famous surgeon—and lived together until 1883 when they legally separated. "A wife's want of sympathy with her husband's work ruined Dickens's married life, mine too, & hundreds of others besides," he commented in 1888.[27] Bernard Shaw offered a different explanation: "When a faithful secretary of his died he not only broke up his societies by insisting on their sharing in his demonstrations of grief, but actually separated from his wife because she objected."[28] The "faithful secretary" was Teena Rochfort-Smith (who figures in a number of Browning's letters to Furnivall), but what had actually happened was more complex than Shaw supposed. Miss Rochfort-Smith was in fact Furnivall's mistress and had been installed in his house during the early part of 1883, possibly on the pretext that she was a friend who had taken ill while visiting London. The Furnivalls' document of separation, not unexpectedly, is dated June 1883. In August, when Miss Smith's dress accidentally caught fire, Furnivall hovered near her deathbed in Yorkshire. Afterwards he wrote: "Compared with the mere surface turquoise minds of so many girls, hers was the sapphire depths of the infinite heaven, lit by the multitudinous stars."[29] Throughout his life, Furnivall's strong interest in women's rights was always combined with a desire to surround himself with attractive young girls: in later years he sculled up the Thames with a boatful of them every Sunday.

Even before his marriage disintegrated, the pattern of Furnivall's life was firmly established: he spent most of each day in either the Reading Room or the Manuscripts Department of the British Museum, with a long interval for tea at his favorite A.B.C. tea shop on New Oxford Street, where he held court after the fashion of Dr. Johnson. With his bright pink neckties, baggy suits, and long white beard, he was a familiar sight to both British and foreign scholars in Bloomsbury. On Sundays he sculled fourteen miles with his working girls from Hammersmith to Richmond and back, usually punctuated with a leisurely picnic on an island near Richmond. Until a few months before his death on 2 July 1910, Furnivall retained his youthful vigor of mind and body. And he kept editing right up to the end; the entries under his name fill nearly eleven columns in the folio *Catalogue of the Printed Books* of the British Museum.

The most appropriate epitaph was supplied, I think, by *The Times* obituary: "Other scholars have played with their learning; Furnivall romped with his. All his life he remained a boy at heart, and his introductions have the blunt, even slangy, speech, the rollicking spirits, the phonetic spelling (though he used it, of course, as a matter of principle, not of accident), and the intense concentration of a boy, combined with the learning and the wisdom of an exceptionally gifted and industrious man."[30]

II

Robert Browning, after the death of his wife in 1861, had also settled into a comfortable routine in London. His valet, William Grove, has left us a precise account of his daily schedule during the later years:

He used to get up at seven o'clock every morning, and stayed in his bedroom till eight. He read during that time generally French and Italian works, and he invariably ate a plate of fruit which had been left in his room overnight— strawberries or grapes, by preference, oranges and other fruits in their season. From eight till half-past he had a bath, and at nine came down to breakfast. This took about twenty minutes, and he would then turn his chair to the fire and read the morning papers till ten o'clock. He read the *Times* and *Daily News* in the morning, and in the evening he read the *Pall Mall* [*Gazette*] and the weekly and fortnightly reviews. From ten till one he spent the time in his study writing. . . . At one o'clock he had lunch. His breakfast and lunch were very light meals, the latter generally consisting of some pudding only, but he always ate a good dinner. . . .

After lunch he would go out to pay afternoon calls or to the private views, frequently walking across Kensington-gardens. He came back at half-past five or six to dress for dinner, which was at seven o'clock, and he went to bed at half-past ten or eleven. During the season he dined out a great deal. I have seen him out every evening for three weeks, but however late he was, and he was seldom later than half-past twelve, he invariably got up at the same time in the morning. . . .

He took three months' holiday, generally in Italy, and spent the rest of the year in London, with the exception of an occasional visit of a week or so to Oxford or the country.[31]

His deepest passions buried in Florence with Elizabeth, Browning was assuming that façade of the urbane, bland man of the world which so puzzled and annoyed Henry James.

Furnivall had narrowly missed meeting both of the Brownings at Denmark Hill in 1855;[32] like most of his contemporaries, he then knew and extravagantly admired Mrs. Browning's poetry (which had been to him at Cambridge, he said, "an entirely new revelation of the possibilities and capabilities of woman's nature"[33]) but not her husband's. Probably during the autumn of 1873 Furnivall and Browning finally encountered one another,[34] and it seems safe to say that the poet's existence was never fully tranquil thereafter. Furnivall was bristling with suggestions: Browning, he said, should write a poem on Victorian life, preferably on the dishonesty of Disraeli, because *The Ring and the Book* (one of the longest poems in the language) was "too small for you, & too far off every one." Browning should reveal more of himself in his poetry. Browning's publisher should issue a Shilling Selection of his works. (Furnivall's maddening insistence upon this latter point eventually drove George Smith, the good-natured publisher of the poet, into helpless rage.) Edmund Gosse, whose testimony is perhaps not entirely trustworthy, reported that "F. used to go to Warwick Crescent . . . and shout and gesticulate and chatter till B. would admit anything and assent to anything for the sake of getting the terrible fellow out of the house."[35]

Browning's letters to Furnivall are, as one might expect, polite, tactful, and often slightly evasive. (Of course the letters that are missing may have been different in character. We have Gosse's word, in a letter to Theodore Watts of 13 March 1881 [printed in Appendix A, below], that during Furnivall's quarrel with Swinburne, Browning wrote to Furnivall "expressing his extreme displeasure at the language F. had used." That letter—and perhaps others like it—has not survived, and such gaps in the correspondence must also be taken into account in evaluating the relationship between the two.) As Furnivall admitted, "His skill in fence was very great; you couldn't get under his guard."[36] Still, Furnivall's eccentric behavior frequently provoked significant emotional responses, and he managed also to elicit a good deal of factual information about Browning's life and poetry, which information he usually printed at once, without attribution, in the Browning Society's transactions or in the literary gossip column of the *Academy*.

It was in the *Academy* that Furnivall announced in July 1881 that he and Miss Hickey were forming a Browning Society, the first (and only one) of his societies to be devoted to the study of a living writer. Browning, still doubtless rather shell-shocked from the previous spring's mayhem in the New Shakspere Society, viewed this latest offspring of Furnivall's fertile imagination with circumspect caution. To Edmund Yates, Browning declared: "I had no more to do with the founding it than the babe unborn; and as Wilkes was no Wilkeite, I am quite other than a Browningite."[37] From a discreet distance Browning observed the sometimes rancorous monthly meetings of the Society, its ambitious publications, its entertainments and performances of his plays. That there was a "grotesque side to the thing"[38] he saw clearly enough; but Browning still expressed pleasure that at last he had found some readers whose genuine enthusiasm discredited the strictures of his critics.

At the opening meeting of the Browning Society, on 28 October 1881, Furnivall had observed: "But to avoid appearing under false pretences, one thing I dezire to state: and that is, that I do not affect to share Browning's religious views . . . but though these beliefs underlie his whole work, I do heartily desire the spread of the study and influence of Robert Browning."[39] It was on precisely this question that the Browning Society eventually foundered. Agnostics like Furnivall, Shaw, and Edward Gonner lined up on one side of the issue, the clerics and maiden ladies formed ranks on the other side, and the Society's meetings in Gower Street increasingly resembled a bloody battlefield. Membership declined, papers failed to be read on schedule; finally in 1892, two and a half years after Browning's death, the Society ceased to exist.

Furnivall's own contributions to the Society's meetings—mostly informal remarks rather than papers—reveal his alarming deficiencies as a literary critic. He was especially preoccupied with the notion of Browning's "manliness" ("Rabbi Ben Ezra" and "Prospice" were his favorite poems), and his speeches were accordingly filled with clumsy sporting figures: "To put forward Aprile [in *Paracelsus*] as representative of the Renaissance spirit seemed to him like taking a smart young man you meet in Hyde Park as a representative of the best sculler or the best football player in England."[40] Or: "When you were rowing or hunting for the first time, you wanted hints as to which bank to steer by, or which way the quarry was likely to take. Well, those who had studied Browning knew that he was hindered in getting hold of people by a good many obscurities, and it was the Society's duty to face these obscurities, to acknowledge them and to investigate their causes."[41]

As the last sentence suggests, Furnivall was not an uncritical admirer of Browning's poetry. In February 1889, for example, he offered this trenchant observation: "If he [Browning] could condescend to put his verse into a different form, as he easily could, it would be much easier for people to understand. Dr. F. maintained that this was what the poet ought to do, and what they had a right to ask him to do."[42] He thought Browning's poetic form was "execrable"[43] and lacking in music, and he "was afraid posterity would judge Browning hardly for it."[44]

Nor was Furnivall pleased with Browning's subject matter. He deplored the poet's tendency to "whitewash a blackguard," dismissing Browning's psychological explorations of villainy in these words: "It seemed to him that Browning delights to take one of these scamps, and then sit down to work with the remark, 'Now let us see what excuses we can make for him.' "[45] The solution, Furnivall believed, was for Browning "to leave off for a time the study of far-off characters in the Middle Ages [sic], and give to the world some impressions of the people he had met in his early days,—some more 'Waring.' There was no man who could give a better study of Victorian society than Browning."[46] Even Browning's habitual use of the dramatic mode annoyed Furnivall, as he explained in his "Foretalk" to the Browning Society's edition of the *Essay on Shelley*: "The interest lay in the fact, that Browning's 'utterances' here are *his*, and not those of 'so many imaginary persons' behind whom he insists on so often hiding himself, and whose necks I, for one, should continually like to wring, whose bodies I would fain kick out of the way, in order to get face to face with the poet himself, and hear his own voice speaking his own thoughts, man to man, soul to soul. Straight speaking, straight hitting, suits me best."[47] Ironically, when Browning partially complied with this request by writing a semi-autobiographical poem, *Parleyings with Certain People of Importance in Their Day* (1887), Furnivall took a strong dislike to it.

Furnivall read only two papers to the Browning Society. The first (25 February 1887) was a "grammatical analysis" of a passage in *The Ring and the Book*, which he offered as an alternative to the endless discussions of Browning's religious views: "I have therefore tried my hand at one of our poet's gnarly pieces, a lyric which it seems profanation to dissect like a dead body, so full of life and love is it."[48] But dissect it he did, and the results were not particularly illuminating. Furnivall's second paper (28 February 1890) was entitled "Robert Browning's Ancestors." Immediately after Browning's death in December 1889 Furnivall began writing to relations of the poet and studying Browning wills and tombstones. His two chief conclusions—that Browning's earliest known ancestor was a butler, and that his father was half-Creole—were not calculated to please the poet's admirers and family.

In the years that followed, Furnivall increasingly fell into the bad graces of Browning's sister and son. Not content with supplying two distinct blots for Browning's 'scutcheon, he further annoyed the family by publicly attributing to the poet a biography of Strafford published in 1836 under John Forster's name, by helping to publish a photograph of Browning taken after his death, and by listening to a recording of the poet's voice in what Sarianna described as an "indecent seance."[49] Sarianna, in fact, was so incensed by Furnivall's behavior that she and Pen commissioned an authorized biography of Browning by Mrs. Sutherland Orr, evidently in order to forestall a life by Furnivall.[50] Edmund Gosse reported, probably without exaggeration, that Furnivall was "perfectly loathed by the family of Mr. Browning."[51]

Though Furnivall's relationship with Browning—and later with his family—was always fraught with tensions, it is evident that there were genuine respect and affection between the two men. Moreover, Furnivall's "peculiarities and defects" (as Browning phrased it), his remarkable idiosyncrasies, must have held much fascination for one who loved to probe psychological aberrations in his dramatic monologues. Through the awkward, often amusing, clash of two differing temperaments, the correspondence between Browning and Furnivall offers us edifying glimpses of the face of the aging poet behind the expressionless public mask.

NOTES

1 Collins, p. 38.
2 For a much fuller account of the Browning Society than I am able to provide here, see my *Interrogating the Oracle: A History of the London Browning Society* (Athens, Ohio, 1969).
3 *Furnivall*, p. 166.
4 Wilfred Partington, *Thomas J. Wise in the Original Cloth* (1946), pp. 316-17.
5 *Furnivall*, p. 10.
6 *Ibid.*, p. 43.
7 My sketch of Furnivall's career is based primarily upon John Munro's Memoir in

Furnivall and his unpublished diaries. The following diaries are extant: (1) 20 Mar. 1840-21 May 1840; (2) 9 Oct. 1841-17 Aug. 1842; (3) 19 Aug. 1842-9 Mar. 1843; (4) 10 Mar. 1843-14 Oct. 1843; (5) 20 Oct. 1843-14 Jan. 1844; (6) 1848; (7) 1851.

8 *Furnivall*, p. 11.

9 Furnivall's review of *Memoir of Daniel Macmillan* by Thomas Hughes, in the *Academy*, 22 (12 Aug. 1882), 112.

10 See Christopher Kent, "The Whittington Club: A Bohemian Experiment in Middle Class Social Reform," *Victorian Studies*, 18 (September 1974), 31-55.

11 For Furnivall's own account of his relationship with Ruskin, see his "Forewords" to Ruskin's *Two Letters Concerning "Notes on the Construction of Sheepfolds"*, [ed. T. J. Wise] (privately printed, 1890).

12 *Furnivall*, p. 20.

13 John Llewelyn Davies, ed., *The Working Men's College 1854-1904* (1904), pp. 41-42. Another eyewitness description of Ruskin as an art teacher at the W.M.C. is provided by Thomas Sulman, "A Memorable Art Class," *Good Words*, 38 (August 1897), 547-51.

14 *Letters from John Ruskin to Frederick J. Furnivall . . . and Other Correspondents*, ed. T. J. Wise (privately printed, 1897), pp. 70-71.

15 Davies, p. 60.

16 Derek Hudson, *Munby: Man of Two Worlds* (New York, 1972), p. 26.

17 C. Edmund Maurice, ed., *Life of Octavia Hill as Told in Her Letters* (1913), pp. 150-55.

18 *Furnivall*, pp. 122-35. For a more recent account, see K. M. Elisabeth Murray, *Caught in the Web of Words: James A. H. Murray and the 'Oxford English Dictionary'* (New Haven, 1977).

19 The *Oxford English Dictionary* records only one use of "Foreword" or "Forewords" earlier than Furnivall's.

20 *Political, Religious, and Love Poems* (E.E.T.S., No. 15, 1866), p. ix.

21 *The Stations of Rome* (E.E.T.S., No. 25, 1867), p. viii.

22 FJF to T. R. Lounsbury, 29 Oct. 1887 (Yale).

23 FJF to Edward A. Parry, 11 Apr. 1903 (Bodleian, uncatalogued).

24 FJF to C. H. Pearson, 21 Jan. 1876 (Bodleian MS. lett. d. 187).

25 Hudson, pp. 123-24.

26 Bodleian MS. Eng. misc. f. 380.

27 FJF to Mrs. Walter Slater, 8 Sept. 1888 (ABL).

28 Partington, p. 317.

29 [Furnivall], *Teena Rochfort-Smith: A Memoir* (1883), p. 10. My assertions about her relationship with Furnivall are based upon scattered clues in the *Memoir* and family sources.

30 *The Times*, 4 July 1910, p. 12.

31 "Robert Browning at Home," *Pall Mall Gazette*, 16 Dec. 1889, p. 3.

32 *Letters from John Ruskin to Frederick J. Furnivall*, pp. 55-57.

33 *BSP*, II, 339*.

34 See Appendix B, Article 1, n. 2. Tennyson had begun living at Seamore Place—where Furnivall met Browning—in late October 1873.

35 *Oracle*, p. 179.

36 See Appendix B, Article 1.

37 *LRB*, p. 212.

38 *Ibid.*

39 *BSP*, I, 2*.

40 *Ibid.*, II, 289*.

41 *Ibid.* II, 323*.

42 *Ibid.*, II, 324*.

43 *Ibid.*, III, 100*.

44 *Ibid.*, I, 74*.
45 *Ibid.*, II, 160*.
46 *Ibid.*, II, 339*-40*.
47 *Ibid.*, I, 3.
48 *Ibid.*, II, 165.
49 See *Oracle*, pp. 29-30.
50 *Ibid.*, p. 169.
51 *Ibid.*, p. 30.

BROWNING'S TRUMPETER

19. Warwick Crescent, W / Jan: 27. '72.

Dear Sir,

You are quite welcome to make the use you mention of the notice of Chaucer in the Essay on the British Poets—which, by the way, you will find reprinted in the 4th volume of the writer's works: permission to reprint is therefore is [*sic*] quite in my competency to grant you, nor need you trouble yourself to apply to the "Athenaeum".[1]

I don't know whether you are aware that the same writer contributed to the "modernization of Chaucer" in company with Wordsworth and others:[2] there is a Sapphic triplet relating to him in "A Vision of Poets".[3]

I am, Dear Sir, / Yours very truly / Robert Browning.

F. J. Furnivall Esq.

MS: HEH.

1 EBB's *The Greek Christian Poets and the English Poets* (1842), first published serially in the *Athenaeum* between February and August 1842. The section on Chaucer was printed in the Chaucer Society publication, *Essays on Chaucer, His Words and Works*, Part II [1874], pp. 157-64, with this introductory note by FJF: "It is well for all lovers of Chaucer to hear a woman's opinion on him, and specially well when that woman is one, pure of spirit and noble of soul, our great Victorian poetess, Elizabeth Barrett Browning. She wrote this opinion before she married, in 'The Book of the Poets,' in the *Athenaeum* of 1842; it was reprinted in her *Greek Christian Poets and English Poets*, 1863, p. 110, &c., and taken thence now by leave of her husband, the poet, Robert Browning, who says that she took part, with Wordsworth and others, in modernizing some of Chaucer's Tales" (p. 156). FJF had founded the Chaucer Society in 1868.

2 EBB contributed "Queen Annelida and False Arcite" to *The Poems of Chaucer Modernized*, ed. R. H. Horne (1841). Other contributors to the volume included Wordsworth, Leigh Hunt (1784-1859; *DNB*), and Richard Monckton Milnes (1809-85; *DNB*).

1

3 "And Chaucer, with his infantine / Familiar clasp of things divine; / That mark upon his lip is wine" ("A Vision of Poets" [1844], ll. 388-90). FJF also reprinted these lines in *Essays on Chaucer*, p. 155.

FJF TO RB, 27 JANUARY 1872

3, St. George's Sq., Primrose Hill, London, N.W.* /
27 Jany. 1872

My dear Sir

I'm greatly obliged to you for your leave to reprint the Chaucer bits of Mrs. Barrett Browning's Essay, & for your reference to the other Chaucer works of hers. I did not know of her having helpt in the modernisation of Chaucer. Evidently she loved him. How she goes back to him in that Essay, after she seems to have finisht with him—first after Gower,[1] next after Spenser, & then again to his *Benedicite* in Wordsworth.

It's a great pleasure to see how her pure & beautiful soul takes to Chaucer, notwithstanding the few stains of his time, which are all that some small women can see in him.

May I say one thing to you which I've often thought of, but never had a notion of getting at you to say,—& that is, ask you to publish a shilling selection from her works, to sell by the million if possible, & let her name be known in every household in England? Just because Longfellow &c are 1/- they're all over the land; & because Mrs. Browning is many shillings, even the Selections 5/- (?),[2] comparatively few know her. She's the first great poetess we've had, the only one; why shouldn't she get into every body's heart? And a shilling edition is the only way to do it. Tell the story of her life in it; & then let the book work.

I remember well how the book was a revelation to me of the depth & beauty of woman's nature, & know it stirred up Gerald Massey[3] & other fellows at our Tailors' Assocn. & Workg. Men's Coll. when I lent it 'em, & lectured 'em on it.[4] And I should have liked then, & shd. like now, to see it sown all over England.

Do think of it. Let the book go at cost of paper & print only, & get all the largest-circulation publishers to work it. Why is she to wait 50 years till her rightful reputation & honour are got for her?

2

Don't think this impertinence or interference. It's not meant for that.

Very tr[ul]y yrs / F. J. Furnivall

MS: Folger. Address: Robert Browning Esq / 19 Warwick Crescent / W. Postmarks: LONDON NW 7 JA 29 72; LONDON W B7 JA 29 72.

1 John Gower (1325?-1408; *DNB*), English poet and friend of Chaucer.
2 *A Selection from the Poetry of Elizabeth Barrett Browning*, with a prefatory note by RB, was first published by Chapman & Hall in 1866 and was frequently reprinted by Smith, Elder. The price of the Smith, Elder reprint was 7/6.
3 Gerald Massey (1828-1907; *DNB*), Christian Socialist poet and journalist, whose career suggested that of George Eliot's Felix Holt. EBB regarded his work as "poetical, but effeminate—somewhat feeble really" (*Elizabeth Barrett Browning's Letters to Mrs. David Ogilvy, 1849-1861*, ed. Peter N. Heydon and Philip Kelley [New York, 1973], p. 133).
4 The Working Men's College was founded in London by a group of Christian Socialists under the leadership of the Rev. F. D. Maurice (1805-72; *DNB*) in 1854. FJF taught classes in English literature and grammar at the College from its founding for more than a decade, and in the early years he had also been one of the leading figures in the institution's social activities. Shortly after the opening of the College, the Council for the Society for Promoting Working Men's Associations opened an adult school in the Hall of Association, Castle Street, Oxford Street, sharing the premises with the Working Tailors' Association. (J. Llewelyn Davies, ed., *The Working Men's College: 1854-1904* [1904], *passim*.)

RB TO FJF, 12 DECEMBER 1873

19 Warwick Crescent, W. / Dec. 12. '73.

Dear Mr. Furnival,[1]

Thank you very much for the honor you offer me,—I am obliged to decline it from a habit I have. I could do nothing for the Society, and why should I pretend to "preside" over it, "*vice*" my friend the Laureate whose help will be help indeed?[2]

Ever faithfully yours / Robert Browning.

MS: HEH.

1 RB occasionally misspelled FJF's name in this way for many years.
2 During November 1873 FJF had called upon Tennyson "about the Shakespeare Society he wished to found, and to make A.[lfred] president. This honour he has declined, hating to push himself forward as a learned Shakespearean, but he has agreed to join the Society." On 19 Dec., when RB dined with Tennyson, the latter wrote to Gladstone: "As to Furnivall I believe him to be a hard-working, painstaking, conscientious man. . . . I have refused the Presidency and even a Vice-Presidency of the Shakespeare Society. I am now merely a subscriber, though I have promised, if need be, to give them a donation." (Hallam Tennyson, *Afred Lord Tennyson* [1897], II, 152-54.) In the first prospectus of the New Shakspere Society, dated 28 Mar. 1874,

FJF announced that "the Presidency of the Society will be left vacant till one of our greatest living poets sees that his duty is to take it"—meaning, presumably, either Tennyson or RB.

FJF TO RB, 13 DECEMBER 1873

3, St. George's Square, Primrose Hill, London. N.W.* /
13 Decr. 1873.

Dear Mr. Browning

Isn't it a bad habit that makes you decline to help fellows who want help in learning their Shakspere?[1] You *must* know 10 times as much about him as we others do.

I wish you'd have a talk with me over it. I'll try to look in on you about 3 on Sunday afternoon, if you'll let me in. If not, leave word when I may come.

In the evening I read Henry VI Pt. 2 with some of our Working Men, their wives & sisters.

Always tr[ul]y yrs / F.J.F.

MS: Folger.

1 RB had declined the presidency of the New Shakspere Society. Before the end of the year Charles Darwin (1809-82; *DNB*), Herbert Spencer (1820-1903; *DNB*), and Matthew Arnold (1822-88; *DNB*) had also declined the office (in letters to FJF dated, respectively, 6 Dec., 9 Dec., and 15 Dec. 1873 [HEH]); Tennyson, of course, had also refused it (see RB to FJF, 12 Dec. 1873, n. 1).

FJF TO RB, 17 DECEMBER 1873

3, St. George's Square, Primrose Hill, London, N.W.* /
Wedny. 17 Decr. 1873.

Dear Mr Browning

Unless you stop me, I shall avail myself tomorrow, Thursday, of your sister's kind leave to come to luncheon with you some after 1, & have a Shakspere chat.

If you haven't seen the enclosed summary of our Chaucer work up to last March,[1] pray look at it.

Sincy. yrs, / F.J.F.

MS: Folger. Address: Robert B[row]ning Esq / 15 [*sic*] Warwick Crescent / *W.* / Furnivall [in lower left corner]. Postmark: [LONDO]N NW [. . .] 17 [. . .].
1 Most of FJF's societies, including the Chaucer Society, issued prospectuses and reports at regular intervals.

FJF TO RB, 24 JANUARY 1874

3, St. George's Square, Primrose Hill, London. N.W.* /
24 Jany. 1874.

Dear Mr. Browning

May I come over for another short Shakspere Society talk some day next week, & bring with me my friend Prof. Seeley[1] (Prof. of Modern Histy at Cambridge) who tells me that he sees you often at the Athenaeum,[2] & whom I want to know you better—not only because he always has about a dozen good subjects for historical dramas in his head—but because he is the keenest & ablest man I know.

He will be lecturing in the North next Tuesday & Wednesday, but any other day would walk over with me.

Sincerely yours / F.J.F.

MS: Folger.
1 Sir John R. Seeley (1834-95, *DNB*), author of *Ecce Homo* (1865) and close friend of FJF, had unsuccessfully attempted to persuade RB to lecture at University College, London, in 1867 (*IG*, p. 37).
2 RB was elected a member of the Athenaeum Club in 1863 (*IG*, pp. 29-30).

RB TO FJF, 3 FEBRUARY 1874

19. Warwick Crescent, W / Feb. 3. '74.

Dear Mr Furnivall,

Will you forgive what may have seemed inattention but was simply caused by a press of claims upon my time last week?

I well remember having had the honor of an introduction to Professor Seeley, some years ago, and some kind notice on his part since then. If you and he will choose any day but Thursday or Friday next,—and, I must add, the Monday following,—it will be a great pleasure to my sister and myself: our luncheon is at 2. o'clock.

Pray believe me, Dear Mr. Furnivall,

Very truly yours / Robert Browning.

MS: King's.

FJF TO RB, 4 FEBRUARY 1874

3. St. George's Square, Primrose Hill, London. N.W.* /
4 Feby. 1874.

Dear Mr Browning

Many thanks for your kind note.

Seeley goes to Cambridge tomorrow night, but will be back on Monday, & very happy to come to see you on Tuesday at 2, with

Yours very truly / F.J.F.

MS: Folger.

FJF TO RB, 16 FEBRUARY 1874

3, St. George's Square, Primrose Hill, London. N.W.* /
16 Febry. 1874.

Dear Mr. Browning

The more I think over your suggestion of a poem on this rebellion against Gladstone,[1] the more I like it, & think that you'll be doing an enormous service to Liberalism & political honesty, by writing it. It would bring people to their senses now; & it would be a warning to all English-speaking people hereafter. The same causes as have workt now will always be at work producing like effects, & you'll be quoted hundreds & thousands of years hence. You should take a big subject like this—Ring & Book was too small for you, & too far off every one. Victorian life is the thing. What wouldn't you, & all of us have given for an Elizabethan R.B. writing in her time, & telling us what folk thought about Essex, Leicester, Cecil &c.[2] As to newspaper accounts &c., they don't live, can't. Poetry will, & must. *Do* set to work at it.

6

If you have any poems in your desk, Dr. Appleton of the *Academy*, an admirer of yours, would *very* much like to have them, he says.[3] Are there any lying hid?

Many thanks to you & Miss Browning for all your kindness to Seeley & myself. We both enjoyed our visit to you greatly, & only regretted that his Cambridge train cut it so short.

Most truly yours / F. J. Furnivall

MS: Folger.
1 Following the dissolution of Parliament on 26 Jan., a Conservative majority of forty-eight was returned to the House of Commons, and the cabinet resigned on 16 Feb. Gladstone announced that he would no longer lead the Liberal Party unless it were able to resolve its internal differences. RB evidently did not write the poem to which FJF alludes.
2 Robert Devereux, 2nd Earl of Essex (1566-1601; *DNB*), Robert Sidney, Viscount Lisle and 1st Earl of Leicester of a new creation (1563-1626; *DNB*), and Robert Cecil, 1st Earl of Salisbury and 1st Viscount Cranborne (1563-1612; *DNB*), all important Elizabethan political figures.
3 Charles Appleton (1841-79; *DNB*) founded the *Academy* in 1869 and edited it until his death. FJF contributed regularly to the *Academy*. However, RB had an aversion to publishing his poems in periodicals, and none appeared in the *Academy*.

FJF TO RB, 23 MAY 1874

3, St. George's Square, Primrose Hill, London, N.W.* /
23 May 1874.

My dear Mr. Browning

Last night we had a Paper at the New Shaksp. Soc. by my friend Hales, supporting the genuineness of the Porter's speeches in *Macbeth*.[1] In speaking afterwards I contended for the grim humour of the first speech, & of Shakspere's producing the Scotch Porter, in the normal state of philosophizing drunkenness, to dwell on 2 of the national topics, hell-fire & lechery:—the Hell (as has been often said) with reference to the fiendly [*sic*] murder just committed, (& the *equivocation*, with reference to Macbeth, who'd already begun to find that he couldn't equivocate to heaven.) I also urged that the triple beat of the rhythmic prose

> Here's / a knocking / indeed
> If a man / were porter / of Hellgate

He should have / old turning / the key

was Shakspere's, as in *Coriolanus* I.iii.

When yet / he was but / tender bodied,
& the only / son of / my womb &c

Will you kindly give me your opinion on at least the first of these points? Isn't there truly grim humour in that Porter's speech, worthy of Shakspere?

Always truly yours / F.J.F.

MS: Folger.
1   At the 22 May 1874 meeting of the New Shakspere Society, J. W. Hales (1836-1914; WW), afterwards Professor of English, King's College, London, delivered a paper entitled "On the Porter in *Macbeth*" (printed in *NSST* [1874], pp. 255-69). After the reading of the paper, FJF observed (p. 274):

How *could* a Scotch porter be better hit off? Surely he must be a dull soul who can't see the humour of the character. I should like to have Mr Carlyle's opinion on the point. It is not one on which I think Coleridge's judgment worth much. Lamb's, now would be a different thing: so too Mr Browning's.

[P.S. Sunday, May 24, 1874. Chatting with Mr Browning this afternoon, I askt him his opinion on the point, and he answered: "Certainly the speech is full of humour; and as certainly the humour and words are Shakspere's. I cannot understand Coleridge's objection to it. It's as bad as his wanting to emend *blanket* by *blank height*, in

Nor Heauen peepe through the *blanket* of the darke.
Macbeth, I.v.

As for Lamb, I've no doubt that he held the speech genuine, for he said that on his pointing out to his friend Munden the quality of Porter's speech, Munden was duly struck by it, and exprest his regret at never having playd the part."]

FJF TO RB, 1 JUNE 1874

3, St. George's Square, Primrose Hill, London. N.W.* /
1 June 1874.

My dear Mr. Browning

Please say whether my report of your opinion on the *Macbeth* porter may stand as it's printed. Alter it in any way you like.

As to Lamb: I've looked at his papers on *Munden*, *Old Actors* &c—so has a friend—& we can't find any allusion to M.'s acting the Porter.[1] Perhaps I wrongly put down "in one of his essays", & you know the fact from report. It's an important one for our side.

Our man Fleay—"the industrious (& often furious) flea"[—]

now says that Shakspere wrote only the first 2 Acts of *The 2 Gentlemen of Verona*.[2] Some of us are going to fight the point.

Always sincerely yours / F.J.F.

MS: Folger.

1 Like FJF, I cannot find such a reference in Charles Lamb's writings. Joseph Munden (1758-1832; *DNB*), Lamb's actor friend, never performed *Macbeth* (Thomas S. Munden, *Memoirs of Joseph Shepherd Munden, Comedian* [1844], pp. 234-40).

2 Frederick G. Fleay (1831-1909; *DNB*), Shakespearean scholar who acquired the nickname "the industrious flea" while an undergraduate at Trinity College, Cambridge, and who later dedicated his *A Chronicle History of the Life and Work of William Shakespeare* (1868) to RB. His comments on *The Two Gentlemen of Verona* are found in a paper he delivered to the New Shakspere Society on 12 June 1874, "On Certain Plays of Shakspere" (*NSST* [1874], p. 289); the discussion at the meeting, which was dominated by FJF, is recorded on pp. 318-38.

RB TO FJF, 2 JUNE 1874

19. Warwick Crescent, W / June 2. '74

Dear Mr Furnivall,

It matters very little what I said on a point about which *you* say so much and have common sense on your side. I am quite sure that I have seen a notice of Lamb's to the effect that on his pointing out to Munden the quality of the porter's speech he was duly struck by it and expressed his regret at never having played the part.

Ever truly yours / Robert Browning.

MS: HEH.

RB TO FJF, 13 AUGUST 1875

19. Warwick Crescent, W / Aug. 13. '75

Dear Mr Furnivall,

You never repeated your pleasant visit, and here is your book of plays still, though you may want it.[1] I send you by post accordingly the volume with many thanks. I leave London to-morrow and could not do so without saying thus much—and that I am

Ever truly yours / Robert Browning.

MS: ABL.

1 FJF was notoriously generous in lending books from his personal library. In a letter to an unidentified correspondent (owned by the editor), 14 Feb. 1893, he complained: "My experience in lending books is a sad one. *All* my sets of books have been ruind by loans: Ruskin, Browning, E.[early] E.[nglish] Text, &c."

RB TO FJF, 23 JANUARY 1876

19. Warwick Crescent, W / Jan. 23. '76

My dear Furnivall,

Unluckily, all to-morrow is wanted for engagement after engagement. My son goes, another friend is going,—afterwards I convoy people to some show or other, and so runs away the day of rest.

I am deeply obliged to you for the interest you take in my poems,[1] and the wish you have for their increased circulation; but depend on it, there is no help for what you consider my ill case, and what I am used to acquiesce in as my natural portion. To get your good will is much: get me anybody's good will, and I shall be gladdened proportionably.[2]

Ever truly yours / R Browning.

MS: HEH.

1 On 15 Jan. 1876 RB wrote to George Smith (Murray): "Mr Furnival has quite mistaken the nature of my 'consent.' He was lamenting that my poetry was not sold more cheaply, so as to be more widely circulated,—and I replied that your opinion was that I addressed a certain good but restricted circle, to which circle the price was a matter of indifference. He rejoined that he should like to print a cheap Selection and himself write the preface: whereto I answered that if you agreed to *that*, I should have no objection. What else could I say? Unless things are very much changed, I suppose you will *not* agree!" RB wrote to Smith again on 23 Jan. (Murray): "I got the note I enclose on Friday—and at once replied to it—thanking the writer [FJF] for his zeal on my behalf, assuring him that I believed nothing he could do or suggest would change matters for the better, and regretting that I was too much engaged to see him to-day. I am quite sure that we both of us,—that is, you & I,—are agreed on every point about our friend & his counsels: nor did I wait for your note to act upon my opinion." (For an account of FJF's prolonged effort to secure an inexpensive edition of RB's poems, see *Oracle*, pp. 35-40; see also RB to FJF, 26 July 1881, n. 4, and 24 Dec. 1883, n. 1.)
2 FJF's first published comment on RB's poetry appeared shortly after this: "Mr. Browning's *Inn Album*," *Notes and Queries*, 5th Ser., 5 (25 Mar. 1876), 244-45. In June FJF attempted to arrange for some of RB's newest poems to be published in the *Athenaeum* (*LRB*, p. 172).

RB TO FJF, 26 JANUARY 1876

19. W. C. Jan 26. '76

Dear Mr Furnivall,

Don't tempt me, I beseech of your goodness. Here is the current of my friends' kindnesses beginning to set upon unworthy me, and I dine, dine till I could believe the word is just the Greek Δίγη—a whirlpool! Yesterday, to-day, to-morrow—but "I'll see no more", like your Macbeth.[1] Bear with this and all other infirmities from

Yours truly ever / R Browning

MS: HEH. Address: F. J. Furnivall Esq / 3. St. George's Square, / Primrose Hill, / NW. Postmarks: LONDON SW 4 JA 26 76; LONDON NW JO JA 26 76.
1 "I'll go no more" (Shakespeare, *Macbeth*, II.ii.50).

RB TO FJF [DECEMBER 1878]

Dear Mr. Furnivall,—

I always took the "mark of wine" to be a proof of the geniality and joviality of Chaucer. But I have only my own opinion to give you; I never thought of becoming better informed about it. ⟨. . .⟩

Remember, you have only my impression, which amounts, however (for many reasons I could give), to a conviction, I must allow.

⟨. . .⟩

Text: "Notes and News," *Academy*, 14 (28 Dec. 1878), 601. The letter was accompanied in the *Academy* by the following explanation: "Mrs. Browning's lines on Chaucer in her *Vision of Poets*, 1844 . . . [quoted in RB to FJF, 27 Jan. 1872, n. 3] have often raised doubts in the minds of her readers. Did she mean by the 'mark' the stain of *quasi*-Bacchanalian licence which is found in some of Chaucer's works, or only the sign of the innocent jollity produced by wine that maketh glad the heart of man? The question was at last referred to Mr. Browning; and by his leave we give his answer:—[Here the letter is quoted.] We are sure that all lovers of Chaucer will gladly accept Mr. Browning's opinion as conclusive."

FJF TO RB, 5 MARCH 1879

3, St. George's Square, Primrose Hill, / London, N.W.* /
5 March 1879.
Dear Mr. Browning

As the New Shakspere Society has now finished its first five
year's work, & shown itself worthy of support, its Committee have
charged me again to ask you to become President of the Society.[1]
They recognize in you a closer kinship—in power, life, analysis of
character &c—to Shakspere, than in any other modern poet. They
think that when they've kept the post of honour for a poet,—&
not a prince or the like,—one ought to be willing to take it for
Shakspere's sake. They would most gladly—as would every member of the Society—see you take it, & they trust you will.

They do not wish to make any call on your time; & they will
make any statement you approve, to remove from you any responsibility for any of their acts or books.

But they do heartily wish to have you as their Head, even if it
be only in name.

In the hope that you will accede to their request, I am,

Very truly yours / F. J. Furnivall

MS: Folger. Address: Robt. Browning Esq. / 19 Warwick Crescent / W. Postmarks:
LONDON NW A5 MR 5 79; PADDINGTON 5 [. . .] 79 3.
1   See FJF to RB, 13 Dec. 1873, n. 1.

RB TO FJF, 12 MARCH 1879

19. Warwick Crescent, W. / March 12. '79.
Dear Mr Furnivall,

If I could say much about the honor the Society proposes to do
me, I should show the more plainly how little I deserved it: but I
do feel—I think—as deeply as I ought how prodigious and exorbitant an honor it is. How can I refuse it? If I asked rather "How
can I accept it?"—the objections would come too thickly. But I resolve only to say "It is even a greater piece of kindness than honor
—and I *cannot* refuse the combination". Pray commend my reply
to the Committee in such gracious words as you will conceive

should be,—but are *not*,—at the disposal of

Yours truly ever / Robert Browning.

MS: HEH. Address: F. J. Furnivall Esq. / 3. St. George's Square, / Primrose Hill, / N.W. / Robt. Browning. Postmark: PADDINGTON W 5 MR 12 79 K. Note in FJF's hand on envelope: "Presidency / N. Sh. Soc."

FJF TO RB, 12 MARCH 1879

3, St. George's Square, Primrose Hill, / London, N.W.* /
12 March 1879.

Dear Mr. Browning

Thank you heartily for your note. It makes me very happy, & will, I am sure, rejoice our Committee & all our Members.

May I have 10 minutes' talk with you on the relations you would like to subsist between you & us?

I shall be close to your house tomorrow, Thursday, about 1 o'clock; & will take the chance of finding you in. If you are not, will you leave word when it will suit you to see me? I can come at any time—except our Meeting hours on Friday evening 7.30-11.

Gratefully & sincerely yours / F. J. Furnivall

MS: Folger. Address: Robt. Browning Esq. / 19 Warwick Crescent / W. Postmarks: LONDON NW A7 MR 13 79; LONDON W W7 MR 13 79.

FJF TO RB, 14 MARCH 1879

3, St. George's Square, Primrose Hill, / London, N.W.* /
14 March 1879.

My dear Mr. Browning

Your kind letter accepting the Presidency of the New Sh. Soc. was read by me at the meetings of our Committee & our Members tonight. The Committee were greatly pleas'd with it, & chargd me to give you their hearty thanks for taking the headship of the Society. The Members passt a Resolution "That this Meeting receives with great pleasure the announcement that Mr. Browning has accepted the Presidency of the Society." One & all were greatly delighted at it.

I told the Committee what you said about reading thro' Shakspere again, & they said they hoped you *would* find something to give the Society a chat or a Paper about, or even a note.[1]

If ever you can spare an evening of a 2nd Friday in a month— next year, perhaps—all our folk will rejoice to see you among them.

Sincy. yrs / F.J.F.

MS: Folger. Address: R. Browning Esq. / 19 Warwick Crescent / W. Postmarks: LONDON NW A11 MR 15 79; P[ADDING]TON [. . .] MR 15 79 3.

1 See FJF's "Recollections" (Article 1, Appendix B, below): "He promised, during one vacation, to read through Shakspere again in the chronological order that I had assigned to his plays and to tell me if anything special occurred to him." RB never read a paper to the New Shakspere Society.

FJF TO RB, 15 MARCH 1879

3, St. George's Square, Primrose Hill, / London, N.W.* /
15 March 1879.

Dear Mr. Browning

When you have time, I *do* hope that you'll read O'Connor's *Life of Lord Beaconsfield*.[1] It is most admirable material for a poem. What couldn't you make of it, if you liked! Hohenstiel Schwangau wd be nothing to it.[2]

Don't trouble to answer; but I can't help writing.

Sincy. yrs / F.J.F.

MS: Folger. Address: R. Browning Esq. / 19 Warwick Crescent / W. Postmarks: LONDON NW A7 MR 17 79; LONDON W W7 MR 17 79.

1 T. P. O'Connor's *Lord Beaconsfield: A Biography* was published in 1879. FJF recalled in 1889: "After Mr. Disraeli's death [1881], I was very anxious that Browning should vivisect him in a Blowgram [*sic*] poem. He admitted that the subject would suit him; but he had kept aloof from English politics; and how could he treat such a character without offending almost all his Tory friends, many of whom he valued?" (See Appendix B, below.) However, in the "George Bubb Dodington" section of *Parleyings with Certain People of Importance in Their Day* (1887) RB did make at least an oblique attack upon Disraeli's character, as he admitted to Mrs. Orr (*A Handbook to the Works of Robert Browning* [1913], p. 351; DeVane, *Browning's Parleyings: The Autobiography of a Mind* [New Haven, Conn., 1927], pp. 150-57, 164-65).

2 RB's *Prince Hohenstiel-Schwangau* (1871) portrayed the duplicity of Louis Napoleon.

RB TO FJF, [DECEMBER 1879]

⟨. . .⟩ Surely the right reading is

> The complexion of the element
> Is Mavors. . . . . .
> Most bloody, fiery and most terrible,

the notion being of planetary influence, 'Sanguineo orbe rubens—Rutilanti sidere Mavors.'[1] ⟨. . .⟩

Text: *Athenaeum*, 27 Dec. 1879, p. 849.
The excerpt from RB's letter was accompanied by the following note in the *Athenaeum*:

The Director of the New Shakspere Society sends us the emendations of his President, Mr. Robert Browning, on the word "Fauors" in 'Julius Caesar,' Act i. sc. 3, l. 129:—

> for now this fearefull Night,
> There is no stirre, or walking in the streetes;
> And the Complexion of the Element
> Is Fauors, like the Worke we haue in hand,
> Most bloodie, fierie, and most terrible.

It is known that the aspect of the planet Mars was most bloody, fiery, and terrible. 'Batman vpon Bartholome' says (lib. viii. cap. 25, leaf 130 back) that Mars "hath mastry over cholar, fire, and cholericke complection," "Vnder him is contayned warre, battel, prison, & enmitie; & he betokeneth wrath, swiftnesse, and woundes, and is *redde*, and vntrue, and guylefull." The word Mars is only a contraction of Mavors; and Mr. Browning says, [here RB's letter is quoted]. Shakspeare speaks in 'Antony and Cleopatra' of "the ill aspects of planets"; in 'Richard II.' of how

> Men judge by the complexion of the sky
> The state and inclination of the day,

and that complexion surely was, the night before Caesar's murder, that of the planet Mars or Mavors, god of battle, though nowhere else does Shakspeare use the long form of the god's name. Mr. Browning's conjecture deserves at least registration. If [William and Isaac] Jaggard's compositor saw "Mavors" in his "copy" he would certainly have altered it to "Favors."

J. O. Halliwell-Phillipps offered the following comment: "Did you ever know anything so utterly childish as Browning's Julius Caesar emendation(?) in this week's Athenaeum?" (Halliwell-Phillipps to C. M. Ingleby, 27 Dec. 1879 [Folger]). For a more temperate (but also unfavorable) opinion of RB's emendation, see the Variorum Edition of *Julius Caesar*, ed. Horace H. Furness (Philadelphia, 1913), p. 70.

1 "Mavors [Mars] becoming red in a bloody world, in a glowing star."

RB TO FJF, 20 MAY 1880

19, Warwick Crescent, / W.* / May 20. '80.

My dear Mr Furnivall,

I never have been to see the "Merchant of Venice" at the Lyceum: is not that the proper way of protesting against the abuses you mention?[1] This circumstance, I have little doubt, is well known to Mr Irving (with whom I was speaking about *Venice*, last Sunday, and *not* about his revival of the play)—and he would justly retort that one, at least, of his critics might as well become acquainted with what he took on himself to criticise.

Ever cordially yours RB.

MS: Texas.

1 It had been announced that for the 20 May benefit performance for Ellen Terry (1848-1928; *WW*) at the Lyceum Theatre, Henry Irving (1838-1905; *DNB*) would do a truncated version of Shakespeare's *The Merchant of Venice*: the fifth act was to be deleted in order to allow time for a new version of *King Rene's Daughter*, renamed *Iolanthe*, by William G. Willis (1828-91; *DNB*). FJF protested against this violation of Shakespeare's text by writing a private letter to Irving on 10 May and, with a number of other Shakespearean scholars, signing a public letter to Irving which was printed and widely discussed in the press. (Lawrence Irving, *Henry Irving: The Actor and His World* [1951], p. 357; "The Stage," *Academy*, 17 [22 May 1880], 393.) Irving nevertheless went ahead with the production, and during the remainder of its run the *Merchant* appeared in this abbreviated version. FJF had quarreled earlier with Irving and never forgave him for tampering with Shakespeare (*Furnivall*, pp. 20, 203).

FJF TO RB, 7 FEBRUARY 1881

3, St. George's Square, Primrose Hill, / London, N.W.* /
7 Febry 1881.

My dear Mr. Browning

I *must*, at the risk of boring you, repeat what a bookseller, a big cheap shop man, Fr. Stephen,[1] at the corner by St Mary's Somerset House told me today. I went in to buy Miss Braddon's *Vixen*;[2] & askt how her books sold. Then I said How does Browning sell? He said 'Oh, fairly; we always keep him in stock; *but the books are such a price!* People often come in & ask for Browning; but when they find how stiff the price is, they go out again. If we could have a cheap edition, the books wd *go like wildfire*.' His exact words. What do you mean, said I, a 1-vol. edn. at 6/- like Tennyson?' 'Yes, that wd be best of all. But we could do with a half-crown edition in a fair no. of volumes.' 'But do you *think*, said I, that yours is the opinion of the trade.' '*Think*', said he, 'I *know* it is. If the books were workt like Tennyson's, they'd have a splendid sale.' May I tell Mr Browning what you say now? 'Yes, I wish you would.'

It was a short thickset man who talkt to me, with a light moustache.

I've long known the shop as doing a great trade, but haven't been into it for years, & my going this afternoon was a mere chance.

I only beg you to test the truth of this man's opinion by any friends in this or any other big shop you like; & to believe what I have so long said, that the *one great* hindrance to your popularity is your insisting—or allowing others to insist—on keeping your books dear.

Always sincy. yrs / F.J.F.

MS: University of Virginia Library. Address: Robt. Browning Esq. / 19 Warwick Crescent / W. Postmark: LONDON NW G7 FE 8 81; [...] .
1 The shop was Steven and Davies, Booksellers' Row, Strand, W.C.
2 *Vixen: A Novel* (1879) by Mary Elizabeth Braddon (1837-1915; *DNB*).

RB TO FJF, 11 MARCH 1881

19. Warwick Crescent, / W.* / March 11. '81.

Dear Mr Furnivall,

I shall be happy to see you at the hour you have appointed next Sunday. Nobody has very much "bothered" me—and I hope the whole affair is nearly over and done with.[1]

I had a kind note from you respecting a "cheap edition" &c.[2] I waited till Smith should return to London, and then made him acquainted with the proposal—whereto he sees objections, but would co-operate were I to desire.

Yours very truly / Robert Browning.

MS: ABL. Address: F. J. Furnivall Esq. / 3. St. George's Square, / Primrose Hill, *N.W.* Postmarks: PADDINGTON W Y4 MR 11 81; LONDON SE 1E MR 11 81; LONDON NW LO MR 11 81. Note in FJF's hand on envelope: "cheap ed."
1 During the early months of 1881 RB had been caught in the middle of a New Shakspere Society quarrel between FJF and Swinburne. For a detailed account of the episode, see Appendix A, below.
2 RB wrote to George Smith on 5 Mar. 1881 (Murray): "You thoroughly explained to me, some time ago, the nature of that mistaken proposal about the 'cheap edition,'— and I only sent the letter as a funny instance of the writer's [FJF's] carelessness while such a storm of abuse was raging round him. I want nothing of the sort—(of an edition, I mean) and am quite sure that if you saw any advantage to me in it you would be first to let me know." See also RB to FJF, 23 Jan. 1876, n. 1.

RB TO FJF, 7 APRIL 1881

19. Warwick Crescent, W. / Apr. 7. '81

My dear Furnivall—(if you will kindly let me drop—and yourself drop—the more formal and un-fellow-student-like style of address) —I am greatly obliged to you for your handsome zeal in my behalf. Be assured that I lay all these assurances and suggestions to heart— and sooner or later shall turn them to account,—as indeed I do even now, since such proofs of good will are precious to

Yours truly ever / Robert Browning.

MS: HEH. Address: F. J. Furnivall, Esq / 3. St. George's Square, / Primrose Hill, / N.W. Postmarks: [LOND]ON W [. . .] AP 7 [. . .] ; LONDON NW CO AP 7 81. Note in FJF's hand on envelope: "drop the 'Mr.' "

RB TO FJF, 7 JUNE 1881

19, Warwick Crescent, / W.* / June 7. '81.

My dear Furnival,

I ought not to have so delayed an answer to your letter—but in truth you ought to need no fresh assurance that I am always happy to see you whenever you incline to give me that pleasure, —and Miss Hickey[1] will be welcomed as befits: I hope I value her sympathy as it deserves—it is not for me to find fault with its kind exaggeration.

Ever cordially yours / Robert Browning.

MS: HEH.

1 Miss Emily Hickey (1845-1924) had at this time just published her first volume of verse, *A Sculptor and Other Poems*, and was gradually entering into London literary life under the encouragement and guidance of FJF. When she and FJF called on RB, 3 July 1881, they had agreed on the way to create the London Browning Society, of which Miss Hickey became the first Honorary Secretary (1881-84). She lectured on English literature for eighteen years at the North London Collegiate School for Girls and in 1884 edited an annotated version of RB's *Strafford* to which the poet contributed notes and revisions. (*Oracle*, pp. 16-19; Enid Maud Dinnis, *Emily Hickey: Poet, Essayist—Pilgrim. A Memoir* [1927]).

RB TO FJF, 12 JUNE 1881

19. Warwick Crescent, / W.* / June 12. '81.

Oh, my dear Furnivall, you must not fancy me such a gad-about because I happen to be bound for Balliol next Saturday & Sunday.[1] If you like to give me so much pleasure, the *next* Sunday (that day seeming to suit you best)—or any after that till July ends[2]—will find me here,—therefore no talking about "Autumn or Winter visitations," pray! and so advise Miss H.

I will see what it may be that you refer to in the "Academy", but could not go to the Club yesterday.[3]

Ever yours truly, / Robert Browning.

MS: ABL. Address: Fred. J. Furnivall, Esq. / 3. St. George's Square, / Primrose Hill, *N.W.* Postmarks: LONDON SW 7 JU 13 81; LONDON NW AP JU 13 81.
1 RB returned from Oxford on 20 June (*NL*, p. 263).
2 Note in FJF's hand: "Br. confused! / I say July 3. / F.J.F."
3 A letter from Miss Hickey ("On the Use of the Trochaic Pentameter by Shakspere and Others," *Academy*, 19 [11 June 1881], 432) cited "One Word More" by "our greatest living poet." "The Club" is the Athenaeum.

SARIANNA BROWNING TO FJF [JULY 1881?]

19. Warwick Crescent. / Friday mg

Dear Mr. Furnivall,

I am at all times most happy to see you, but unfortunately on Saturday mornings I am due at a small Home with which I have been connected for many years.[1] If I am absent, there will be no one to take my place,—and though the poor children may not lose much, I can at least set them an example of punctuality.

You are very kind and generous in your efforts to increase the acquaintance with my brother's writings, and you cannot suppose that we are, either of us, insensible or indifferent. I thank you most thoroughly for your warm-hearted appreciation and disinterested endeavour to widen the circle of his readers—yet you must feel that he cannot himself take any part in the matter. He has all his life felt that his duty was to work to the best of his power, and there leave it.

Believe me, dear Mr. Furnivall,

Yours very sincerely, / Sarianna Browning.

MS: HEH (where dated [*c.* 1885?]).
Date: "The founder [FJF] applied to my Sister for 'names of friends who might wish to join' [the Browning Society] —but she resolutely refused to give any information of the kind—saying that I had kept free of all attempts to help myself to a

reputation, except by writing books" (RB to Mrs. FitzGerald, 6 Aug. 1881, in *LL*, p. 119).
1 Not identified.

RB TO FJF 26 JULY 1881

19. Warwick Crescent, / W.* / July 26. '81.

My dear Furnival,

The lines "Eurydice to Orpheus" were written to illustrate a picture by Sir F. Leighton, and appeared in the Academy Catalogue as a motto to that work.[1] It afterwards was included in Moxon's Selection, 1865. The lines "Deaf and Dumb" were similarly intended to illustrate a marble group by Woolner—but were first printed in the Collected Edition, as you suppose.[2] The other pieces originally appeared thus: "Amphibian"—as prologue, and "The Householder" as epilogue, to "Fifine". "Apparitions"—as prologue to "The Two Poets of Croisic"—to which "What a pretty Tale you told me"—served as epilogue. "A Wall" ushered in "Pacchiarotto". I have not got the books for reference, or I would give the dates of publication also.

W. J. Fox was the first noticer of my boyish poems, when I had never seen him. I thereupon saw him once or twice, and lost sight of him for years—till after the publication of "Pauline" which he reviewed so generously. Having thus made acquaintance with his "Repository", I gave it a few poems: "The Boy and the Angel", and some others, I gave to Hood for his magazine.[3]

Certainly I have no objection to your reprinting the Essay, if Moxon permits.[4]

Ever truly yours / Robert Browning.

MS: HEH.
1 FJF's *Bibliography* prints "Orpheus and Eurydice. F. Leighton," as it was originally entitled, and adds this note: "From the Catalogue of the Royal Academy Exhibition, 1864, p. 13, where it is actually printed as prose: a mess—specially in lines 6-8—duly condemnd by *Punch*, May 28, 1864, and the *Observer* before that" (*BSP*, I, 62). See also RB to FJF, 11 Oct. 1881. (Leighton's painting, with RB's lines painted on the frame, now hangs in Leighton House, London.) Sir Frederic Leighton (1830-96; *DNB*), President of the Royal Academy, was an old friend of the Brownings who designed EBB's tomb in Florence. For an account of his relationship with the Brownings, see Martha H. Shackford, *The Brownings and Leighton* (Wellesley, Mass., 1942).
2 FJF, *Bibliography*: "These lines were written in 1862 for Woolner's partly-draped group of Constance and Arthur, the deaf and dumb children of Sir Thomas Fairbairn,

which was exhibited in the International Exhibition of 1862; but the lines did not appear in the Exhibition Catalogue" (*BSP*, I, 64). Thomas Woolner (1825-92; *DNB*), Pre-Raphaelite sculptor and poet, did a wooden plaque of RB in 1856 which today hangs in the Armstrong Browning Library.

3 William Johnson Fox (1786-1864; *DNB*), liberal Unitarian journalist and minister of South Place Chapel, Finsbury. At the age of twelve or thirteen RB sent a volume of unpublished poems, entitled *Incondita*, to Miss Eliza Flower, who showed them to Fox, and she in turn conveyed to RB the praise bestowed upon them by Fox (*LRB*, p. 20). (RB subsequently destroyed most of the poems, but the few scraps that have survived are printed in *New Poems by Robert and Elizabeth Barrett Browning*, ed. F. G. Kenyon [1914].) Fox's generous review of *Pauline* appeared in the *Monthly Repository*, NS 7 (April 1833), 252-62. RB contributed five poems to the *Monthly Repository* and six to *Hood's Magazine*; for a complete list, see BNP, p. 24.

4 A reprint of RB's *Essay on Shelley*, as it is now usually called, was the first publication of the Browning Society in 1881 (*BSP*, I, 1-19). The essay was an introduction to a collection of Shelley letters published by Moxon in 1852 and subsequently withdrawn when the letters were found to be forgeries. FJF's "Foretalk" to the *Essay*, dated 2 Aug. 1881, explained that "the interest lay in the fact, that Browning's 'utterances' here are *his*, and not those of anyone of the 'so many imaginary persons' behind whom he insists on so often hiding himself, and whose necks I, for one, should continually like to wring, whose bodies I would fain kick out of the way, in order to get face to face with the poet himself, and hear his own voice speaking his own thoughts, man to man, soul to soul. Straight speaking, straight hitting suit me best." (*BSP*, I, 3). FJF on other occasions expressed dislike of RB's dramatic method.

RB TO FJF, 29 AUGUST 1881

Hôtel Virard, St. Pierre de Chartreuse, Isère, France.
Aug. 29, '81.

My dear Furnivall,

I received your letter, and at the same time the proof-sheets of your *Bibliography*, in a parcel from home yesterday.[1] What am I to say? This hamlet is close by, and a dependence on, the famous convent founded by St. Bruno as a necessary effect of his hearing a dead man declare "Justo judicio Dei condemnatus sum."[2] Ought I not to set up a pillar, at least, on finding myself—quite as startlingly—called noteworthy; and brought into prominence after this fashion by the—never mind how partial—judgment of an extraordinarily generous friend? I can only repeat—you startle me. Other feelings that are inevitable must continue unexpressed, though they are not easily kept down.

Were I in town, I could perhaps supplement your list of notices of the criticisms on my works by an instance or two you might like to preserve. I can only remember the good natured ones however.

The pencil notes of John Mill which he meant to construct an article upon—till he found he had been forestalled by a flippant line in the Review which he was accustomed at that time to write for—are at the end of the copy of *Pauline* in Forster's Library at Kensington.[3] He had never seen me. *Paracelsus* was *first* reviewed by Forster, in the *Examiner*. He also wrote a paper on it in the *New Monthly Magazine*—in the same month that another by J. Heraud appeared in *Fraser*.[4] The most curious notice I ever had was from Cardinal Wiseman on *Blougram*—i.e. himself. It was in the *Rambler*, a Catholic Journal of those days, and certified to be his by Father Prout, who said nobody else would have dared put it in.[5] My friend Milsand reviewed me in the *Revue des deux Mondes*, and in another French review.[6] But I have a huge shelf-full of reviews of my Father's collecting, which probably contain articles more or less to the point. Many I never read even at the time, and not one since. I only mention the few that rise in my mind as I read your list to show that when you please to say "you shall be grateful" for such an exercise of memory, I am not so ungrateful as to keep silence altogether. Well, you have not had much experience of any "steel"-like quality that may be in me, but let me say once for all, that whenever you have occasion to test it, you are entitled to look for "the ice brook's temper."[7]

Ever yours truly, / Robert Browning.

Come, I ought to say something "sine ullâ solemnitate."[8] Well bestowed as you are in Wales, you would be struck at the extraordinary picturesqueness and beauty of this wild little clump of cottages on a mountain amid loftier mountains. The "Hotel" is the roughest inn, and its arrangements the most primitive, I have yet chanced upon—but my sister bears them bravely. We stay two or three weeks longer, weather permitting, then go to Venice. Early in November you must come and see us, and we will compare our gains in travel. My sister desires me to give my best regards to you and to Mrs. Furnivall, my own accompanying them.

Thank you for the pleasant note which I return: "here are in all three worthy voices gained."[9]

Text: *LRB*, pp. 194-95. Published: *LVC*, 1st Ser., I, 66-70.
1 Beginning with RB's letter of 26 July 1881, most of his correspondence with FJF

during the remainer of this year deals with particulars in FJF's *A Bibliography of Robert Browning, from 1833 to 1881* (*BSP*, I, 21-174), the main portion of which was begun in July and published by the Browning Society shortly before its inaugural meeting on 28 Oct. 1881. RB was awed and faintly alarmed by this prodigious piece of work by FJF: on 6 Sept. he wrote Mrs. FitzGerald that "I have on the table here the proofs of a 'Bibliography of R.B.' 'published for the B. Society by Trübner & Co'—containing the most extraordinary list of every one of my works, from the biggest to the least,—with the minutest description of the same—mentioning every variation in any edition of every line and word that has been altered at any time,— illustrations from letters &c—and yet, at page 32 (as far as the proofs go) only getting to 'Dramatis Personae' published in 1864. I should have thought it would have taken months to get all the work done: whether it be worth doing at all, is another matter. It makes me feel as I look at the thing, as if I were dead and *begun* with, after half a century." (*LL*, pp. 124-25.) For many years FJF intended to publish a fully revised edition of the bibliography, but it was never completed; FJF's interleaved copy, with notes for the revision, is in the Humanities Research Center, the University of Texas.

2   St. Bruno (*c.* 1032-1101), founder of the Carthusian Order, established a monastery (described in Matthew Arnold's poem "Stanzas from the Grande Chartreuse") at Chartreuse in 1084. (RB's account of a visit to the monastery appears in *NL*, p. 267.) The dead man had declared, "I am condemned by the just judgment of God."

3   John Stuart Mill (1806-73; *DNB*) was given a copy of RB's *Pauline* in 1833 by W. J. Fox and submitted a review to the editor of the *Examiner*, who declined it because of its excessive length. Mill then intended to rewrite the review for *Tait's Edinburgh Magazine*, but the August number of *Tait's* alluded briefly to *Pauline* as "a piece of pure bewilderment"; hence Mill abandoned the review and returned his annotated copy of *Pauline* to Fox. Fox gave the book to RB, who, after adding some marginalia of his own, presented it as a gift to his friend John Forster (1812-76; *DNB*), the historian and biographer. (However, this unique copy of *Pauline* was not to be found in the Victoria and Albert Museum; see RB to FJF, 15 Sept. 1881, n. 3.) DeVane (pp. 11, 47) has argued that RB's entire poetic career was altered by the episode, but recently his thesis has been challenged by some scholars. (See William S. Peterson and Fred L. Standley, "The J. S. Mill Marginalia in Robert Browning's *Pauline*: A History and Transcription," *Papers of the Bibliographical Society of America*, 66 [1972], 135-70.)

4   [John Forster], review of *Paracelsus*, *Examiner*, 6 Sept. 1835, pp. 563-65; [Forster], "Evidences of a New Genius for Dramatic Poetry," *New Monthly Magazine and Literary Journal*, 46 (March 1836), 289-308; [John A. Heraud], review of *Paracelsus*, *Fraser's Magazine*, 13 (March 1836), 362-74.

5   RB's "Bishop Blougram's Apology" was widely assumed to be a satirical portrait of Nicholas Wiseman (1802-65; *DNB*) Roman Catholic Archbishop of Westminster. (For a recent discussion of Wiseman's presence in the poem, see Julia Markus, "Bishop Blougram and the Literary Men," *Victorian Studies*, 21 [1978], 171-95.) However, the anonymous review of *Men and Women*—in the *Rambler*, 5 (January 1856), 54-71 —was not by Wiseman but by Richard Simpson (1820-76; *DNB*), Roman Catholic writer and Shakespearean scholar. (Esther R. Houghton, "Reviewer of Browning's *Men and Women* in *The Rambler* Identified," *Victorian Newsletter*, No. 33 [1968], p. 46.) The Rev. Francis S. Mahoney (1804-66; *DNB*), a humorist who wrote under the pseudonym of "Father Prout," was an old friend of the Brownings.

6   Joseph Milsand (1817-86), French critic, reviewed RB's *Poems* (1849) and *Christmas-Eve and Easter-Day* in *Revue des Deux Mondes*, NS 11 (15 Aug. 1851), 661-89; and *Men and Women* in *Revue Contemporaine et Athenaeum Français*, 27 (15 Sept. 1856), 511-46. The two men met in Paris in January 1852 and subsequently often visited each other. (See Th. Bentzon [Mme Blanc], "A French Friend of Browning— Joseph Milsand," *Scribner's Magazine*, 20 [July 1896], 108-20.)

7   Shakespeare, *Othello*, V.ii.253.
8   "Without any solemnity."
9   "There's in all two worthy voices begged" (Shakespeare, *Coriolanus*, II.iii.86).

RB TO FJF, 15 SEPTEMBER 1881

Hôtel Virard, St. Pierre de Chartreuse, Isère, F. /
Sept. 15. '81.

My dear Furnivall,

Many thanks for your kind & pleasant letter: I am sure I ought to be "helpful" to you in such little matters when it is in my power. First, to its questions the replies are—*Karsish* is the proper word, referring as it does to him of the "Epistle"—*Karshook* (*Heb:* a Thistle) just belongs to the snarling verses I remember to have written but forget for whom: The other was the only one of the "Fifty."[1] I wrote the Venice stanza to illustrate Maclise's picture, —for which he was anxious to get some such line or two: I had not seen it, but, from Forster's description, gave it to him, in his room, *impromptu.* Maclise (a friend of my own) painted the whole thing —not the sky merely: when I did see it, I thought the Serenader too jolly somewhat for the notion I got from Forster—and I took up the subject in my own way.[2] Metre: "Hervé Riel" goes mainly in anapests & tribrachs—I fancy—Ŏn thĕ sēa / ănd ăt thĕ / Hōgŭe / Fīftĕen Hūnd/rĕd nĭnetў / twō / Dĭd thĕ Ēng/lĭsh fĭght thĕ / Frēnch / Wōĕ tŏ Frānce/. But the "Toccata" is purely Trochaic: Ō Gāl/ūppĭ / Bāldăss/ārĭ, / thīs ĭs / vērў / sād tŏ / fīnd!/. What you tell me about the copy of "Pauline," interests me much: if "the entry was struck out of the catalogue," I suppose that means—the request I made to the Executor, Mr Chitty, that the book might be returned to me,—which he promised to attend to, but of which I heard no more,—was really complied with *so far*—I shall try if I can recover the copy: the odd thing is—that it was prefaced by some such notice as that given in the "Bibliography" page 16. I may have possibly repeated it for some friend.[3] The "poems on a leaf in the Museum" are merely autographic copies of printed pieces.[4] Looking hastily through the new "Proofs"—I can only see, to observe upon —Page 18. There might be a reference to Lady Martin's account of the circumstances under which the "Blot in the Scutcheon" was produced by Macready—the last of her papers in Blackwood on Shakspearian Characters, during the current year.[5] 19. *23* years ago: I wrote in this and other instances with no copy at hand.[6] 21. Alfred Domett, besides being the Author of the work mentioned, was Prime Minister in New Zealand.[7] 28. "Shelley Letters." When I get home and have a copy before me, I will give you in a few words the true account of the whole transaction—and *perhaps* some remarks on the Essay by a very distinguished personage indeed.[8] (*Don't speak of this*, however.) Also, if on consideration I properly am able, I will give a list of the true names of men, things, and places in "Red Cotton Night-Cap Country."[9]—It is only just that I should do the little I can to show I am sensible of the favours done me—sensible I *am*.

And now, my dear Furnivall, you may hear of me again from Venice: this rough delightful country we leave on the 18th—the day when, by my calculation, this letter reaches you. Remember the address: "Albergo dell' Universo, Venezia": for about a month. I hope you have had weather like ours: to-day ends our five-weeks' stay—during which only one rainy day confined us to the house. All congratulations to Mrs. Furnivall on her climbing feat.[10] What am I to say to Miss Lewis?[11] I hope to do more toward justifying all this sympathy before I leave off.

My sister's cordial greetings to you & Mrs Furnivall.

Ever truly yours Robert Browning.

MS: BL. Envelope: HEH. Address: *Angleterre.* / F. J. Furnivall, Esq. / Castell Farm, / Beddgelert, / N. Wales. Postmarks: ST LAURENT DU PONT ISÈRE 2N 16 SEPT 81; CARNARVON A SP 18 81. Note in FJF's hand on envelope: "R. Browning's / writing. / F.J.F." Published: *LRB*, pp. 196-97; *LVC*, 1st Ser., I, 71-75.

1 In "One Word More," the concluding poem of *Men and Women* (1855), RB listed "Karshook" among his characters, an error for "Karshish." (RB had written a poem entitled "Ben Karshook's Wisdom" in 1854.) FJF pointed out the mistake to RB and wrote a letter to the *Academy* about it (20 [1 Oct. 1881], 260).

2 Late in 1841 RB wrote to Fanny Haworth, "I chanced to call on Forster the other day—and he pressed me into committing verse on the instant, not the minute, in [Daniel] Maclise's [1806-70; *DNB*] behalf—who had wrought a divine Venetian work, it seems, for the British Institution—Forster described it well—but I could do nothing better than this wooden ware . . ." (*LRB*, p. 7). RB had visited Venice in June 1834. Maclise's "The Serenade" (now in the Armstrong Browning Library) appeared in the exhibition of the British Institution for Promoting the Fine Arts in the United Kingdom which opened on 5 Feb. 1842. The *Art-Union* (4 [1 Apr. 1842], 76), in its report on the exhibition, cited RB's lines in the catalogue—later expanded and entitled "In a Gondola"—and offered this observation: "We have quoted the

passage pictured, less to justify the somewhat fantastic air and character of the cavalier, than as an example of exceedingly rich and graceful versification from the pen
of a poet, kindred to Maclise in imagination and mind.''

3 FJF, *Bibliography*:

Mr. R. H. Shepherd [bibliographer, 1842-95; *DNB*] writes:—'On the fly-leaf
of a copy of the original edition of *Pauline*, formerly in my possession, was the
following note in the author's handwriting:—

"*Pauline*—written in pursuance of a foolish plan I forget, or have no wish to
remember; involving the assumption of several distinct characters: the world was
never to guess that such an opera, such a comedy, such a speech proceeded from
the same notable person. Mr. V. A. (see page second) was Poet of the party, and
predestined to cut no inconsiderable figure. 'Only this crab' (I find set down in
my copy) 'remains of the shapely Tree of Life in my fools' Paradise.'

"(I cannot muster resolution to deal with the printers' blunders after the
American fashion, and bid people 'for "jocularity" read "synthesis" ' to the end
of the chapter.)

"Dec. 14, 1838." '

(*BSP*, I, 38.)

This, as RB says, is similar to the note written by the poet in the copy of *Pauline*
given to Forster. FJF learned that the latter book (see RB to FJF, 29 Aug. 1881,
n. 3) was entered in Forster's catalogue of his own library but that the title had been
struck through before the collection reached the Victoria and Albert. In 1900 the son
of Sir Joseph W. Chitty (1828-99; *DNB*), one of Forster's three executors, found the
annotated *Pauline* among his father's effects and offered it to the officials of the V &
A, who placed it in the Forster Collection.

4 T. J. Wise's note: "Some of Mr. Browning's poems, in their author's handwriting, preserved in the British Museum" (*LVC*, 1st Ser., I, 73). It seems more likely, however,
that this is a reference to "a few MS. verses on a single leaf" in the Forster Library,
Victoria and Albert Museum, mentioned in FJF's letter to the *Academy*, 20 (1 Oct.
1881), 260.

5 Helena Faucit, afterwards Lady Martin (1817-98; *DNB*), had known RB for many
years and had played the roles of Lady Carlisle in *Strafford* (1837), Mildred in *A Blot
in the 'Scutcheon* (1843), and Colombe in *Colombe's Birthday* (1853). FJF's *Bibliography* (*BSP*, I, 46) quotes a passage about the *Blot* performance from her article "On
Some of Shakespeare's Female Characters: By One Who Has Personated Them. III.—
Desdemona," *Blackwood's Magazine*, 129 (March 1881), 324-45 (reprinted in her
book *On Some of Shakespeare's Female Characters* [1885]).

6 I have been unable to identify this reference in FJF's *Bibliography*.

7 Alfred Domett (1811-87; *DNB*), an intimate friend of RB's youth who is described in
"Waring," was Prime Minister of New Zealand, 1862-63, and the author of two volumes of poetry—*Ranolf and Amohia, a South Sea Day Dream* (1872) and *Flotsam
and Jetsam* (1877)—the former of which contains a passage alluding to RB (quoted in
BSP, I, 102, 164).

8 RB evidently did not keep this promise, since FJF's introduction to the Browning
Society's reprint of the *Essay on Shelley* is vague and brief (*BSP*, I, 4). Hood suggests
that the "very distinguished personage" was Thomas Carlyle, who praised the essay
lavishly in a letter to RB dated 8 Mar. 1853 (printed in *LRB*, pp. 367-68).

9 FJF, *Bibliography*: "This poem [*Red Cotton Night-Cap Country*] is the story of
Mellerio, the Paris Jeweller, and was studied at the place of his ending, St. Aubyn
in Normandy, from the law-papers uzed in the suit concerning his will. It was put
in type with all the true names of persons and things; but, on a proof being submitted by Browning to his friend the present Chief Justice, [John D.] Lord Coleridge, then Attorney-General, the latter thought that an action for libel might lie
for what was said in the poem, however unlikely it was that such procedure would

be taken. Thereupon fictitious names were substituted for the real ones in every case. . . . I believe that Browning means to restore the true names in his next edition of the poem." (*BSP*, I, 66; cf. *LRB*, p. 309.) The actual names were never restored in the poem, but RB allowed Mrs. Orr to print them in her *Handbook*. See also RB to FJF, 9 Dec. 1882.

10 Memorandum by FJF: "up Snowdon & back, from & to Castell Farm, where we were lodging, some 2 miles south" (BL Ashley B.2567).

11 Miss Mary A. Lewis (d. 1905), daughter of Sir George Cornewall Lewis (1806-63; *DNB*), wrote edifying fiction for the Christian Knowledge Society. In his "Forewords" to the *Bibliography*, FJF quoted an anonymous reader of RB's poetry (identified in FJF's interleaved copy [Texas] as Miss Lewis) as saying that "I bow down before Mr. Browning because I know that he has made me a better woman than I used to be" (*BSP*, I, 26). On 27 Jan. 1882 she delivered a paper to the Browning Society praising the poet's "strong, hopeful philosophy of life" and concluding with this observation: "The best wish we can offer to the remaining years of the 19th century is that future historians may be able to say that whereas Clough, Matthew Arnold, and Carlyle represented the philosophical and religious thought of its central period, Browning became the representative man of its close" (*BSP*, I, 11*-14*; the paper is printed in its entirety in *Macmillan's Magazine*, 46 [July 1882], 205-14). RB, writing to Mrs. FitzGerald in July 1882, described Miss Lewis' paper as being among the few that were "the kindest notices I have had, or at all events those that have given me most pleasure" (*LL*, p. 144).

RB TO FJF, 1 OCTOBER 1881

Albergo dell' Universo, Venezia, Italia. Oct. 1, '81.

My dear Furnivall,

Just as I was leaving St. Pierre, in a wild mountain pass, the postman recognized me, and gave me your letter—and here I found another—"proofs" down to page 58—for all of which my best thanks.

Yes, the autograph was a mere quotation. The "W.M. the younger" was poor William Macready's eldest boy—dead, a few years ago. He had a talent for drawing, and asked me to give him some little thing to illustrate; so, I made a bit of a poem out of an old account of the death of the Pope's legate at the Council of Trent—which he made such clever drawings for, that I tried a more picturesque subject, the Piper. I still possess the half dozen of the designs he gave me. If you cared to have the Legend of the Legate I am sure you are welcome to it, when I can transcribe it from the page of the old book it remains upon, unprinted hitherto —which I mention to show how equally welcome you are to reprint the other "unconsidered trifles" you speak of.[1] I am bound to let any similar insignificances be of what use they may in giving a touch of, at least novelty, to a labour of love like yours.

A King lived long ago was given to the *M. Repository*.[2] You will find a strophe of a chorus out of Euripides in the book he gives name to, published lately by Mahaffy; I translated it at his desire.[3] Nothing else occurs to me at this moment. We are still in the disturbance of arrival here, and I must be brief: I shall not let your suggestions drop to the ground, depend upon it!

My sister repeats her kind regards, and all wishes that your Welsh excursion may have done good service to Mrs. Furnivall and yourself. We count on remaining here for a week or two. I did not know you had the glory of a "boy."[4] I congratulate you, and am

Ever truly yours, / Robert Browning.

Text: *LRB*, pp. 197-98. Published: *LVC*, 1st Ser., I, 76-78.

1 During the illness in May 1842 of young William C. Macready, Jr. (1832-71), afterwards of the Ceylon Civil Service, RB wrote two poems for him: "The Pied Piper of Hamelin" and "Crescentius" (the latter published in *Asolando* [1889] under the title "The Cardinal and the Dog"). Macready's seven pencil drawings to illustrate the poems (*Browning Collections*, Lot 252) are now in the Armstrong Browning Library. RB's literary source for both poems was Nathaniel Wanley's *Wonders of the Little World* (1678), presumably the "old book" into which he had written one of them. Despite RB's offer, FJF did not print the "Legend of the Legate" (i.e., "The Cardinal and the Dog") in *BSP*.

2 "A King lived long ago," *Monthly Repository*, NS 9 (November 1835), 707-08; reprinted (with alterations) in *Pippa Passes*, Part III.

3 RB contributed a translation of a lyric by Euripedes to John P. Mahaffy's *Euripedes* (1879), p. 116. Mahaffy (1839-1919; *DNB*), Professor of Ancient History at Trinity College, Dublin, promised a paper on "Browning's Transcripts and Translations from the Greek" for the Browning Society (*BSP*, I, xii), but it was never delivered.

4 Percy Furnivall (1868-1938; *WW*), FJF's only son, was, like his father, active in sports and later became a well-known surgeon (obituary, *Lancet*, 234 [14 May 1938], 1137).

RB TO FJF, 2 OCTOBER 1881

Albergo dell' Universo, Venezia. / Oct. 2. '81.

My dear Furnival,

Thanks for the letter that comes a few days after another which obliged me in the fashion you make me accustomed to. The lines about the wind certainly *are* somewhere in the "Repository":[1] I retained no copy of them, and when, many years afterward, I wanted to include them in "James Lee", I applied to Mrs Fox,— who copied and sent the poem—possessing as she did the series of magazines. I never contributed a line to the "Atlantic Monthly":

its publisher—and, perhaps, at that time, Editor—was the late James Fields who had bought proofs in advance, and chose to dispose of the poems you mention as he pleased, without reference to me.[2] I think the metre / ---- / - ~~~ / -- / - // is continued throught [sic] the savage-soliloquy.[3] As for Hegel—I am rejoiced if our wits should jump—but I never read a word of his—caring as little as you for elaborate metaphysics: I am greatly interested, however, in Mr Bury's letters. How the grain which one seems to scatter with small result comes up and bears fruit in unguessed places![4]

With respect to the "Personal notices from newspapers"[5]—I am not sorry they are so few—amusingly few, when I remember certain passages in my life which have been attended with far more important results—if *these* be at all noteworthy. I shall not "draw my pen" through any *fact*: and although it was not incumbent on me to furnish an atom of what is unknown,—nor have you, in your delicacy, required anything of the kind,—still you were quite justified in questioning me about what *was* known more or less imperfectly: and I should be a poor creature indeed if I pretended to play the indifferent to all your kindness and labour—spontaneous as were both. Of course, I cannot endorse one single word of the appreciation which it is my proper business to simply do my best to deserve: but whoever pleases is free to know that I value and—making the inevitable abatement—gratefully lay it to heart: so—enough of me!

I cannot engage to be in London before the very beginning of November: the unseasonably cold and stormy weather may somewhat shorten our stay in Venice, and I forego a visit to a friend, in the neighbourhood, which was to have followed it.[6] I will notify to you the time of our departure so as to hinder any communication from you "coming tardy off".[7] So, "in a little month,"—to go on Hamletizing,[8]—we may meet, I trust. Meantime, and ever, my dear Furnivall, believe me

Yours truly / Robert Browning.

Oh, I remember the juvenile son,—but, in head-muddle, I connected the gentleman in question with my own mature young man.[9] I write in so comfortless a condition,—my chin, at this moment, resting on the extravagantly high old table just to be reached and kept steady on both arms (not elbows) from the as absurdly low sofa whom [sic] the depths of which I rise,—that "all these things," as the Patriarch said, "are against me."[10] The other evening,—by way of contrast,—I wrote my name in an album on the desk left by Byron in the Mocenigo palace,—an honor done me by its young and charming Mocenigo mistress.[11] Byron wrote the last Canto of Childe Harold, Beppo, and other poems on what Ruggles' Ignoramus calls "descâ suâ"—a capital one of its kind.[12]

My sister sends her kindest regards—over my shoulder—to Mrs Furnivall and yourself.

I believe there is a very genuine regret on the part of the Italians for Garfield's loss, and as true a sympathy with his wife.[13] The papers were demonstrative on the subject.

MS: HEH.

1 The lines beginning "Still ailing, Wind? Wilt be appeased or no?" first appeared in the *Monthly Repository*, NS 10 (May 1836), 270-71, and were quoted ironically in Section VI of "James Lee's Wife."

2 In return for £100, RB supplied to James T. Fields (1817-81; *DAB*), editor of the *Atlantic Monthly* (1861-71), advance proofs of *Dramatis Personae* (1846) and permission to print several of the poems in his magazine (James C. Austin, *Fields of 'The Atlantic Monthly': Letters to an Editor 1861-1870* [San Marino, Calif., 1953], p. 401). "Gold Hair" was printed in the May 1864 issue of the *Atlantic*; "Prospice" and Section VI of "James Lee's Wife" appeared in the June issue.

3 The "savage-soliloquy" is the Epilogue to *Fifine at the Fair* (beginning "Savage I was sitting in my house, late, lone").

4 John B. Bury (1861-1927; *DNB*), in 1881 a student at Trinity College, Dublin, and afterwards a well-known classical historian, was at this time preparing a paper on "Browning's Philosophy"—read to the Browning Society on 6 May 1882 (*BSP*, I, 259-77)—which compared RB's ideas with those of G. W. F. Hegel (1770-1831), the German philosopher. RB examined a proof of the paper (see RB to FJF, 25 Apr. 1882), which was one of Bury's earliest literary efforts, and wrote the author that his name was "one of whom I have heard but lately, but henceforth am little likely to forget" (Norman H. Baynes, *A Bibliography of the Writings of J. B. Bury* [Cambridge, England, 1929], p. 47). Bury was also the Honorary Secretary of the Trinity College Browning Society (*BSP*, I, vii), delivered a second paper to the London society on *Aristophanes' Apology*, 29 Jan. 1886 (*BSP*, II, 79-86), and was a member of its Committee from 1882 to 1887. Of the *Aristophanes* paper FJF wrote: "Bury's Paper slight, tho good" (FJF to "My dear C." [James Dykes Campbell?], 16 Jan. 1886 [Folger Y.c.994 (162)]).

5 Appendix V of FJF's *Bibliography* was entitled "Personal Notices."

6 The friend was John Ball (1818-89; *DNB*), scientist and politician, who had a villa near Bassano (*LL*, p. 120). RB arrived back in London on 4 Nov.

7 Shakespeare, *Hamlet*, III.ii.28.

8 *Hamlet*, I.ii.147.

9 Robert ("Pen") Wiedeman Barrett Browning (1849-1912), RB's only child, was the object of the poet's constant concern during his later years. Pen unsuccessfully attempted to enroll at Balliol College, Oxford, matriculated instead at Christ Church, and finally abandoned academic life in 1871. During the 1870s he became interested in painting and sculpturing, but after his father's death in 1889 Pen led an eccentric,

withdrawn existence in Asolo, the scene of *Pippa Passes*. (Maisie Ward, *The Tragi-Comedy of Pen Browning* [New York, 1972] ; Getrude Reese, "Robert Browning and his Son," *Publications of the Modern Language Association*, 61 [1946], 784-803.)

10 "And Jacob their father said unto them, . . . all these things are against me" (*Genesis* 42:36).

11 The Mocenigo Palace (now known as the Palazzo Robilant) is actually four contiguous Venetian palaces, one of which was leased by Byron for three years in 1818. The owner in 1881 was the Countess Mocenigo, whom RB described as "young, pretty and of the prettiest manners" (*LL*, p. 38).

12 In *Ignorāmus*, a farcical Latin play by George Ruggle (1575-1622; *DNB*) performed before James I in 1614, there is a comic dialogue involving the word *desk* (IV.vii). The Latin equivalent is *mensa scriptoria* rather than *dêsca*, which is a characteristic transliteration by Ignorāmus.

13 James A. Garfield (1831-81; *DAB*), twentieth President of the United States, died on 19 Sept. 1881, having been shot by an assassin on 2 July.

RB TO FJF, 3 OCTOBER 1881

Albergo dell' Universo, Venezia. Oct. 3, '81.

Ah, *no*—my dear Furnivall! Your proposal, kind and ingenious as it is, would give the notion of sending out a "sample," as is the wont of dealers in stuffs and Printed cottons. Your agency already does all that fair human endeavour can do: better be content with *that*.

I wrote two days ago. The notion of such a selection as you describe is well worth considering, and consideration it shall have when Smith and I can talk it over on my return.[1]

Ever truly yours, / Robert Browning.

Text: *LRB*, p. 198. Published: *LVC*, 1st Ser., I, 79.

1 During the summer of 1881 FJF had been once again agitating for an inexpensive selection of RB's poems. He evidently approached George Smith directly, for on 8 July RB wrote to Smith (Murray): "I return the unwise letters of Furnivall. He has written to me—engages to 'never write to you again, nor allude to the subject in his [Browning Society] prospectus'—whatever that may mean. I can only suppose that the whole thing is a quite mistaken way of showing his satisfaction at my refusing to side with his enemies the other day. So, pray overlook what, under the circumstances, you might well be angry about."

RB TO FJF, 8 OCTOBER 1881

Albergo dell' Universo, Venezia, / Oct. 8. '81.

My dear Furnivall,

You will have received ere this the letter I dispatched in answer to yours concerning "Ben Ezra"—(depend on it, you are not likely to put a question which I leave altogether unreplied to). I wish I saw any way to permit you to go your own in that matter—but I do not, frankly,—I must not be accessory to any "hawking my wares"—much as I am bound to you for thinking that their display would so advantage their author. Your benevolence is doing enough—if not too much—for me already—so, you will "spare my chameleon blushes"[1] on that point, I know.

The lines were simply styled "Lines" in the Repository and were printed very soon after the pieces which you have ascertained to be there,—within a couple of years, probably. Fox handed over the Editorship to others—for whom I did nothing.[2]

Oh, the un-Venetian cruelly cold and rainy weather we are underdergoing! I look forward to "Beef and a Sea-coal fire"[3] with a complacency I never felt before: and these I trust to have the enjoyment of at the end—but very end—of the month. I am omitting to say that the proof you last sent came safely: I see nothing to "strike out"—as I told you beforehand: of course you questioned me about a few facts, and equally of course I did not hold my tongue.

My sister's best regards to you and Mrs Furnivall go with those of

Yours truly ever / Robert Browning.

I received yesterday a mad letter from an American lady desiring me to propose that the Sh. Society furnish her with funds that she may promulgate in England her discovery that the Plays were written by Bacon—doubly mad, inasmuch as she evidently thinks this a sprout of her own brain,—ancient madness as it has got to be. Even a month ago, I was entreated by "Edward J. Collings", of Bolton, to favor a Club he is connected with by giving my views of the "attempt to prove that all our knowledge of Shakespeare tends to show that he was a most unlikely man to write such plays,—while all our knowledge of Bacon tends to show that he was just *the* man who could and would write them". Textually thus: "He had been informed I had treated of this question."[4]

MS: HEH. Address: *Inghilterra.* / Frederick J. Furnivall, Esq. / 3. St. George's Square, / Primrose Hill, / London, / N.W. Postmarks: VENEZIA 8 10-81 5S; LONDON NW XX OC 10 81. Note in FJF's hand on envelope: " 'Lines' in / Fox's / Journal."
1 "Pardon my Cameleon blushes," says Mrs. Malaprop in Richard Brinsley Sheridan's

The Rivals (1775), V.iii. The word *Cameleon*, however, appears only in the earliest extant version of the play, the Larpent MS, which was not published until this century (*The Rivals . . . edited from the Larpent MS.* by Richard L. Purdy [Oxford, 1935]); and since the MS was in private hands throughout the nineteenth century, it it not clear how RB could have been familiar with this variant reading. Cf. RB to FJF, 11 Nov. 1884, n. 2.

2 Another reference to "Still ailing, Wind? Wilt be appeased or no?"; see RB to FJF, 2 Oct. 1881, n. 1. W. J. Fox was editor of the *Monthly Repository* from August 1828 until June 1836. His successor was Richard H. Horne (1803-84; *DNB*), once a correspondent of EBB.

3 Not identified.

4 RB's curt reply to Collings, dated 24 Aug. 1881, is in the Armstrong Browning Library. (In a letter to William Hale White, 24 Aug. 1881 [Folger], RB identifies Collings as a "member of a Debating Society at Bolton.") In fact, RB was more interested in the Shakespeare-Bacon controversy than his letter to FJF suggests. In 1889 he spoke to Hiram Corson "of talks he had had with his friend, James Spedding, the editor and biographer of Lord Bacon, [and] the opinion which Spedding had expressed that the composition of the Plays was entirely beyond Bacon's powers, great as those powers were of their kind" (Corson, "A Few Reminiscences of Robert Browning," *Cornell Era*, 40 [May 1908], 364-65). In June 1888 RB received a presentation copy of Sir Theodore Martin's pamphlet *Shakespeare or Bacon?* (Folger).

RB TO FJF, 11 OCTOBER 1881

Albergo dell' Universo, Venezia. Oct. 11, '81.

My Dear Furnivall,

Your last letter, of the 6th, seemed in the main to have been answered by anticipation the day before—so I waited till we could regain the proper pace, my foot after yours.

You will let the "sample"[1] alone, I know,—never mind how foolish I may be in my apprehensions, and I can go at once to the few *corrigenda* in the "proofs" which arrived this morning. Maclise's picture undoubtedly *was* in the Academy Exhibition, together with my verse in the Catalogue, and you have missed it for the funny reason that it was printed as *prose!*[2] I remember beseeching the secretary, Mr. Knight,[3] at the Academy dinner, to get the lines into good order again, but to no purpose: or—*wait!* I am confounding —it strikes me all at once—the verse I wrote for Leighton's work, when this accident befell, with the verse in question for Maclise's picture, which was exhibited in some more or less private adventure in the way of a Gallery—*what* Gallery might be found by referring to the periodical which Mr. S. C. Hall edited in those days, for there was a notice both of picture and verse therein.[4] The mist cleared off from my memory on the circumstance starting up vividly in it that Mr. Knight excused his oversight by observing that Leighton was so very poetical a painter that there was no knowing whether the same quality might not have got the better of his prose!

Next. How have I overlooked hitherto that my school was at Peckham—not Dulwich—that of the Rev. Thomas Ready.[5]

Last, about my being "strongly against Darwin, rejecting the truths of science and regretting its advance"—you only do as I should hope and expect in disbelieving *that*. It came, I suppose, of Hohenstiel-Schwangau's expressing the notion which was the popular one at the appearance of Darwin's book[6]—and you might as well charge Shakespeare with holding that there were men whose heads grew beneath their shoulders, because Othello told Desdemona that he had seen such.[7] In reality, all that seems *proved* in Darwin's scheme was a conception familiar to me from the beginning: see in *Paracelsus* the progressive development from senseless matter to organized, until man's appearance (*Part* v).[8] Also in *Cleon*, see the order of "life's mechanics,"[9]—and I daresay in many passages of my poetry: for how can one look at Nature as a whole and doubt that, wherever there is a gap, a "link" must be "missing"—through the limited power and opportunity of the looker? But go back and back, as you please, *at* the back, as Mr. Sludge is made to insist,[10] you find (*my* faith is constant) creative intelligence, acting as matter but not resulting from it. Once set the balls rolling, and ball may hit ball and send any number in any direction over the table; but I believe in the cue pushed by a hand. When one is taunted (as I notice is often fancied as an easy method with the un-Darwinized)—taunted with thinking successive acts of creation credible, metaphysics have been stopped short at, however physics may fare: time and space being purely conceptions of our own, wholly inapplicable to intelligence of another kind—with whom, as I made Luria say, there is an "everlasting moment of creation,"[11] if one at all,—past, present, and future, one and the same state. This consideration does not affect Darwinism proper in any degree. But I do not consider that his case as to the changes in organization, brought about by desire and will in the creature, is proved.[12] Tortoises never saw their own shells, top or bottom,

34

nor those of their females, and are diversely variegated all over, each species after its own pattern. And the insects; this one is coloured to escape notice, this other to attract it, a third to frighten the foe—all out of one brood of caterpillars hatched in one day. No—I am incredulous—and *you*, dear patron and friend, are abundantly tired; so, thus much shall serve, scribbled as it has come to pass.

Our weather is mending somewhat, but continues a month behind hand, and very little characteristic of Venice. I walk, even in wind and rain, for a couple of hours on Lido, and enjoy the break of sea on the strip of sand as much as Shelley did in those days.[13] Good bye; all good wishes to you and yours, from

Yours truly ever, / Robert Browning.

Text: *LRB*, pp. 198-200. Published: *LVC*, 1st Ser., I, 80-85.

1 See RB to FJF, 3 Oct. 1881.

2 FJF, *Bibliography*:

'I have searched the Royal Academy Catalogues from 1835 to 1847 in vain, either for the title of the picture or the verses.'—R.[ichard] H. S.[hepherd].

[FJF then adds:] The picture...is not mentioned in [William J.] O'Driscoll's *Memoir of Daniel Maclise, R.A.*, 1871, and cannot have been in the Academy.

(*BSP*, I, 24)

The reason Shepherd and FJF were unable to locate the reference is that Maclise's painting was exhibited at the British Institution rather than the Royal Academy (see RB to FJF, 15 Sept. 1881).

3 John P. Knight (1803-81; *DNB*), portrait-painter, Secretary of the Royal Academy, 1848-73.

4 On Maclise's painting, see RB to FJF, 15 Sept. 1881, n. 2, where a passage from the article by Samuel C. Hall (1800-89; *DNB*), editor of the *Art-Union* (afterwards the *Art Journal*), is also quoted.

5 Before he entered, at 8 or 9, the small school operated by the Rev. Thomas Ready (d. 1886), at 77 Queen's Road, Peckham, RB was given instruction by Ready's two sisters. RB remained at the school until the age of 14. Ready, author of *Thoughts on the Divine Permission of Moral Evil* (1845) and various edifying tales, became Vicar of Mountnessing, Essex, in 1841 (obituary, *Gentleman's Magazine*, 221 [November 1886], 703).

6 See *Prince Hohenstiel-Schwangau*, l. 986. After receiving RB's letter, FJF inserted the following note in *BSP* (I, 198): "The sneer at 'modern Science' is not Browning's own, of course, but just the popular chaff of the day put into Louis Napoleon's mouth.—F." For discussions of evolutionary ideas in RB's poetry, see Georg Roppen, *Evolution and Poetic Belief* (Oslo, 1956), Chap. 2, and William Harold, "Robert Browning and Evolution," *Wisconsin Studies in Literature*, No. 4 (1967), pp. 56-65.

7 Shakespeare, *Othello*, I.iii.43-44.

8 *Paracelsus*, V.638-711. The passage expresses a vaguely Tennysonian faith in the movement upward of all created beings, including man, on an evolutionary path that leads ultimately to God.

9 "Cleon," l. 202.

10 "Mr. Sludge, 'The Medium,' " ll. 814-16.

11 *Luria*, V.233, slightly misquoted.

12 RB evidently did not understand Darwin's principle of natural selection, for Darwin, unlike Lamarck (1744-1829), did not assert that genetic change was "brought about by desire or will in the creature."
13 Shelley visited Venice during September and October 1818.

RB TO FJF, 21 OCTOBER 1881

Albergo dell' Universo, Venezia. Oct. 21, '81.
My dear Furnivall,

You very well know I can say nothing about this extraordinary halo of rainbow-hues with which your wonder-working hand has suddenly surrounded my dark orb. As with the performances of the mosaicists I see at work here—all sorts of shining stones, greater and smaller, which hardly took the eye by their single selves— suddenly coalesce and make a brilliant show when put ingeniously together—as my dazzled eyes acknowledge, pray believe! I will correct any mistake as to fact I may observe on going hastily through the proofs. Two thirds of the reviews and other notices I never saw till now, while many that stay in my memory are absent here, by the way.

Page 109: I am astounded at the notion, as to how it could possibly arise, that there was ever the slightest "falling out" between Carlyle and myself. Nothing of the kind ever happened during our long acquaintance.[1]

Page 110: *Mrs.* Ritchie: her husband was not present. This minute incident took place not at *Freshwater*, where (for all Tennyson's repeated invitations of the kindest sort) I never yet have been, but at Twickenham, on the day of the christening of Hallam, whom his father trusted me with, straight out of the baby's bed.[2]

I do not stop for misprints. Page 92: "Shirley" is not Charles Lever, but a living writer[, whose] name escapes me at the moment: he sent me his book with a letter some time ago.[3] Page 109: Miss Blagden: she was devoted to, but never in any way "nursed the poetess in her final illness."[4] Page 106: All about the vernacular of the epitaph on *Pietro di Albano* [*sic*] is pure fun of Father Prout's.[5] I told him of the thing at Florence, and did it *impromptu* into this doggerel:—

Studying my cyphers with the compass,

36

I gather I soon shall be below ground,
Because of my lore men make great rumpus,
And war on myself makes each dull rogue round.

He must have thought it worth remembering. In the text—*con* should be *col,*—sotterra, not *sotto terra*, sap*er*, for *ir*, gran, *without d*, m' hanno, for *nei h*.

And now, the stay here is hardly likely to last much longer. The weather is again abominable and *un-Venetian*. I suppose we may count on being back in London by the end of the first week in November—when we will talk by the fireside, I hope. Meanwhile and always, with truest regards to Mrs Furnivall and yourself from us two stay-aways, believe me, ever gratefully yours,

Robert Browning.

The pin-pointed iron pen, the table whereon my chin rests, and the seat from the depth of which I strain upwards must account for and excuse the scrawly scribble. The paper seems damp too.

Text: *LRB*, pp. 200-01. Published: *LVC*, 1st Ser., I, 86-89.

1 FJF, *Bibliography*: "1878. 'Belfast News-Letter,' Aug. 20, from the 'Pictorial World.' 'Mr. Carlyle, the philosopher, and Mr. Browning, the poet, are said to be once more friends again, after their little falling-out of a year or two back.' (*BSP*, I, 112.) RB and Thomas Carlyle (1795-1881; *DNB*) had long enjoyed a warm friendship: in 1846 Carlyle declared that "he had more hopes of Robert Browning than of any other writer in England" (*Elizabeth Barrett Browning: Letters to Her Sister, 1846-1859*, ed. Leonard Huxley [1929], p. 9). The main source of tension in their relationship was Carlyle's view of the uselessness of poetry, but RB told William Allingham in 1881, "I never minded what Carlyle said of things outside his own little circle (drawing a circle in the air with his forefinger)—what was it to me what he thought of Poetry or Music?" (*William Allingham's Diary*, ed. H. Allingham and D. Radford [Carbondale, Ill., 1967], p. 310). For a detailed discussion of the relationship, see C. R. Sanders, "The Carlyle-Browning Correspondence and Relationship," *Bulletin of the John Rylands Library*, 57 (1974-75), 213-43, 430-62.

2 This paragraph deals with two distinct but similar occasions. On 5 Oct. 1852 RB served as a godfather at the christening of Hallam Tennyson, the poet's first son, in Twickenham. On 27 Jan. 1879 RB was again present as a sponsor, this time in Henry VII's Chapel, Westminster Abbey, for the christening of Tennyson's grandson, Alfred Stanley Browning Tennyson. Among those present were Anne Thackeray Ritchie (1837-1919; *DNB*), daughter of W. M. Thackeray and novelist in her own right, to whom RB dedicated *Red Cotton Night-Cap Country*.

3 FJF, *Bibliography*: "1865. 'A Campaigner at Home.' By Shirley [Charles Lever, the Irish Novelist?] London: Longmans, &c., 1865, pp. 274-283. 'Robert Browning,' a reprint of the article in 'Fraser's Magazine,' Feb. 1863." (*BSP*, I, 94; the bracketed phrase is FJF's.) "Shirley" was Sir John Skelton (1831-97; *DNB*), Scottish statesman and writer. The Brownings had known Lever (1806-72; *DNB*), in Italy.

4 FJF, *Bibliography*: "1873. 'Dublin Express,' Jan. 29. 'Miss Blagden. There has just died at Florence, a lady well known in the world of letters. . . . Miss Isa Blagden,

the authoress of "Agnes Tremorne" . . . was linked to Mr. *Browning* and his illustrious wife by the ties of closest friendship. She nursed the poetess in her final illness' " (*BSP*, I, 111.) Though Isabella Blagden (1817?-73) did not nurse EBB, she did pay a visit shortly before EBB's death, and afterwards she cared for RB and Pen while they recovered from the shock of the event (*DI*, pp. xxiv-xxv).

5 In a letter to EBB, 8 Feb. 1846, RB quotes a quatrain "said, I believe truly, to have been discovered in a well near Padua some fifty years ago" (*The Letters of Robert Browning and Elizabeth Barrett Barrett 1845-1846*, ed. Elvan Kintner [Cambridge, Mass., 1969], I, 444) and allegedly written by Pietro di Abano (1250-1320), physician and magician. RB's translation was published as a note appended to "Pietro of Abano," *Dramatic Idyls*, 2nd Ser. (1880), but a garbled version by Father Prout appeared earlier in *The Reliques of Father Prout* (1860), p. iv. (See *BSP*, I, 93, 114.)

RB TO FJF, 25 OCTOBER 1881

Venice, Oct. 25., '81.

My dear Furnivall,

This is just a word to apprise you that we leave, on Nov. 2., for London—where we hope to arrive at the end of the week. You must not let me lose a letter by directing it to this place after you get the present warning: for "lose" I should say—"find delay in receiving"—since such a letter would be sent home in the end: I wrote acknowledging your last. The weather is cold and we are mainly warmed by socialities which abound here: but there are the old friends we want to see again.[1] And, in the hope of soon seeing you among them, believe me ever

Yours truly / Robert Browning.

MS: HEH. Address: *Inghilterra*. / Frederick J. Furnivall, Esq. / 3 St. George's Square, / Primrose Hill, / London, / N.W. Postmarks: VENEZIA 25 10-81 3S; [L]ONDON NW MM OC 27 [81]. Note in FJF's hand on envelope: "leaving Venice."

1 Among the friends that RB saw in Venice were Daniel Sargent Curtis (1825-1908), an American painter, and the sons of W. W. Story (*LL*, pp. 127-29); on Story, see RB to FJF, 8 Dec. 1881, n. 4.

RB TO FJF, 12 NOVEMBER 1881

19, Warwick Crescent, / W.* / Nov. 12, '81.

My dear Furnivall,

I have been back some days, but found the inevitable accumulation of matters to be forthwith disposed of: the first pleasure-letter, so to speak, goes properly to you—though how is it to run

19. Warwick Crescent, W.
March 12. '79.

Dear Mr Furnivall,

If I could say much about the honor the Society proposes to do me, I should show the more plainly how little I deserved it = but I do feel — I think — as deeply as I ought how prodigious and exorbitant an honor it is. How can I refuse it? If I asked rather "How can I accept it?" — the objections would come too thickly. But I resolve only to say "It is even a greater piece of kindness than honor — and I cannot refuse the combination." Pray commend my reply to the Committee in such gracious words as you will conceive should be, but are not, at the disposal of
        Yours truly ever Robert Browning.

By courtesy of the Huntington Library

Browning's letter to Furnivall of 12 March 1879 (see p. 12).

By courtesy of the Ashmolean Museum, Oxford

In Max Beerbohm's famous drawing, "Mr. Robert Browning Taking Tea with the Browning Society," Frederick J. Furnivall is the bearded figure standing to the left of Browning (who is seated).

now that I am about it? Of your care, trouble, and the strange kindness of it all, I cannot speak, let me try my best. You will get little for your pains beside the consciousness of your own utterly disinterested generosity—indubitable, however you may exceed in your estimate of what I have been able to do.[1] I daresay it disconcerts my critics, in a series for many a year, that people are disposed to reconsider the old convenient verdict on my poetry—"unintelligible". Had they confined themselves to "Bad"—no absolute refutation would be possible—so long as the law "De gustibus"[2] is in force: but one may prove one's power of understanding the alleged nonsense, when "the whirligig of Time brings round his revenges".[3] I daresay also that you mind foolish laughter as little as I —or you *would*, with fifty years' experience. What have I next to speak about? Please insert in your list of subscribers the name of *Mrs Bronson*,[4] *Cà Alvise, Venice*: her subscription is in my hands together with enough for postage-stamps, if you will direct the "Bibliography" to the above address. Next,—the writer of the lines you send me, *is* known to me, by name at least.[5] I had a letter from her just before I left Venice, which I shall reply to presently. Nothing else occurs to me at the moment. Well,—I rather think Sunday morning is the "breathing-time of the" week with you: and every Sunday morning finds me at home. Will you find me too whenever a good spirit prompts you? I shall be happy to see you.

All regards to Mrs Furnivall from my Sister: she comes back with a bad cold unluckily. For myself, I hope you are as well as

Yours truly ever / Robert Browning.

MS: HEH. Address: Frederick J. Furnivall, Esq. / 3 St. George's Square, / Primrose Hill, / N.W. Postmarks: LONDON SW 5 NO 12 81; [LON]DON NW KO NO 12 81. Note in FJF's hand on envelope: "Bibliography."

1 RB is alluding to the generally hostile reaction in the press to the formation of the Browning Society and to its first meeting on 28 Oct. 1881.

2 "De Gustibus—" is the title of a poem in *Men and Women*. The Latin expression *De gustibus no est disputandum* means that there is no accounting for tastes.

3 "And thus the whirligig of time brings in his revenges" (Shakespeare, *Twelfth Night*, V.i.[396]).

4 Katherine Colman (DeKay) Bronson (1834-1901), a wealthy American who frequently played hostess to RB in her Venetian home (see "Browning in Venice"). She remained a member of the Browning Society until it disbanded in 1892. In a memorandum explaining a reference to her in RB's letter to FJF, 28 Sept. 1884, FJF wrote: "*Mrs. Bronson*—lives at Ca Alvisi, Venice. Browning used always to stay with her there; & if he had gone to her house instead of the beastly cold Rezzonico Palace that his daughter-in-law bought for his son, he might have been alive now." (BL Ashley B.2567.)

5   Elizabeth Dickinson West, daughter of the Dean of St. Patrick's, Dublin, and afterwards the second wife of Edward Dowden (1843-1913; *DNB*), first corresponded
with RB in 1871 when she sent him a copy of her published essay entitled "Browning
as a Preacher" (*LRB*, pp. 148-51; *IG*, pp. 54-55). The lines that FJF had sent RB were
Miss West's poem "To Robert Browning, on Re-reading Some Poems Long Unread"
(*Academy*, 20 [17 Dec. 1881], 455), of which RB wrote to her, "Your Sonnet is
dear to me, you must know" (*LRB*, p. 202).

FJF TO THE ACADEMY, *20 NOVEMBER 1881*

3 St. George's Square, N.W.: Nov. 20, 1881.
A most interesting fact has just happened to me in connexion
with this touching "twilight" poem ["Andrea del Sarto"]. Last
night came here a letter from an art member of our new Shakspere
Society, now in Florence, Mr. Ernest Radford,[1] saying:—

In the gallery of the Pitti Palace, numbered in the catalogue 118, and
painted by Andrea del Sarto, is a portrait of himself and his wife. I think no
one can look at this picture, with Browning's most beautiful poem in his
mind, without being deeply moved, and without feeling at the same time
sure that it was from this picture that the poet received the *impulse* to his
work. [Mr. Radford then describes the picture, and adds:—] Really, while
looking at it, the words of the poem come little by little into your mind, and
it seems as if you had read them in Andrea's face. And so now, when I read
the poem in my room, the picture is as vividly before me almost as when I am
in the gallery. So completely do the two seem complementary.

This morning I asked Mr. Browning whether the Pitti picture
had suggested his poem to him, and, to my delight, he said, yes, it
had. His friend, and his wife's friend, Mr. Kenyon,[2] had asked him
to buy him a copy of this picture. None could be got, and so Mr.
Browning wrote his poem of "Andrea del Sarto" from the picture,
and sent it to Mr. Kenyon instead of the copy of the Pitti original.
He added that no one could know what Andrea del Sarto was, as a
painter, till he had seen Lord Cowper's splendid collection at Panshanger.[3]

There is some worth, then, in art-criticism—in Mr. Radford's,
at least. And there is some worth and life in a poet's "Men and
Women"—in Mr. Browning's, at least.

F. J. Furnivall

40

Text: "Mr. Browning's 'Andrea del Sarto,' " *Academy*, 20 (26 Nov. 1881), 403. (The bracketed sentence is FJF's.)

1   Ernest Radford (1857-1919), barrister and poet, active in the Rhymers Club, and a Cambridge University extension lecturer. In 1885 he delivered the introductory address to the Scarborough Browning Society (*BSP*, II, 104*), and he read two papers to the London Browning Society, neither of them published: "The Browningite of the Future" (24 June 1887) and "Andrea del Sarto in Poetry and Fact" (25 Mar. 1892). At one time he intended to write a book entitled *Browning and Renaissance Romance* (Radford to FJF, 26 Nov. 1881 [HEH]). The del Sarto painting to which Radford refers in his letter was reproduced in both Parts I and II of the Browning Society's *Illustrations* series (1882-83); Part I contains a "Notice of the Artists and the Pictures" by Radford.

2   John Kenyon (1784-1856; *DNB*), EBB's cousin and benefactor. Julia Markus, in "Browning's 'Andrea' Letter at Wellesley College: A Correction of DeVane's *Handbook*," *Studies in Browning and His Circle*, 1 (Fall, 1973), 52-55, expresses doubts about the reliability of FJF's anecdote; she also prints the letter from Browning to Kenyon, dated 17 Mar. 1853, in which he speaks of the difficulties in having the Andrea painting copied.

3   Panshanger, Herts., was one of the country homes of Francis Thompson de Grey Cowper, 7th Earl Cowper (1834-1905; *DNB*), who owned five works attributed to del Sarto (H. Guiness, *Andrea del Sarto* [1901], p. 70). RB's *Balaustion's Adventure* was dedicated to Countess Cowper.

RB TO FJF, 8 DECEMBER 1881

19, Warwick Crescent, / W.* / Dec. 8. '81.

My dear Furnivall,

I assure you I shirked no labour but took down and piled up scores of old dead and gone reviews[1] as stale as the dust on them —"read" them I could not pretend to attempt, so did the sight of their very outsides sadden me—the word is not too strong. So much misconception at best—ignorance at middling, and malice at worst, in those old slaps on my face in order apparently to keep some fellow's critical hands warm! Yourself and those like you are the best suffumigators after this old smell: why keep a whiff of it to show how nastily I lived for a long while—sustained abundantly however by many a kindlier breathing from various quarters: only, the "sweet south" "creeps" or "steals" silently, while the unpleasantness is, as Donne phrases it, "a *loud* perfume".[2] No, let us bid goodbye to it all,—not to real conscientious criticism by any any [sic] means,—but to mere mopping and mowing and such monkey-tricks. So, I only send you three characteristic samples, French, Italian, and American: whether the writers praise or blame (which on my honour, I absolutely forget)—they at least have not taken up a book to get done with it on the easiest terms—laughing at what is worth no more serious notice. What a world of width between such people and Mr Kirkman—whose paper I return![3] The only *pain* I ever felt is the profitable one caused by such eulogy: I know *painfully* my own shortcoming and inadequate deserts. All I engage is, that in what of life may be left me, I will try harder than ever to deserve what my best efforts have hitherto failed to do. Enough! As to the one volume edition of E.B.B.'s works—and Story's preface to the same—I never knew of the existence of either.[4] Do not bring her in as if *parenthetically*—illustrative of me and my poems. These, I rejoice with all my heart to know and say, are in no need of any assistance: their popularity keeps ever far in advance of mine, as any Bookseller will inform you, and, as Beethoven said of his music "nothing but good can come to them."[5]

Will you understand and benignantly comply with all this? Yes, — and assure yourself I shall be more than ever

Gratefully as affectionately yours / Robert Browning.

MS: HL. Address: F. J. Furnivall, Esq. / 3. St. George's Square, / Primrose Hill. No Postmark or stamp. Note in FJF's hand on envelope: "my Bibliography & others' Reviews of / B." Published: *LRB*, pp. 205-06; *LVC*, 1st Ser., I, 90-92.

1   FJF originally intended to include in his *Bibliography* extracts from "the chief criticisms on Browning," but he later concluded that "the money wanted for these old criticisms may perhaps be better spent in printing new ones from our Members' point of view" (*BSP*, I, 25). Nevertheless, in both Appendix IV of the original *Bibliography* (*BSP*, I, 89-108) and a supplement dated 31 Dec. 1881 (*BSP*, I, 117-50) FJF quoted lengthy passages from earlier critics, often accompanied by his own sarcastic comments on their deficiencies.

2   John Donne, "Elegie [No. 10]: The Perfume," l. 41.

3   The Rev. Joshua Kirkman (1829-1904), Vicar of St. Stephen, Hampstead (obituary, *Times*, 4 July 1904, p. 13), delivered the "Introductory Address" at the first meeting of the Browning Society on 28 Oct. 1881 (*BSP*, I, 171-90), in which he praised RB as "our nearest to Shakespeare" (p. 172) and "the greatest Christian poet we have ever had" (p. 186).

4   FJF's *Bibliography* quotes a long passage "from W. W. Storey's [*sic*] 'touching and appreciative letter' [about EBB] in the 'Atlantic Monthly,' Sept. 1861, dated Florence, July 5, 1861, and partly reprinted in the very interesting Memoir of E.B.B., prefixt to the American edition of her *Poetical Works*, 2 vols. in 1, Jas. Miller, 779 Broadway, New York, p. 13-14 . . ." (*BSP*, I, 153). The *Atlantic Monthly* article was actually by Kate Field (1838-96; *DAB*), a young American studying music in Florence under the charge of Isa Blagden, and an intimate friend of the Brownings. William Wetmore Story (1819-95; *DAB*), American lawyer, sculptor, and poet, met the Brownings in Italy during the late 1840s and remained a close friend until RB's death in 1889.

5   The body of Beethoven anecdotes is so immense that I have been unable to identify the source of this one.

RB TO FJF, 16 DECEMBER 1881

19, Warwick Crescent, / W.* / Dec. 16. '81.

My dear Furnivall,

I return the Proofs: where do you find that the holiday of Hervé Riel was for "more than a day—his whole life-time?"[1] If it is to be found, I have strangely overlooked it. Yes, Landor was the Friend, and his praise was prompt, both private and public—(in his Satire on Satirists.)[2] "Eyebright"—i.e., "Euphrasia," an early sympathizer still (happily) alive.[3] I do not remember the "Eclectic."[4] Of course I shall be delighted to see Miss Lewis on any day she may please to appoint. Once again, all thanks from

Yours truly ever / Robert Browning.

MS: BL. Note in FJF's hand on letter: "Hervé Riel." Published: *LRB*, pp. 206-07; *LVC*, 1st Ser., I, 93-94.

1 In the "Additions" to the *Bibliography*, dated 31 Dec. 1881, FJF inserts this note on "Hervé Riel": "the facts of the story had been forgotten and were denied at St. Malo, but the reports to the French Admiralty at the time were lookt up, and the facts established. See the account in the *Promenade au Croisic*, par Gustave Grandpré, iii.186, and *Notes sur le Croisic*, par Caillo Jeune, p. 67, a 'Croisic Guide-Book.' Browning's only alteration is that Hervé Riel's holiday to see his wife 'La Belle Aurore,' was not to last a day only, but his life-time: 'ce brave homme ne demanda pour récompense d'un service aussi signalé, qu'*un congé absolu* pour rejoindre sa femme, qu'il nommait *la Belle Aurore.*' " (*BSP*, I, 163.)

2 *Sordello*, III.951. Walter Savage Landor (1775-1864; *DNB*), one of the earliest critics to praise RB's poetry (most notably in his sonnet "To Robert Browning," published in the *Morning Chronicle* [London], 22 Nov. 1845, p. 5), was cared for during his last years by the younger poet. Landor's "Satire on Satirists" (1836) contains a flattering allusion (l. 67) to *Paracelsus*.

3 An allusion in *Sordello*, III.967, to "My English Eyebright" refers to RB's friend Euphrasia Fannie Haworth (1801-83), who lived near Macready's country home and met RB there in the 1830s (*DI*, p. 31; *The Diaries of William Charles Macready*, ed. William Toynbee [1912], I, 118).

4 In the supplement to his *Bibliography*, FJF quotes passages from three articles in the *Eclectic Review* (*BSP*, I, 135-37, 139-43).

RB TO FJF, 20 DECEMBER 1881

19, Warwick Crescent, W. Dec. 20, '81.

My dear Furnivall,

You are undoubtedly right, and I have mistaken the meaning of the phrase—I suppose through thinking that, if the "coasting-pilot's" business ended with reaching land, he might claim as a right to be let go: otherwise, an absolute discharge seems to approach in importance a substantial reward. Still, truth above all things—so treat the matter as you please—believing me ever,

Yours, / R. Browning.

Text: *LRB*, p. 207. Published: *LVC*, 1st Ser., I, 95.

RB TO FJF, 24 DECEMBER 1881

19, Warwick Crescent, / W.* / Dec. 24. '81.

My dear Furnivall,

Forgive a little delay in acknowledging your letter. I might keep a stereotype for "Thanks and best thanks"—so surely do I need that expression. I can have no possible objection to your projected "Tales": I never saw the Sordello Tale,—nor heard of it indeed till I read about it in the Bibliography.[1]

You may have noticed an article in yesterday's "Pall Mall" in which the writer has his doubts whether the B. Society "is altogether without the consent—not to say, approbation of Mr B.,—if it is so, an excuse must be found in the fact that poets' flesh is but frail flesh after all."[2] I conceive that the proper course for Mr B. would have been to write to the Society and ask whether there had really been committed such an outrage as a combined endeavour on the part of certain people not only to read his poems but induce others to do so: because, were such the case, Mr B., who had for so many years been composing what he meant nobody should attend to, must entreat that such proceedings should forthwith stop: it being plainly the duty of an author to submit, for no matter how long, to no matter what abuse of his books—and to make an instantaneous protest against the first non-editorial "We", who, in the shape of a Society, may please to approve rather than condemn. Probably the next step should be that Mr B. stations a detective at Smith & Elder's shop-door to collar the first man who has the look of a B-buyer in his face.

Enough of this nonsense: you know how sincerely I wish you and your Family all the fittest of Christmas wishes. The Browning Society (Limited) is enriched by the arrival of the Painter[3]—whom you must see before he leaves.

We all send kindest regards—and you will believe me ever
affectionately yours / Robert Browning.

MS: ABL. Address: Frederick J. Furnivall, Esq. / 3. St. George's Square, / Primrose
Hill, / N.W. Postmark: PADDINGTON W M9 DE 24 [81]. Notes in FJF's hand on
envelope: "Dec. 24, 1881. / Brg. Soc."

1 FJF, *Bibliography*: "*Sordello*: A Story from Robert Browning, by Frederic May Holland, author of the 'Reign of the Stoics.' New York: G. P. Putnam's Sons, 1881, p.
1-26. Tells the story of the poem, with a few extracts from it; gives 5 or 6 pages of
critical notes, and states the historical basis of the work, with an englisht specimen
of the real Sordello's poetry. Mr. Holland has also in MS. like stories from *The Ring
and the Book, Luria, A Blot in the 'Scutcheon, The Return of the Druses, Colombe's
Birthday, Pippa Passes, Red-Cotton Night-Cap Country*, and *Balaustion's Adventures*,
including the *Apology of Aristophanes*. George Bell & Sons . . . will publish these
'*Stories from Robert Browning*' soon." (*BSP*, I, 148.) *Stories from Robert Browning*,
with an Introduction by Mrs. Sutherland Orr, was issued in 1882. Holland (1836-
1908; *WWA*) was an American writer.

2 In a leader entitled "The Browning Society," the *Pall Mall Gazette* (22 Dec. 1881, p.
11) declared that RB "permits, it appears, or sanctions in some degree, the foundation of a Browning Society. If so, there is, of course, nothing more to be said upon
his part in the matter. It is an ungracious act to reject the advances of admirers, however indiscreet their zeal; and, moreover, the flesh is weak, and poets are made of
flesh as much as other people." FJF sent off an angry reply which was published in
the *Pall Mall Gazette* on 2 Jan. 1882, p. 12.

3 The "Painter" is of course Pen Browning.

RB TO FJF, 5 JANUARY 1882

19, Warwick Crescent, / W.* / Jan. 5, '82.

My dear Furnivall,

I quite understand and appreciate your motive in writing to me
about the report you have heard concerning Robert. It is mere gossip grown out of just this fact that, more than four years ago, he
formed an attachment to a young lady of perfectly unexception-
able character and connections:[1] I objected to a marriage, on many
accounts quite irrespective of these, and communicated with the
lady's father (who—parenthetically—is wealthy) and the project
was dropped on both sides. This occurred at a time when Robert's
pictorial career was just begun, and would have seriously affected
it: and wholly dependent on myself as he was, with little prospect
of becoming otherwise, he had no right so to dispose of his actions
in that matter: and my objections were felt to be reasonable—I believe, on both sides.[2]

Robert continues his residence abroad for certain obvious advantages: English weather does not suit him—born as he was in Italy—and the out-of-door occupation which *does* suit him—as you see by his looks—is easily managed in the charming country by the Black Forest which he makes his summer-quarters—returning to Antwerp in the winter or spring. He has the advantage of capital companionship in the association with three or four young gentlemen in the true as well as the conventional sense of the word—all painters and all pleasantly attached to him: this is the secret of his choosing to *work* abroad—always with an eventual settlement here in prospect. From motives of delicacy, I wish no sort of notice of what is over and done with to be quite uselessly obtruded on him: I have, besides, plenty of such indirect knowledge of past, and present circumstances as makes a direct enquiry unnecessary as well as painful: friends of my son, with vigilant eyes enough, visit him occasionally, and have long ago set my mind at rest. You see into what may be transformed, by gossip, the simple fact that, four years ago, a young man had a project which he found it would be undesirable to carry into effect, and so abandoned it—without a single dishonorable step, retaining, as he does, the friendship of all the parties concerned.

I am sure you will therefore content yourself with letting this idle and mistaken report wear itself out, and leave the event to show how much ground there was for it.

Ever truly yours / Robert Browning.

MS: HEH. Address: Frederick J. Furnivall, Esq. / 3 St. George's Square, / Primrose Hill, / N.W. Postmarks: PADDINGTON W 5 JA 82 J; LOND[ON . . .] J[. . .] JA [. . .] 82. Note in FJF's hand on envelope: "Penini & the innkeeper's / daughter."
1 Note in FJF's hand: "Daughter of the owner of the Hotel at Dinant where R.B.B. stayed." Pen's hostel in Dinant was the Tête d'Or (Collins, p. 30).
2 Encouraged by Sir John Millais (1829-96; *DNB*), Pen Browning became so enthusiastic about an artistic career that he moved to Antwerp and Dinant in order to study under Jean-Arnould Heyermans (b. 1837). Milsand, in some letters to Sarianna written in the autumn of 1877 (ABL), refers to the engagement.

RB TO FJF, 12 JANUARY 1882

19, Warwick Crescent, / W.* / Jan. 12. '82.

My dear Furnivall,

I am beginning to enjoy the results of the institution of the

"Society" (—quite over and above the sympathy and kindness of its promoter & adherents—) in the evident annoyance it is giving my dear old critics who have gone on gibing and gibbering at me time out of mind. If these worthies could point to a single performance in which they had themselves "read and studied" anything of mine,—far less induced others to do so,—there might be a reason for their wrath: but there has never been one such article in the "Saturday" since its existence: as for the "Pall Mall"—the late Proprietor's rule excluded any article upon any work published by "Smith & Elder"[1]—on what principle I fail to see, inasmuch as he might fairly say "Since I publish nothing I do not believe to be of worth in its way,—why should not the Editor of my Journal have the same opinion and express it?"—but at any rate the mouth so reticent before needs not grow loquacious all at once on the other side of the question. I suppose these writers have their pets, and think loyalty to these demands irritation at any fancied intruder on the occupied hero's little plot of ground,—his τέμενος as the Greeks called it. All which amounts to—Pray don't imagine I can't understand the mock compliments to myself pretended to be involved in the censure of those who make so thoroughly appreciated a person "ridiculous": the "*ridiculus mus*"[2] is the inveterate nibbler at—and spoiler of—the fruits of a man's whole life's labour which might otherwise go to the bake house and prove tolerable ship-biscuit. As for you—I shall not waste a word in bidding you mind this gabble as much and as little as does

Yours ever / Robert Browning.

MS: HL. Address: Frederick J. Furnivall, Esq. / 3 St. George's Square, / Primrose Hill, / N.W. Postmarks: PADDINGTON W 4 JA 12 82 [...] ; LONDON NW HO JA 12 82. Published: *LRB*, pp. 207-08; *LVC*, 1st Ser., I, 96-98.
1   George Smith was the proprietor of the *Pall Mall Gazette* from 1865 to 1880 as well as head of Smith, Elder. See also RB to FJF, 24 Dec. 1881, n. 2.
2   "Ridiculous mouse."

RB TO FJF, 17 JANUARY 1882

19, Warwick Crescent, / W.* / Jan. 17. '82.

My dear Furnivall,

Thank you very much for your friend's information, though I

was already in possession of it. I had some weeks ago directed that every possible reparation should be made, and I will at once write to urge expedition in the matter. I have an old friend there who, for many reasons, will not be found wanting in zeal, I know.

Ever truly yours RB.

MS: English Poetry Collection, Wellesley College Library. Note in FJF's hand on verso of letter: "I forget what this refers to. / F.J.F. 18/5-93."

RB TO FJF, 23 JANUARY 1882

19, Warwick Crescent, W. Jan. 23. '82.

My dear Furnivall,

I return Mr. Radford's letter with many thanks. I never heard nor dreamed there had been any such notion at any time of a Moorish Front for the Duomo—it was altogether a fancy of my own illustrative of the feelings natural to Luria and Braccio each after his kind.[1] As for *Aristophanes*—the allusions require a knowledge of the Scholia, besides acquaintance with the "Comicorum Graecorum Fragmenta," Athenaeus, Alciphron, and so forth, not forgotten.[2] But I wrote in France, at an out of the way place, with none of these books.[3]

How good you are, and how unable am I to do more than gratefully recognize it! I am reading Miss Lewis's novel—have got through only the first volume, and like it much: my sister promises me that I shall like the second volume still more.[4]

Ever yours, / Robert Browning.

Text: *LRB*, p. 208. Published: *LVC*, 1st Ser., II, 3-4.

1 FJF, *Bibliography*: "Mr. Ernest Radford has made another interesting discovery about Br.'s sympathy with Art. In *Luria*, I.121-7, the Secretary tells Braccio that Luria drew the charcoal sketch that attracted his notice, a Moorish front to the unfinisht Duomo or Cathedral of Florence, typifying Luria's leadership of the Florentine army. And Br. makes Braccio say, 'I see: A Moorish front, nor of such ill design!' Br. had instinctively felt that the lines of the Duomo lent themselves to eastern treatment. Well, Mr. Radford, poking about, went to a small and rarely visited museum, cald the *Opera del Duomo*, containing drawings and models relating to the Cathedral, and there his eye was caught by a drawing of the Duomo completed by a Moorish front (drawn in 1822, and given to the Museum in 1833). Some architect or artist had been moved by the same feeling as Br., and had carried it out on paper. Br. had of course never seen or heard of this drawing." (*BSP*, I, 163.)

2 RB's literary borrowings in *Aristophanes' Apology* (1875) are discussed by Carl N. Jackson, "Classical Elements in Browning's 'Aristophanes' Apology,' " *Harvard Studies in Classical Philology*, 20 (1909), 15-73, and Thurman L. Hood, "Browning's Ancient Classical Sources," *Harvard Studies in Classical Philology*, 33 (1922), 79-180. The only reference to *Aristophanes' Apology* in FJF's *Bibliography*—to which RB may possibly be responding—is an excerpt from the review in *The Times* (*BSP*, I, 145).
3 RB's note in the manuscript of the poem reads: "Begun about August 11—ended Saturday, Nov. 7. '74. Mers, Picardy" (DeVane, p. 376).
4 The second volume of Mary A. Lewis' *Two Pretty Girls* (1881) contains a flattering reference to RB (*BSP*, I, 107).

RB TO FJF, 17 FEBRUARY 1882

19 Warwick Crescent, / W.* / Feb. 17. '82.

My dear Furnivall,

Pardon a delay in replying to your first note—which this second shall not have to apologize for—

If "B" has "no sense of humour," he ought to shut up poetical shop, or, better, never have opened it. The mistake grew out of a word on the want of sympathy and understanding he confessed to respecting "practical jokes"—wherein he failed to see "humour" at all. He rather fancied his love of humour led him into scrapes of indecorousness occasionally, when occupied on serious matters. Who knows?

The little pamphlet[1] was printed by Arabel Barrett for a Bazaar to benefit the "Refuge for young destitute girls" which she set going all those years ago—the first of its kind, I believe, and still in existence.

Ever truly yours / Robert Browning.

MS: BL. Note in FJF's hand on letter: "Mrs. Orr said, B if askt, wd. confess that he had 'no sense of humour'. I thought this such a tremendous joke that I askt B. about it. F." Published: *LRB*, p. 209; *LVC*, 1st Ser., II, 5-6.
1 *Two Poems* (1854), a pamphlet containing "A Plea for the Ragged Schools of London" by EBB and "The Twins" by RB, was sold for sixpence in May 1854 at a bazaar for the benefit of a "Refuge for young destitute girls" established by Arabella Barrett (1813-68), EBB's sister.

RB TO FJF, [24 FEBRUARY 1882]

Page 198. beauties in tights—not fights![1]

In utmost haste / *RB*

MS: HEH. Address: F. J. Furnivall, Esq. / 3 St. George's Square, / Primrose Hill, / N.W. Postmarks: PADDINGTON W L1 FE 24 82; LONDON NW EK FE 24 82. Note in FJF's hand on envelope: "Press corrn."
1 RB is correcting an amusing typographical error in the proofs of J. T. Nettleship's paper on *Fifine at the Fair*, which was delivered to the Browning Society on 24 Feb. The sentence appears (corrected) in *BSP*, I, 201.

RB TO FJF, 11 MARCH 1882

19, Warwick Crescent, / W.* / March 11. '82.

My dear Furnivall,

The story of "Old Tod," as told in Bunyan's "Life & Death of Mr Badman", was distinctly in my mind when I wrote "Ned Bratts"—at the Splugen, without reference to what I had read when quite a boy. I wrote "Ivan Ivanovitch" at the same place and altitude.[1]

The "Saint" by "Haste-thee-Luke!"—i.e., "Luca-fa-presto," as Luca Giordano was styled—somewhat disparagingly—from his expeditious way of working.[2]

No "bother"—so, no forgiveness from

Yours ever / Robert Browning.

MS: HL. Address: F. J. Furnivall, Esq. / 3 St. George's Square, / Primrose Hill, / N.W. Postmarks: PADDINGTON 4 MR 11 82 H; LONDON NW HK MR 11 82. Note in FJF's hand on envelope: "Ned Bratts & old Tod." Published: *LRB*, p. 209; *LVC*, 1st Ser., II, 7-8.
1 "Ned Bratts" and "Ivàn Ivànovitch"—both published in *Dramatic Idyls*, 1st Ser. (1879)—were written in the Splügen Pass of Switzerland during August or September 1878. However, in Venice shortly afterwards RB consulted a Russian woman about the names in "Ivàn Ivànovitch" (Orr, p. 312), and upon his return to London in November he read his personal copy of Bunyan's *Works* (Edinburgh, 1771). For an analysis of RB's borrowings from Bunyan, see DeVane, pp. 442-44.
2 The reference is to "In a Gondola," l. 188. Luca Giordano (1634-1705) was one of the most important Italian decorative painters of the latter seventeenth century.

RB TO FJF, 5 APRIL 1882

19. Warwick Crescent, W. / Apr. 5. '82.

My dear Furnivall,

I have been receiving favour after favour from you, letters and enclosures, and you get not even a grunt from the pig I must seem! I find so much to letter-write about just now—but repose is at hand. I will briefly say that "Browning" (the Bishop) is a misprint for "Brownrig"[1]—and that I have not yet examined the "Tales"[2]—but will do so. The photograph represents very inadequately Andrea's highly-finished picture: is it indeed from the picture itself?[3]

Ever yours / Robert Browning.

MS: HEH. Address: Frederick J. Furnivall, Esq. / 3. St. George's Square, / Primrose Hill, / *N.W.* Postmarks: PADDINGTON W M5 AP 5 82; LONDON NW JK AP 5 82. Notes in FJF's hand on envelope: "Book Catal. / & Andrea foto / B. a pig."
1 Ralph Brownrig (1592-1659; *DNB*), Bishop of Exeter.
2 The "Tales" are probably *Stories from Browning* by F. M. Holland, which at this time was in preparation for the printer. See RB to FJF, 24 Dec. 1881, n. 1.
3 In the first part of *Illustrations to Browning's Poems* the Browning Society published a photograph of the painting by Andrea del Sarto which supposedly inspired RB's poem. (See FJF's letter to the *Academy*, 20 Nov. 1881, above.) Two copies of the photograph were also distributed to every member of the society, though FJF had earlier complained that "the negative will have to be much toucht. The pure photo is a mere blotch." (*BSP*, I, 161.)

RB TO FJF, 25 APRIL 1882

19. Warwick Crescent, W. / Apr. 25. '82

My dear Furnivall,

I return the "proof"[1]—and should be exacting indeed if I were "dissatisfied" with the only too kind study by one, hitherto unknown to me, even by name—but whom I am little likely to forget henceforward.

At page 266 are some misprints which may be corrected.

I take the opportunity of saying, once for all, that I never read a line, original or translated, by Kant, Schelling, or Hegel in my whole life—nor even know the name of any book of theirs—except the "Critique of Pure Reason" which stares one in the face at every turn of a printed leaf now-a-days.[2]

Ever yours / Robert Browning.

MS: ABL. Address: F. J. Furnivall Esq. / 3. St. George's Square, / Primrose Hill, / N.W. Postmarks: PADDINGTON W 5 AP 25 82; LONDON NW JK AP 25 82. Note in FJF's hand on envelope: "Bury's / Paper."
1 Note in FJF's hand: "of Bury's Paper / on B.'s Philosophy." The proof is that of J. B. Bury's Browning Society paper, "Browning's Philosophy" (*BSP*, I, 259-77). (See RB to FJF, 2 Oct. 1881, n. 4.)
2 Friedrich W. J. von Schelling (1775-1854) and Immanuel Kant (1724-1804), German philosophers. Kant's *Kritik der reinen Vernunft* was published in 1781. See also RB to FJF, 2 Oct. 1881, n. 4, for a discussion of Hegel.

RB TO FJF, 8 MAY 1882

19, Warwick Crescent, / W.* / May 8. '82.

My dear Furnivall,

I should have done better had I tried at once yesterday to say what I could of what I felt on receiving that Present:[1] the complete inspection of it, the more thorough understanding of the immense kindness involved in it,—all this makes the delay which I thought might help me to a more adequate acknowledgement, rather a hindrance, so thick and fast do the considerations follow which I would find some sort of expression for if I could. After all, you will believe a simple word as well as—or better than—words many and elaborate,—and that word shall be truth itself—that I never was so honored, so gratified by any action of any approach to a similar nature, that ever happened to me in the course of my life. But how could it be otherwise, and why should I be concerned to assure you of what you must intimately know?

Will you communicate this, or the substance of it to my "Hundred and two" friends—not one of whom shall slip from the grateful memory of, my dear Furnivall,

Yours affectionately and gratefully ever / Robert Browning.

MS: HEH. Address: Frederick J. Furnivall, Esq. / 3. St. George's Square, / Primrose Hill, / N.W. Postmarks: PADDINGTON W M4 MY 8 82; LONDON NW HK MY 8 82. Note in FJF's hand on envelope: "birthday. / gift." Published: untitled circular by FJF dated 8 May 1882.

1 FJF sent out a "private and confidential" printed appeal, dated 7 Apr. 1882, urging members of the various Browning societies to contribute subscriptions to a gift for RB's seventieth birthday on 7 May. In a second circular, dated 8 May 1882, FJF reported to the 102 subscribers that the previous day he had given to RB, in their name, a specially bound set of RB's works in an oak case with carved figures suggested by his poems. (The set and case comprise Lot 458 in *Browning Collections*.) FJF offered this account of RB's reaction: "You will be pleazd to hear that our Birthday-present toucht the Poet, and gave him real pleazure. He thrice told me that it was the prettiest and most gratifying prezent ever made to him, and that he thankt heartily every friend who had joind in it. He said he would send me a note saying so." After quoting RB's letter, FJF summarized his own reply: "In answer I had said that our one wish was to acknowledge by some slight token that might gratify him, the help and pleasure that he for so many years has given us; and that this end being attained, all is well." The inscription which appeared in the books is printed below in Appendix B, Article 1. Two additional gifts for RB, which had to be presented to him on his following birthday because of their tardy arrival, were an improved reproduction of del Sarto's self-portrait (see RB to FJF, 5 Apr. 1882, n. 3) and a copy of *Jocoseria* in matching binding, the latter from FJF and Teena Rochfort-Smith ("Notes and News," *Academy*, 23 [12 May 1883], 327).

RB TO FJF, 14 MAY 1882

19, Warwick Crescent, / W.* / May 14. '82

Dear Furnivall,

That mistake of Hawthorne's—or rather of Hawthorne's inform-
ant—has long amused me.[1] There was never any sort of allusion to
the Apennine (Statue, or the mountains' self) in the diminutive
"Penini",—which was simply the little fellow's first attempt at
pronouncing his own second Christian name of Wiedemann—the
maiden-name of his Grandmother—by which it was at first proposed that he should be called to the avoiding the ambiguous
"Robert": not proposed by the "Robert" who is ever

Yours truly RB.

MS: HEH. Address: F. J. Furnivall, Esq. / 3. St. George's Square, / Primrose Hill, W.
Postmarks: PADDINGTON W 7 MY 15 82 K; LONDON NW AL MY 15 82. Notes in
FJF's hand on envelope: "on his boy's name *Pen*. / Browning."
1 Nathaniel Hawthorne (1804-64; *DAB*) recorded in his journal on 9 June 1858 that
Pen Browning was called "Pennini for fondness. The latter cognomen is a diminutive
of Apennino, which was bestowed upon him at his first advent into the world because he was so very small, there being a statue in Florence of colossal size called
Apennino." (*Passages from the French and Italian Notebooks of Nathaniel Hawthorne* [Boston, 1883], pp. 293-94.) Pen himself offered to William Lyon Phelps (in
1904) this explanation of his nickname: "When he was a child, he stuttered (he stuttered, indeed, in telling me about it), and in trying to pronounce 'Nini'—the name
Italians give their children—he said 'P-n-n-n-nini.' English visitors called it 'Pen-n-nini,'
and this led to 'Pen.' " (Phelps, *Autobiography with Letters* [New York, 1939], p.
454.)

RB TO FJF, 29 JUNE 1882

19, Warwick Crescent, / W.* /June 29. '82.

My dear Furnivall,

You give me opportunity which I gladly catch at to inform Mr
Brace[1] that I duly replied to an obliging invitation he addressed to
me nearly a fortnight ago,—and that my reply—altogether in ac-
cordance with the address of his letter—was returned to me by the
Post Office. I enclose it—begging you to explain the matter to Mr
Brace who must have wondered at my silence.

Ever truly yours / Robert Browning.

MS: English Poetry Collection, Wellesley College Library. Address: Fred. J. Furnivall,

Esq. / 3 St. George's Square, / Primrose Hill, / N.W. Postmarks: PADDINGTON W 2
JU 29 82 J; LONDON NW FK JU 29 82.

1   Charles Loring Brace (1826-90; *DAB*), founder of numerous charitable enterprises in
New York. In June 1882 Brace and his wife were in London on a visit (Emma Brace,
The Life of Charles Loring Brace [New York, 1894], pp. 377-78). RB's letter to
Brace, dated 18 June 1882 (HEH), reads in part: "I should be happy to meet you at
Mr. Neill's to-morrow were I not precluded by an engagement: pray have the kindness
to thank that gentleman on my part. If you will do me the further service of inform-
ing me of the time when you and Mrs Brace are most likely to be found at home I
will do my best to procure myself the pleasure of calling—but you understand already, I have no doubt, the many hindrances to which we are subject, this busy season, and will make allowance for any delay in obeying you." The letter was addressed
to 19 Seymour Street, Portman Square, W., and was returned marked "Not known."
Mrs. Brace's maiden name was Neill.

RB TO FJF, 28 JULY 1882

19, Warwick Crescent, / W.* / July 28. '82.

My dear Furnivall,

The time is very near when we two go our several ways from
London, and that must not be without a hand-shaking between us,
and "goodbye" more plainly spoken, on my side, than much that I
feel decidedly enough but say little or nothing about. Could you
lunch here at 1. o clock next Sunday? I & my Sister would be delighted to see you, if a word tells us we may hope to do so.

Ever truly yours / Robert Browning.

MS: HEH. Address: Frederick J. Furnivall, Esq. / 3. St. George's Square, / Primrose
Hill, / N.W. Postmarks: PADDINGTON W L3 JY 28 82; LONDON NW CK JY 28 82.
Note in FJF's hand on envelope: "lunch."

RB TO FJF, 15 AUGUST 1882

Hôtel Virard, St. Pierre de Chartreuse, / Isère, France.
Aug. 15. '82.

My dear Furnivall,

Let me thank you at once for Professor Corson's only too kind
paper:[1] I had no notion, from the reports, that there was so much
to be grateful for—and, in my eyes at least, if this were the only
product of your Society I should be abundantly obliged to it. The
one misprint that I notice is at page 317: *patronage* is set down
personage. As for Mr Lang's explanation,—it is indeed useless to

observe on the logic which deduces the rendering, of three ordinary Latin words by twice as many out of the way English ones, from "literal translation"—and then says "Anyhow, the Agamemnon is *harsh*"—which is quite another matter.[2]

I wish with all my heart I could content you about the "Selections":[3] those in use at present *sell*, and a second selection from them would, I suppose, act as a sucker from the main trunk and flourish at its expense: sooner or later, you will at all events get a condensed and cheaper edition of the "works"—of *that* there is no doubt. What a pleasant profitable article is that of yours in the "Academy"![4] I received the Book itself just before leaving town, and had no time to even cut the leaves: I shall do more than that when I return. To-day ends the second week out of England. It is often a disappointment to try a second experience of such a place as this whence I write—but, through a little change in the management of the "Hôtel", things are much for the better—and the beautiful wild country remains the same—which is all one could desire of it. The weather was perfect till yesterday,—to-day is rainy and all the cooler: I hope you may be as well off at the end of the month, and that meantime the health of Mrs Furnivall is restored. Tell me, when you write. By the bye, where is Professor Corson?[5] He was also bound for France, I think. If you have any communication,—tell him, however unnecessarily, how I feel his indulgence and sympathy—and tell yourself, my dear Furnivall, that I am ever
affectionately yours, RB.
My sister desires her kindest regards. The Bill which abolishes our house has *passed*, we see, so your photographs have some reason for existence![6]

MS: HEH. Address: *Angleterre.* / F. J. Furnivall, Esq. / 3. St. George's Square, / Primrose Hill, / London. N.W. Postmarks: ST LAURENT DU PONT 2E 16 AOUT 82 (37); LONDON NW XX AU 17 82. Note in FJF's hand on envelope: "Corson. / Shilling / Selection."

1 Hiram Corson (1828-1911; *DAB*), Professor of English Literature at Cornell University and the leading American Browningite (*Oracle*, pp. 91-96), delivered a paper entitled "The Idea of Personality, as Embodied in Robert Browning's Poetry" to the Browning Society on 23 June 1882 (*BSP*, I, 293-321). FJF wrote to Corson on 8 Aug. 1882 (Cornell University Library): "Mrs. Fitzgerald said yesterday that Browning told her he liked your Paper better than anything else that had been written on him since the Society started."

2 "Where Virgil describes the death of Troilus, 'et versâ pulvis inscribitus hastâ' ('and his reversed spear scores the dust'), Mr. Morris has 'his wrested spear a-writing in the

dust,' and Troilus has just been 'a-fleeing weaponless.' Our doomful deed is that to be a-translating thus is to write with wrested pen, and to give a rendering of Virgil as unsatisfactory as it is, technically, literal. In short, Mr. Morris' *Aeneid* seems on a par with Mr. Browning's *Agamemnon* [*of Aeschylus* (1877)]." (Andrew Lang, "The Poetry of William Morris," *Contemporary Review*, 42 [August 1882], 216-17.) Lang (1844-1912; *DNB*) in his writings regularly attacked the Browning Society and expressed dislike of most of RB's works except for *Men and Women*.

3 FJF was riding his favorite hobbyhorse again: see RB to FJF, 23 Jan. 1876, n. 1.

4 FJF reviewed Thomas Hughes' *Memoir of Daniel Macmillan* (1882) in the *Academy*, 22 (12 Aug. 1882), 112.

5 Corson, after reading his paper to the Browning Society and visiting RB in June, spent the rest of the summer in Guernsey (Corson, "A Few Reminiscences of Robert Browning," *Cornell Era*, 40 [April 1908], 302).

6 The Browning Society had photographs taken in 1882 of the interior and exterior of 19 Warwick Crescent "in consequence of the passing of the Bill which enables the property to be taken for a Railway" (*BSP*, I, iv; see also "Notes and News," *Academy*, 21 [10 June 1882], 413). However, RB did not move to 29 De Vere Gardens until 1887 (see RB to FJF, 27 June 1887), and his Warwick Crescent house was not pulled down until 1960. In a memorandum dated 16 May 1887 (Murray) RB clarifies what happened: he had taken 19 Warwick Crescent on lease in March 1862 at a rent of £92 10s. per annum, and in 1881 he became a yearly tenant. In 1882, however, he received notice that the property would be required by the Docks and Canal Company. But the proposed railway was postponed, only to be temporarily revived in March 1887. Hence Browning bought the house at De Vere Gardens, even though his lease at Warwick Crescent would not have expired until 24 June 1888.

RB TO FJF, 22 AUGUST 1882

Hôtel Virard, St. Pierre de Chartreuse, / Isère, France.
Aug. 22. '82.

My dear Furnivall,

It is always a pleasure to hear your voice & shake your hand across the distance. I think you over-estimate the power in my poems to become popular: to be sure, so much popularity as they have already obtained is a mystery to me—though nothing is plainer than that your helping has pushed them faster than, of their own force, they would have got forward. I think there is no great objection to the bringing out a *small* "Shilling Selection" such as you speak of—"Hervé Riel & some Idylls"—at all events I engage to speak about it to Smith when I return to London. By the bye, that is a very kind (too kind by far in some respects) notice of Hervé Riel—for which, I make no sort of doubt, I am as usual indebted to *you*. The translation is capital,—with an exception or two, no faults: but "Le vent du nord s'apaise" is a mistake turning on the word "Still": it should be, on the contrary, "Le vent du N. souffle toujours"—and assists the manoeuvre. Then, "sous les remparts du Solidor, les belles chevauchées le long de la Rance!"—"pleasant riding" means "riding at anchor"—not that the Captains were about to gallop backward & forward on horseback. "Sure as fate" applies to the coming of the English, not the action of Hervé Riel. I think it worth while to point out these little oversights because I am much gratified at the fine achievement of Hervé Riel being recognized and authenticated so thoroughly by M. Darmesteter: do thank him heartily from me if you have the opportunity—you who reach in so many directions.[1]

I believe I mentioned that, on our stay here expiring, we were bound for Ischia on a visit to a friend: but a dreadful accident has happened to a guest of his,[2] and he breaks up his establishment and leaves the the [sic] place—his offer of the house to us (which came along with your letter yesterday) is not to be thought of: we shall accordingly spend the rest of our time in the north of Italy, and so get to Venice by degrees,—nor stay there very long—since at last a new abode *must* be sought out—if not, entered into. This "Cartusia" is a very satisfactory "lodge in the wilderness":[3] by some new regulation, we get the newspaper the day after its publication—a godsend in these stirring times.[4] The fine weather, wild scenery, and general quiet are eminently *restorative*, and my Sister profits by them to the full as much as I do. I rejoice that your account of Mrs Furnivall and her walking feats is just as satisfactory. All regards to her,—and to you, from both of us. As for Professor Corson—I have no more to say—but much to feel & remember with respect to him: what I would say if I could, you can better interpret, I am sure.

Ever affectionately yours / Robert Browning.

MS: HEH. Address: *Angleterre.* / F. J. Furnivall, Esq. / 3. St. George's Square, / Primrose Hill, / London. N.W. Postmarks: ST LAURENT DU PONT 2E 23 AOUT 82 (37); LOND[ON . . .] . Note in FJF's hand on envelope: "Shilling Selection / Darmesteter." Published: *Furnivall,* pp. lxix-lxx (inc.).

1 The following note in the *Academy* (22 [19 Aug. 1882], 134) was undoubtedly written by FJF: "Mr. Browning's spirited poem, 'Hervé Riel' has at last had justice done to it in France. Dr. James Darmesteter [1849-94], the well-known Zend scholar and editor of 'Macbeth,' one of the vice-presidents of the New Shakspere Society, has, in *Le Parlement* of August 15, given an article of over four columns to an account of Mr. Browning and the Browning Society, a translation of 'Hervé Riel,' a statement of the historical facts on which Mr. Browning founded his poem, and a feeling appreciation of the generous spirit in which the English poet came forward, at the time of

France's greatest despondency after the German War, to show her . . . the heroism and true nobility of the poor Breton pilot. . . . [Darmesteter] calls on his country-men to set up a statue of Hervé Riel on the banks of the Rance, in front of the tower of Solidor. . . ." FJF had sent the *Parlement* article to RB (*LL*, p. 150), and Darmesteter acknowledged in his article that he had received information about the poem from FJF. When Darmesteter reprinted it in the following year, he incorporated the corrections suggested by RB in this letter (Darmesteter, *Essais de Littérature anglaise* [Paris, 1883], pp. 249-67).

2 The friend was Reginald Cholmondeley (1826-96); his guest, the daughter of the Rev. Nugent Wade (1845-91), climbed the mountain of Epomeo, behind Cholmondeley's house, in order to watch the sunset and sketch, and fell over a precipice. She never regained consciousness and died the following day. (*LL*, pp. 149-51.)

3 "Oh for a lodge in some vast wilderness . . ." (William Cowper, *The Task* [1785], "The Time Piece," l. 1).

4 In order to put down a military revolt in Egypt led by Arabi Bey, an Anglo-French fleet had bombarded Alexandria in June, and throughout August British troops occupied Egypt.

RB TO FJF, 29 AUGUST 1882

Hôtel Virard, St. Pierre de Chartreuse, / Isère, France. / Aug. 29. 82.

My dear Furnivall,—"wisely but slow—they stumble who run fast."[1] What I said was simply that I saw nothing objectionable in proposing such a Shilling Edition to Smith as would suit your purpose so kindly intended: but you have only to take it as a thing concluded on, and talk about it being a work of the Society's, to get it knocked on the head at once. If Smith allows it, you may be sure I will gladly relegate to you the business of picking and choosing,—but if we begin by that natural ending—there will be objection enough: I really want to do something in accordance with the views of one who has done so much for me—and for that very reason, I would take the right way to get it done. Pray believe in my experience in this matter—as I believe in your zeal and kind intentions. I got your letter—or rather Professor Corson's, with your redirection: his is only too generous,—as is everybody! I hope you will profit by the holiday you so richly deserve. The weather here is broken,—still we get good out of the intervals, and shall stay on as long as we are able. All regards to you from my Sister and from

Yours affectionately, / Robert Browning.

MS: HEH. Address: *Angleterre.* / Frederick J. Furnivall, Esq. / care of W. G. Stone, Esq. / Walditch, / Bridport, / Dorset. Postmarks: ST LAURENT DU PONT 2E 30

RB TO FJF, 12 SEPTEMBER 1882

St. Pierre de Chartreuse, Isère, F. / Sept. 12. '82.

My dear Furnivall,

The weeks have gone by "insensibly and noiselessly,"[1] and next Monday, Sept. 18, will most likely see us depart for Chambéry —whence we go to Venice, stopping (as we are at present minded) for a little at Bergamo and Vicenza: but if you have any word to bestow on me, it will preferably find me at Venice, *poste restante*. I remember, when on this very 18th last year we were fairly started, meeting by a good chance the postman—who stopped us "to deliver something" which proved to be a missive of yours:[2] such a chance may not recur, and, although I shall give proper direction for letters to be forwarded, still such is the isolation of this place that I put little trust in recovering property of this kind. A telegram to me was certainly lost a fortnight ago, as a subsequent message assured me. I hope you are enjoying yourself at the pleasant house and neighbourhood you describe. The weather is broken here, but we have taken advantage of all that was favorable in it. My Sister's kind regards go with mine to Mrs F. and yourself.

Ever truly yours / Robert Browning.

MS: ABL. Address: *Angleterre.* / F. J. Furnivall, Esq. / W. G. Stone, Esq. / Walditch, / Bridport / Dorset. Postmarks: ST LAURENT-DU-POINT 2E 13 SEPT 82 (37); BRIDPORT A SP 15 82. Note in FJF's hand on envelope: "going to / Venice."
1   Not identified.
2   See RB to FJF, 1 Oct. 1881.

RB TO FJF, 7 OCTOBER 1882

19, Warwick Crescent, / W.* / Oct. 7. '82.

My dear Furnivall,

I have got, I believe, all the letters with which you obliged me at Venice: the last arrived yesterday. Why do you always manage to give me so much pleasure—as by the account of Miss Beale's paper,[1]—and why cannot I reciprocate by at least doing some poor little thing that you think is in my power? Indeed, the Preface for which you are so kindly urgent, is quite out of it: tell Mr Bell so,[2] pray, with many thanks for thinking better of my abilities than they deserve,—or, at all events, of my "sweet reasonableness" when wise counsels would benefit me.

How glad I am that you so evidently enjoy yourself! This fine summer of Saint Martin does indeed cast the other half of his charitable cloak around us: I am too warm in the sun at this moment.

Come and see us when you can and whenever you can. We are disappointed doubtlessly at this stop to our progress,—and certain people, whom we much wanted to see, are flatteringly sorry they do not see us: but we did well to return, I believe. Don't return before you can help,—and get your collating work done: I like the samples of it I have seen—(in the Academy)—very much indeed.[3]

Ever yours affectionately / Robert Browning.

MS: ABL; envelope: Yale. Address: F. J. Furnivall, Esq. / P. Smith's, Esq. / 7. Lansdowne Crescent, / Cheltenham. Postmark: PADDINGTON W 5 OC 7 82 N. Note in FJF's hand on envelope: "This is Robert Browning's / handwriting. / F. J. Furnivall / 27 April 1895." Published: *LRB*, pp. 211-12; *LVC*, 2nd Ser., I, 78-80.

1 Miss Dorothea Beale (1831-1906; *DNB*), Principal of Cheltenham Ladies' College, delivered a paper on "The Religious Teaching of Browning" at the 27 Oct. 1882 meeting of the Browning Society (*BSP*, I, 323-38). In the paper she described RB as "a prophet whom God has given to our storm-tost age, a pilot who has learnt by long experience the hidden rocks and sandbanks on which the vessel of faith may be wrecked, now that the old anchor chains are burst asunder" (p. 326). She explained at the meeting that the purpose of her paper had been "to bring out from the poems some of the treasures by which we feel our spiritual nature has been enriched" (*BSP*, I, 47*).

2 Memorandum by FJF: "the *Preface* was one to Shakspere's Works, which George Bell the publisher, thru me, offered Browning £100 to write" (FJF's copy of *LVC* [King's]). Bell (1814-90; *MEB*) was on very close terms with FJF (Edward Bell, *George Bell, Publisher* [1924], p. 125).

3 A letter from FJF about the alterations in the First Folio text of *Much Ado about Nothing* appeared in the *Academy*, 22 (30 Sept. 1882), 243-44, and in a review published in the 22 July 1882 issue (pp. 60-61) he had similarly advocated the superiority of the First Quarto text of *Hamlet* to the First Folio text.

RB TO FJF, 5 NOVEMBER 1882

19, Warwick Crescent, / W.* / Nov. 5. '82.

My dear Furnivall,

I return Mr Symons' letter and the annexed Poem[1]—of which,

—pray assure him,—I never heard before and never wrote a word of —nor indeed have had the patience to read even now: it is a "holy fraud" apparently.

Ever truly yours / Robert Browning.

MS: HEH. Address: F. J. Furnivall, Esq. / 3. St. George's Square, / Primrose Hill, / N.W. Postmarks: PADDINGTON 7B NO 6 82; LONDON NW 7W NO 6 82. Note in FJF's hand on verso of letter: "My dear Sir [Arthur Symons] / Thanks for your scraps. I thought you'd rather have R.B.'s answer than mine. And here it is. / Very try yrs / F.J. F. / 6/11-82." Published: *NL*, pp. 280-81.

1 Arthur Symons (1865-1945; *DNB*), poet and critic, was during the 1880's an ardent Browning enthusiast (*Oracle*, pp. 71-79). To a friend he wrote on 17 Nov. 1882:

... November the 7th should be marked with red in my Calendar: it will always be to me a Red-letter-day. To explain I must tell you that about a week before that day, I had sent a few Browning scraps [for publication in the Browning Society's transactions] to Mr. Furnivall and among them a poem [entitled "Unanswered Yet"] (cut out of an American paper) signed 'Robert Browning'.

This poem I had not found in his works, nor was it at all in his style; so I wished an explanation. [Symons then quotes the messages from RB and FJF, which he received on the 7th.]

Is not that a treasure for me? I have long wanted to get Br.'s autograph and *now have it* under such interesting circumstance, the note being written solely for my benefit. (Roger Llombreaud, *Arthur Symons: A Critical Biography* [Philadelphia, 1964], p. 23.)

When the poem was again attributed to RB after his death, the *Pall Mall Gazette* on 7 May 1890 printed denials from Symons and another correspondent who claimed the author was a Miss F. G. Browning (reprinted in *BSP*, III, 97*).

RB TO FJF, 9 DECEMBER 1882

19, Warwick Crescent, / W.* / Dec. 9. '82.

My dear Furnivall,

I find you propose to publish that little friendly scribble I added to a young lady's Album two years' ago[1]—never dreaming that any use would be made of it in the way which took me by surprise at the Club, when I came on what I thought was an advertisement and found was my very own handwriting[2]—though cramped to suit the tiny book. The poem,[3] as a thing for the purpose it was written for, is *spoiled* by this excrescence,—though suitable enough for the young Lady's purpose. I should be very glad if you would omit it, and all reference to it in your "Scraps" or elsewhere, and to reward you for your complacency—if you care to have it, I will give you the list of *real* names and places to be substituted one day for the sham words which saved—problematically—the "Red Cotton

N. C. C" from going to grief.[4] I suppose it is safe by this time.
Ever yours truly but hurriedly / Robert Browning.

MS: HEH.

1 In the *Century Illustrated Monthly Magazine*, NS 3 (November 1882), 159-60, the editor, Richard Watson Gilder (1844-1909; *DAB*), printed two poems inscribed by RB and Henry W. Longfellow (1807-82; *DAB*) in the album of an American girl. RB's contribution—dated Venice, 14 Oct. 1880—was a revision of the Epilogue to *Dramatic Idyls*, 2nd Ser. Apparently because of a reference to "Edith" in Longfellow's poem, both BNP (p. 21) and DeVane (p. 458) assert that the album belonged to Longfellow's daughter Edith (1853-1915), wife of the third Richard Henry Dana (1851-1915; *WWA*). But in fact the girl in question appears to have been Edith Bronson (1861-1956), daughter of RB's Venetian hostess (see RB to FJF, 12 Nov. 1881, n. 4). Mrs. Bronson was Gilder's sister-in-law. Despite RB's protests in this and the following letter, FJF reprinted his poem in *BSP*, I, 48*, though in later issues of Part IV of the transactions the last ten lines were cancelled (T. J. Wise, *A Complete Bibliography of the Writings in Prose and Verse of Robert Browning* [1897], p. 50).
2 Note in FJF's hand: "Scribner's Century Mag. Nov 1882."
3 Note in FJF's hand: "Touch him ne'er so lightly: Dram Idylls 2nd Ser. end."
4 See RB to FJF, 15 Sept. 1881, n. 9. FJF did not take advantage of RB's offer.

RB TO FJF, 13 DECEMBER 1882

19, Warwick Crescent, / W.* / Dec. 13. '82.
My dear Furnivall,

Thank you for your kindness. The scrap may have gone forth past recall—but I rely on you to prevent it being stereotyped: you know I never interefere, if I can possibly help, in the doings of the Society: but this was an exceptional case. A trifle written for a very young person from whose mother I had received a great deal of benevolence, and attention of every sort: I still think the printing, without any application to me, must have been the effect of some editorial manœuvre: at any rate,—my feeling towards the family remaining quite unchanged by what I shall treat as an accident or the result of a misconception,—*I want nothing more to be said on the subject*,—giving useless pain and obtaining no good: only, your Society ought not to countenance the "conveyance—as the wise it call"[1] by incorporating my "*grateful*" tribute: did you really think—or, rather, the transcriber—did *he* think I ever did, could, would or should call my own fancies "graceful"?[2]

In a few days—as I promised—I will get out the proof sheets of the "Red C. N. C."—and get you an exact list of "*mutanda*"[.][3] I doubt if I shall do this for the Poem itself, when reprinted,—so that your paper may be in request with whoever cares to know the "rights" of my performance.

Ever yours truly / R Browning.

MS: HEH. Note in FJF's hand on letter: "not to print addition to 'tree & cleft' lines."
1 " 'Convey' the wise it call" (Shakespeare, *The Merry Wives of Windsor*, I.iii.30).
2 FJF corrected this typographical error in *BSP*, I, 65*.
3 "What must be changed" (Latin).

RB TO FJF, 9 JANUARY 1883

19, Warwick Crescent, / W.* / Jan. 9. '83.

My dear Furnivall,

I have been overwhelmed with your kindnesses in these last weeks: the papers, the illustrations,—and now comes this really charming print.[1] I probably saw the original picture in a favorable *darkness*—it was blackened by taper-smoke, and one fancied the angel all but surrounded with cloud,—only a light on the face. By the bye, that picture of Lippi's, mentioned by Mr Radford,—with the saints in a row—has,—either that or its companion, "*the Annunciation*", also in the National Gallery,—the Arms of the Medici above the figures,[2]—and in all likelihood both pictures were painted during Lippi's stay, enforced or otherwise, in the Medici Palace.

I have given (this afternoon) Smith my new book to print. It is a collection of things gravish and gayish—hence the title "Jocoseria"—which is *Batavian* Latin, I think. There are some eleven of these pieces,[3] little and big,—the main of them being the Deer-stalking Poem you remember, "Donald," Solomon & Balkis, Christina & Monaldeschi, Ixion, Mary Wollstoncraft & Fuseli, and a long "Hakkadosch Jochanan"- a Rabbinical story: Eleven pieces in all. May some morsels of this Olla Podrida take your taste!

Ever truly yours—with belated but very sincere New Year wishes— / Robert Browning.

MS: ABL. Address: F. J. Furnivall, Esq. / 3. St. George's Square, / Primrose Hill, / N.W. Postmarks: PADDINGTON W ZA JA 9 83 V; LONDON NW AL JA 10 83. Note in FJF's hand on envelope: "Guardian Angel / preview." Published: *LRB*, p. 213; *LVC*, 1st Ser., II, 11-13.
1 *Illustrations to Browning's Poems*, Part I (1882), with an Introduction by Ernest

Radford, contained "Photographs of *a*. Andrea del Sarto's Picture of himself and his Wife, in the Pitti Palace, Florence, which suggested Browning's poem *Andrea del Sarto* [see FJF to the *Academy*, 20 Nov. 1881, above]; *b*. Fra Lippo Lippi's 'Coronation of the Virgin,' in the Accademia delle belle Arti, Florence (the painting described at the end of Browning's *Fra Lippo*); *c*. Guercino's 'Angel and Child,' at Fano (for *The Guardian Angel*). . . ." The Society had also issued "An Engraving (by Dawson's process) of Mr. C. Fairfax Murray's drawing of Andrea del Sarto's Picture named above. . . ." (*BSP*, I, xv.)

2   Radford had written (p. vii): "But this juxtaposition of the pure and impure, of heavenly and earthly, is the *note* of the painter [Fra Filippo Lippi (*c*. 1406-69), subject of one of RB's best-known dramatic monologues]. In no picture can it be seen better than in a small work in the National Gallery, which now I can only imperfectly recall. There are monks seated in a row, and amongst them is one with a young face full of beauty, of earnestness and intense devotion. There are others that I remember little, but at the extreme end of the row is a face which seems, without being a caricature, to be the fleshly embodiment of all that is distinctively ungodly in man's impulses." The painting to which Radford refers is *St. John the Baptist with Six Other Saints*; in the companion piece, *The Annunciation*, the device of Cosimo de' Medici is visible on a parapet. Both paintings were formerly in the Medici-Riccardi Palace before being acquired by the National Gallery in the nineteenth century.

3   *Jocoseria* contains only ten poems. The poem which RB decided to omit was "Gerousios Oinos" (DeVane, pp. 459, 565-66).

RB TO FJF, 4 FEBRUARY 1883

19, Warwick Crescent, / W.* / Feb. 4. '83.

My dear Furnivall,

You are very good to care about my opinion concerning what you know far better than anybody.[1] I like the suppressed syllable after the emphatic "wild thyme"—as if "thymé"—so well that I would not stick in the "on" that used to be supplied to "where": but the beat of the verse is so regular, as one notices in all rhymed passages, that I should keep the old curtailment "lush"—which is, besides, a better epithet, I think. "Slow lush and lusty the grass grows!"—(in the 2d act of the "Tempest")—Oberon's intention being to describe the secrecy and appropriateness of the place where Titania "sleeps over-canopied": the odours are not unattended to, for he goes on to the "sweet musk-roses"—but "sweet" comes weakly after "luscious", does it not? And to scan it is impossible.

("was there ever a more lively line, to eye and ear, written than Donne's

And like the tender stalk at whose end stands

The woodbine quivering, are her arms and hands.[2]

one follows up the stalk on to the final flower.)

My business with "proofs" is all but done,[3] and I don't feel sure there is much to care about in what you will soon see. How odd that "Blackwood" should have regularly reviewed that old Book of Melander's from which I took the title![4] My edition is in three volumes—of which I only possess the latter two—bound in one: a gift from my Father when I was young—and it is mentioned in a note to "Paracelsus".[5] The title is Dutch Latin, and barbarous—one would preferably say "Jocososeria"—indeed the first of my volumes is headed "Jocosum atque Seriorum Tomus Secundas"[6]—but all the pages have "Jocoseria", as if the same thing.

All love to you and yours: I have not seen you this long while.

Ever yours truly / Robert Browning.

MS: HEH. Address: F. J. Furnivall, Esq. / 3. St. George's Square, / Primrose Hill. / N.W. Postmarks: LONDON W 7 FE 5 83; LOND[ON] W AL FE 5 83. Note in FJF's hand on envelope: "B. [J. R.] Seeley & [Edwin A.] Abbott [1838-1926; *DNB*] on / Luscious woodbine in / *M N Dream*. B on *Jocoseria*."

1 FJF had polled several friends, including Tennyson, for their opinion of how Shakespeare's lines (in *A Midsummer Night's Dream*, II.i.249-52) should be scanned.
2 John Donne, "Elegie VIII. The Comparison," ll. 27-28.
3 *Jocoseria* was published on 9 Mar. 1883. FJF's presentation copy (Berg) from RB is inscribed: "F. J. Furnivall, Esq / with all gratitude and / esteem from / Robert Browning. / March 9. '83." Above "Donald" is the following note in FJF's hand: "On R.B.'s sending this vol. to Tennyson, T. told him that he too had written a poem on this same story. C. K. Paul (8 April 1883) to whom RB told it. R.B. afterwards told me too. F." The volume also contains other notes in FJF's hand: the annotation of "Adam, Lilith, and Eve" is based on a conversation with RB, 8 Apr. 1883.
4 An article on Otto Melander's *Jocoseria* (1597) was published in *Blackwood's Magazine*, 133 (February 1883), 267-76; the anonymous author was John Dowden (1840-1910; *DNB*), Bishop of Edinburgh (*The Wellesley Index to Victorian Periodicals*).
5 RB's note referred to "such rubbish as Melander's 'Jocoseria.' "
6 "Humorous and serious matters, second book." The Latin is indeed barbarous; it is based upon Cicero's phrase "joca et seria" ("jokes and serious things").

RB TO FJF, 12 FEBRUARY 1883

19, Warwick Crescent, / W.* / Feb. 12. '83.

My dear Furnivall,

Though it is a matter of course that, when you signify that you will visit me, I take for granted that you know I am delighted to hear it,—yet I do not think I may so easily dispense with telling you that your kindness makes me very grateful. I am happy that you are interested in these new things, and that they also interest *our* charming young friend.[1] Take, both of you the truest thanks of

Yours ever affectionately / Robert Browning.

MS: HEH. Address: F. J. Furnivall, / 3. St. George's Square, / Primrose Hill, / N.W. Postmarks: PADDINGTON W 4 FE 12 83 J; LONDON NW HK FE 12 83. Note in FJF's hand on envelope: "Teena—Ixion &c."

1 The "new things" were some of the poems that would appear in *Jocoseria*, and the "charming young friend" was Miss Mary Lilian ("Teena") Rochfort-Smith (1861-83), an attractive and scholarly young member of both the New Shakspere Society and the Browning Society. (See RB to FJF, 9 Sept. 1883.) Note in FJF's hand following "young friend": "Teena R. Smith." For a discussion of FJF's relationship with Miss Smith, see Introduction.

FJF TO HIRAM CORSON, 19 FEBRUARY 1883

[London]

This is good news indeed.[1] Well done you! I send your note to R.B. to let him see how you're working for him. Miss Hickey 'll send you the Prospectusses [*sic*], & also some to the Baltimore folk. On Sunday week R.B. read to my friend Teena Rochfort-Smith & me 8 out of the 11 pieces in his new vol. I wrote a few lines on it in last *Academy*.[2] You'll like the vol, I think. *Ixion* is a magnificent poem, & *Donald* is most pathetic.

I do hope that Prest. Gilman 'll get the money for the *Book*.[3] It'll be such a gratifying thing for the University to produce it. Nothing could be happier.

We go on quietly here, but are always in want of money to print & illustrate. Still, if we keep going, we shall do all we want in time. That infernal publisher, Geo. Smith, still stands in the way of a *shilling Selection* here. B. will not do anything that S. doesn't like. Mrs. Orr's *Primer* goes on well.

F.J.F. 19/2-83

MS (postcard): John M. Olin Library, Cornell University. Address: Prof. Hiram Corson / The Cornell University / Ithaca / N.Y. / U.S.A. Postmark: LONDON NW J7 FE 20 83.

1 Corson's letter was doubtless similar to the one he addressed to the *Literary World* (Boston), 14 (21 Apr. 1883), 127, in which he described the numerous Browning

clubs he and others had recently founded in the United States, including one at the Johns Hopkins University in Baltimore, Md.

2 See FJF's paragraph in "Notes and News," *Academy*, 23 (17 Feb. 1883), which described *Jocoseria* as RB's "best production since 'The Ring and the Book.' " For FJF's accounts of the visit, see *BSP*, I, 96*, and Appendix B, Article 2, below.

3 Daniel Coit Gilman (1831-1908; *DAB*) was the first president of the Johns Hopkins University. "The *Book*" is the Old Yellow Book (see RB to FJF, 29 Jan. 1884, n. 1).

RB TO FJF, 20 FEBRUARY 1883

19. Warwick Crescent, W. / Feb. 20. '83

My dear Furnivall,

I return Professor Corson's very kind (and indeed surprising) letter with all thanks to him—and to you who set this stone rolling![1]

There is nothing in any part of the "Ring & the Book" that, properly speaking, is not wholly *mine*—that is, my imaginary deduction from certain naked *facts* recorded in the original collection of documents. These stop abruptly (the official ones) before any judgment that must have been pronounced on the whole: and but for an expression superscribed on the last paper or two,—to the effect that they relate to the "quondam" Guido,—I should never have known how the sentence really went, did not there follow the M.S. letters mentioning that all the criminals had suffered the same day. I obtained, a long while afterwards, a M.S. account of the story with particulars of the execution. That Caponsacchi and Guido severally were examined is certain from the reports of their evidence and statements: and, guessing at the way each may have spoken, from the *facts* undoubtedly in the mind of each, I raised the whole structure of the speeches, such as it is. For instance—in the last speech to which you refer—the *fact* is that the two ecclesiastics passed the night preceding his execution with Guido: and, knowing as he did the innocence of his wife, what so likely as that, in his last utterance of despair, *her* name with an appeal to it, should suggest itself?[2]

I had such a gracious letter from Miss Rochfort-Smith that I dared not reply to it at once; as Johnson said, "was it for me to bandy compliments with my Sovereign?"[3] Be my interpreter with her, if I need one, and believe me

Ever truly yours / Robert Browning.

MS: HEH. Published: *Furnivall*, pp. lxx-lxxi (inc.).

1 See FJF to Corson, 19 Feb. 1883, n. 1, above.
2 RB's *The Ring and the Book* was based primarily upon the "Old Yellow Book," a collection of legal documents describing a seventeenth-century Roman murder trial, which he purchased in Florence in June 1860. The issue to which RB addresses himself in this letter—the relationship between poetic imagination and historical fact in the poem—is also discussed in Books I and XII of *The Ring and the Book* and has continued to vex Browning critics to this day. In particular RB is defending his invention of Guido's second monologue, which ends with these words: "Pompilia, will you let them murder me?" (XI.245). The so-called "Secondary Source" which RB saw in 1862 was supplied by his friend Mrs. Eric Baker (*LRB*, p. 351; *DI*, p. 124) and is included in C. W. Hodell's edition (Washington, D.C., 1908) of the OYB.
3 "It was not for me to bandy civilities with my Sovereign" (*Boswell's Life of Johnson*, ed. G. B. Hill and L. F. Powell [Oxford, 1971], II, 35).

RB TO FJF, 1 MARCH 1883

19. Warwick Crescent, W. / March 1. '83

My dear Furnivall,—These new remittances from America should properly go to you[1]—Dulce decus et præsidium meum—(not that the verse quite runs thus.)[2] I return your own kind and pleasant letter: don't return what I myself send. I shall write to Prof. Moss.[3]

All regards to Miss Meta[4] and to you—from yours ever

Robert Browning.

MS: Yale. Published: *NL*, p. 282.

1 RB wrote to J. D. Williams in April: "This little 'Jocoseria' . . . has had the usual luck of the little-deserving,—got itself sold (as Carlyle would say) at the rate of 2000 very early, and is now reprinting. It all comes of the Browning Societies." (Collins, p. 28.) An American edition of *Jocoseria* was published by Houghton Mifflin.
2 "My splendor and protector," an adaptation of Horace's *Odes*, I.i.1-2.
3 Not identified. Possibly Henry Whitehead Moss (1860-1917), Headmaster of Shrewsbury, 1866-1908. (RB's handwriting is ambiguous, and the name may be Ross.)
4 Not identified.

RB TO FJF, 10 APRIL 1883

19. Warwick Crescent, W. / Apr. 10, '83.

My dear Furnivall,

I did indeed translate that little song for Mrs. Bell,[1]—never dreaming anybody would suppose there was "another hand" in her work. See now! I should have thought it very mean had I told anybody "That's mine"! and she herself unnecessarily tells it— from sheer honesty, I have no doubt, on somebody observing "what, you versify?"

You amuse me by what Mr Garnett[2] proposes to do with that No. 9 of the Railway Indicator: we have all of us been obliged to him in our time. Will he accept for the Museum all the numbers I possess—from 1. to 18. inclusive—the missing links being No. 2.— and that same 9 which *he* possesses? They shall be put aside here for you when you next please to call: I could send them—but—you may as well call!

Innocent XII was not the first to be tolerant in that direction,— but if his predecessor's clemency had been sufficient, there would have needed no supplementary "Bull" on the subject, you see! A Pope *adds* to the efficacy of another Pope's measure,—does something on his own account.[3]

I got an American paper, last night, wherein there is repeated that Jochanan revived by "a transfusion of blood": there is not a word about such a thing,—on the contrary, the account in the poem makes it impossible. How could the "transfusion" bring experiences with it—or how could the boy's gift—"which he threw and it stuck" be taken in that manner? This comes of the critics reading attentively the criticisms of their brethren, and paying no attention at all to the text criticized. The writer of the article in the "Times" made the mistake first—and even the Academy-article must needs follow him.[4] The whole story is a fiction of my own— with just this foundation, that the old Rabbins fancied that *earnest wishing* might add to a valued life. Could you say a word on the subject and set this right?[5]

Ever yours / *RB*.

MS: HL. Address: F. J. Furnivall, Esq / 3. St. George's Square, / Primrose Hill, *N.W.* Postmarks: PADDINGTON M6 AP 10 83; LONDON NW KK AP 10 83. Note in FJF's hand on envelope: "Ry. print of B's / poems." Published: *LRB*, pp. 216-17; *LVC*, 1st Ser., II, 14-16.

1 RB had anonymously supplied a translation of a lyric which appeared in Clara Bell's English version of the novel *The Hour Will Come* by Wilhemine von Hillern (Leipzig, 1879). RB's contribution was disclosed in the *Whitehall Review*, 1 Mar. 1883, and the poem was promptly reprinted by FJF in *BSP*, I, 410.

2 Richard Garnett (1835-1906; *DNB*), Superintendent of the British Museum Reading Room. For an explanation of the "Railway Indicator," see RB to FJF, 14 Jan. 1885, n. 2. The British Library set of the timetables is now complete except for Part 2. The BL copy of Part 9 is inscribed to FJF over the date 8 Apr. 1883; on the cover of Part 1 RB wrote a passage from Aristophanes' *Birds* ("most noble city in the air...") with an implied comparison to Chicago (*LRB*, p. 370).

3 In the *Literary World* (Boston), 14 (10 Mar. 1883), 76-77, a letter from "H.," of Baltimore, Md., was printed under the heading "A Question for the Browning Society."

The correspondent asserted that RB's treatment of Innocent XII (Pope 1691-1700) in *The Ring and the Book* was historically inaccurate, because that Pope did not abolish nepotism and the persecution of Molinists and Jansenists. The letter concluded: "Will Professor Corson, or some other Browning student, tell us whether the poet purposely attributed to the Twelfth Innocent the good deeds and characteristics of his predecessors? And if so, was it not a blemish to give his poem in these particulars an unveracious historical basis?" FJF's reply, dated 9 Apr. and printed in the *Literary World*, 14 (5 May 1883), 145, declared that "Browning is a scholar and has a scholar's accuracy, and deserves a little more work from any one objecting to his statement than H. has given. A day's search would have saved H. from this mess."

4   The reference is to "Jochanan Hakkadosh" in *Jocoseria*. See *The Times*, 8 Mar. 1883, p. 8; John Addington Symonds, *Academy*, 23 (31 Mar. 1883), 213.

5   "We owe to Mr. Browning an apology for having (in common, we believe, with all his other critics) said that the lover, poet, soldier, and statesman each transfuse their blood into the veins of his Jochanan Hakkadosh. We confess there is not one word or hint in the poem about such a transfusion, and that we did not know the fancy of the old Rabbins that earnest wishing alone could transfer part of one life to another valued one." ("Notes and News," *Academy*, 23 [14 Apr. 1883], 255.)

RB TO FJF, 15 APRIL 1883

19. Warwick Crescent, W. / Apr. 15, '83.

My dear Furnivall,

By all means, if Miss "Teena"[1] kindly cares to come, bring her next Sunday, and don't be under any apprehension that we shall kill a fatted calf on your account or on hers; we shall as easily content you both as we shall ourselves be contented, and much more, by your visit.

My poor friend, Miss Haworth, was the first to call my attention, long ago, to the existence of the old ballad of *Johnnie Faer*—which I was in total ignorance about when I wrote the poem some years before.[2] There was an odd circumstance that either mended or marred the poem in the writing—I fancied the latter at the time. As I finished the line—which ends what was printed in Hood's Magazine as the First Part[3]—"and the old one—you shall hear!" I saw from the window where I sat a friend opening the gate to our house—one Captain Lloyd[4]—whom I jumped up to meet, judging from the time of day that something especially interesting had brought him,—as proved to be the case, for he was in a strange difficulty. This took a deal of discussing,—next day, other interruptions occurred, and the end was I lost altogether the thing as it was in my head at the beginning, and, subsequently, gave it to Hood as a fragment: some time afterwards, I was staying at Bettisfield Park in Wales,[5] and a guest, speaking of early winter, said "the deer had already to break the ice in the pond"—and a fancy struck me, which, on returning home, I worked up into what concludes the story—which originally all grew out of this one intelligible line of a song that I heard a woman singing at a bonfire on Guy Faux night when I was a boy—"Following the Queen of the Gypsies, O!":[6] From so slender a twig of fact can these little singing birds start themselves for a flight to more or less distances[.]

Ever yours / RB.

MS: HL. Address: F. J. Furnivall, Esq / 3. St. George's Square, / Primrose Hill, / N.W. Postmarks: PADDINGTON 7B AP 16 83; LONDON NW LA AP 16 83. Note in FJF's hand on envelope: "Flight of the / Duchess." Note in FJF's hand on letter: "return / this to me." Published: *LRB*, p. 217; *LVC*, 1st Ser., II, 17-19.

1 Note in FJF's hand: "Rochford [*sic*] Smith."
2 DeVane (p. 172) suggests that this was "probably one of the many variations of the Scotch ballad, *The Gypsy Laddie*, the story of Johnny Faa and the Countess of Cassilis." "The poem" to which RB refers is his "The Flight of the Duchess."
3 The first nine sections of the poem appeared in *Hood's Magazine*, 3 (April 1845), 313-18.
4 Not identified. William R. O'Byrne's *A Naval Biographical Dictionary* (1849) lists thirteen Lloyds, several of whom were captains.
5 During September 1842 RB spent a week at the Flintshire home of Sir John Hanmer, Baron Hanmer (1809-81; *DNB*), statesman and poet (Frederic G. Kenyon, ed., *Robert Browning and Alfred Domett* [1906], p. 44).
6 During his childhood RB often saw groups of gypsies camping in the Dulwich woods, near his home in Camberwell.

RB TO FJF, 24 JUNE 1883

19, Warwick Crescent, / W.* / June 24. '83.

Dear Mr Furnivall,

I have heard by accident of your intended kindness in the matter of the works of my wife which you wish should be presented to me next year by the members of the Society.[1] How kind your wish is, I know sufficiently and need not say: but I shrink from any fresh appeal of this nature—which might easily grow into an annual tax on the generosity I have had such abundant proof exists: besides, one touches the appointed term of man's life only once,—and there is no need to remind me, year by year, that so much is taken from my stay among the true friends—among whom I shall ever count you!

Affectionately yours / Robert Browning.

MS: HEH. Address: Frederick J. Furnivall, / 3. St. George's Square, / Primrose Hill, / N.W. Postmarks: PADDINGTON 7C JU 25 83; LONDON NW JU 25 83. Note in FJF's hand on envelope: "proposed gift of Wife's works."

1 FJF, in a printed appeal dated 9 May 1883, proposed that "on May 7, 1884 [RB's birthday], thoze who think with me should give the Poet the Works of ELIZABETH BARRETT BROWNING in a carvd oak case, with appropriate designs, to hang by his own Works. . . ." Because of RB's objections, the bookcase and books (described in *Browning Collections*, Lot 423, and now in the Clark Library, University of California at Los Angeles) were presented instead to Pen Browning on 9 Mar. 1884.

RB TO FJF, 25 JUNE 1883

19, Warwick Crescent, / W.* / June 25. '83.

My dear Furnivall,

You are wrong, I assure you. The intelligence came to my sister three weeks ago from quite another person than the one you suppose. My sister doubted whether any good would be done by telling me about what had already taken place. She felt exactly as I did—and now more than ever do—that it is objectionable to solicit subscription from people who certainly *may* refuse (as who may *not?*) but thereby lay themselves under the imputation of indifference, or ill-will, or merely *stinginess*. The first gift had all the grace of being spontaneous—a thing called out by an occasion never to recur—and which would establish no sort of precedent for renewed declarations of feeling. Besides, the first case was peculiar: I really had no copy of my own books nor cared to have—that is, of my own procuring. But my wife's works have never been out of my possession: I want no other copy.

Surely it is for me—imperatively for *me* who have received so much kindness from you and your friends—to stay your hand when you are still further extending it. I should have been greatly embarrassed if the gift had taken me by surprise: for, by a parity of reasoning, why should not one be followed by another—a purchase of my wife's poems by—well, one of her son's paintings? It is so wise to stop short of the one step *past* the summit—for, as Donne says admirably,—

> Love is a growing or still-constant light:
> And his short minute after noon is—night.[1]

and not otherwise with the performances of Love. Pray do not go on with what,—in the prospect of [what] may follow from it,—greatly distresses me—whom its desire was,—I well know,—to gratify. And by conceding this you will gratify me most effectually. You can easily recall the invitations by a word that shall apprise the recipients of them, that Mr B. has somehow got wind of the project, and it is consequently abandoned, as the intended surprise would be no surprise at all.

I need not say—your "Private" shall remain private indeed. I have explained that you are mistaken altogether as to how the other "privacy" became none. Pray—let all (in your own words) be as if it had not been, and account me ever affectionately

Yours / Robert Browning.

MS: HEH. Address: Frederick J. Furnivall, Esq / 3. St. George's Square, / Primrose Hill, / N.W. Postmarks: PADDINGTON W [...] X JU 25 83; LONDON NW KL JU 25 83. Notes in FJF's hand on envelope: "Wife's Books &c / declines gifts of em."
1 Donne's "Lecture upon the Shadow," ll. 25-26, slightly misquoted.

FJF TO RB, 3 JULY 1883

3, St. George's Square, Primrose Hill, / London, N.W.* /
3 July 1883.

My dear Browning

Dykes Campbell has a copy of the 1833 volume of your wife's *Poems*, with several pen corrections, & two new stanzas in the *Prometheus Bound*.[1]

May he leave the volume at your house, or call with it some morng., & ask you if the handwriting is your wife's? The stanzas added read like hers.

Yrs / F.J.F.

MS: Scripps College Library. Address: R. Browning Esq. / 19 Warwick Crescent / W. Postmarks: [LON]DON NW 4 JY 3 83; PADDINGTON 4 JY 83 3. Note in RB's hand on envelope: "*Verse omitted in a Poem by E.B.B.*"
1 James Dykes Campbell (1835-95; *DNB*), retired businessman, bibliophile, and the second Honorary Secretary (1884-86) of the Browning Society. His wife offered this explanation of the following letter: "My husband had always been a great admirer and student of the writings of both Mr. and Mrs. Browning, and amongst his early 'finds,' when book-hunting, he had picked up a small volume by E.B.B. in which there were a number of notes in a very fine handwriting which he always hoped was that of the authoress. He showed the book one day to his old friend Dr. Furnivall, who could not be *sure* that the notes were by Mrs. Browning but said he would ask Mr. Browning,

which he did. [This] letter conveys a request to my husband that he would show the book to Mr. Browning, and to his great joy the notes were pronounced to be indeed by Mrs. Browning. Thereupon an acquaintance ensued and a friendship followed which was one of the greatest events of both our lives." (William S. Peterson, "An Unpublished Memoir of Robert Browning," *Victorian Poetry*, 7 [1969], 148.)

RB TO FJF, 4 JULY 1883

19, Warwick Crescent, / W. / July 4 '83.
My dear Furnivall,

I have no doubt the verses are by my wife, and the corrections also. The Book will, in all likelihood, have been the presentation-copy to some friend. If Mr. Campbell pleases to call with it, any morning, I shall be glad to see it, and can possibly guess at the person to whom it was originally given: if the book is simply left with me (for I may be out) it shall be promptly returned.

Affectionately yours / Robert Browning.

Typescript: BL Add. MS. 49526. Address (also typescript): F. J. Furnivall, Esq, / 3. St. George's Square, / Primrose Hill, N.W. Published: William S. Peterson, "An Unpublished Memoir of Robert Browning," *Victorian Poetry*, 7 (1969), 148n.

RB TO FJF, 29 AUGUST 1883

Hôtel Delapierre, Gressoney St. Jean, Val d'Aosta. Italia.
Aug. 29, '83.
My dear Furnivall,

I have just got my letters from London and yours among them. Of course, I was sure some reason was for your silence, and that you would have kindly given me a farewell sight of you had it been in your power.

We arrived here a week ago, and are in a beautiful place indeed, a paradise of coolness and quiet, shut in by the Alps; just under the Monte Rosa with its glaciers. The reaching this rest was rough work however. From Jura to Port St. Martin by two hours carriage-drive, and thence seven continued hours of clambering and crawling on mule-back; even our luggage needing to be carried on a couple of the poor creatures after the same fashion. And just so shall we have to descend, when time comes and snow falls—which, they say, will be soon enough. We are very well off, however, in a quite perfect "Hotel"—with every comfort desirable, and no drawback of any kind.[1] When the snow comes, whither we go is uncertain. I greatly hope the determination will not be forced on us before another fortnight.

My sister sends her kindest regards with mine. I wish you may be in the enjoyment of anything like our glorious weather.

Ever affectionately yours / Robert Browning.

My very handwriting is affected by the lumpy ink and skewery pen. You will decipher it, I daresay. I have received *from home* some newspapers, but no literary journal of any kind—*yet.*

Text: *LRB*, pp. 220-21. Published: *LVC*, 2nd Ser., I, 83-85.

1 According to the 1843 edition of Murray's *Handbook to Switzerland* (p. 255), the Hôtel Delapierre offered its guests "a harpsichord, German music, a tolerable library of Latin, German, and some French authors, portraits of Joseph II. and Maria Theresa, and a formidable array of many generations of the [owner's] half-length ancestors. . . ." The 1879 edition of Murray (p. 349) omitted these details but still described it as a "very good" inn.

RB TO FJF, 9 SEPTEMBER 1883

Hôtel Delapierre, Gressoney St. Jean, / Val d'Aosta, Italia. / Sept. 9. '83

What am I to say, my dear Furnivall, to your appalling letter?[1] I tried but could say nothing yesterday: and, to my great relief, the evening brought the second note with Mr Grant White's letter and book.[2] If I had read the dreadful account in a newspaper as relating to a stranger—even an animal—I should have felt its horror thoroughly: but when the victim proves to be the dear and charming young creature I was privileged to know,—who was so good and frank in her sympathy with my poorest attempts to please her,— well, there is little good in attempting to speak even while one knows and says that adequate speech is impossible. I never had such an awful piece of news come to me,—so utterly to be rather disbelieved in than simply not expected. You will know I feel for you in every nerve, my dear Friend: but you must help yourself like the strong man you are—I know of no manner of comfort from without: you must justify the the [*sic*] affection of your sweet lost intimate,—do so, like a brave as well as loving heart!

You may suppose how my Sister was shocked by the dreadful contents of the letter. She wishes me to say for her—just what I am unable to say for myself, and associates with me in the little I contrive to say.

May you—as Coleridge writes—"grieve down this blow!"[3] Ever most truly yours

Robert Browning.

I will of course write to Mr Grant White in a day or two. I hope to remain here a fortnight longer: under other circumstances I should have had much to tell you of its beauty.

I am writing some poetry which will be much influenced by this experience, I do not doubt. [4]

MS: HEH. Note in FJF's hand on letter: "on Teena's death."

1 Miss Rochfort-Smith suffered severe burns when her dress caught fire on 28 Aug. in Yorkshire, and she died on 4 Sept. ([FJF], *Teena Rochfort-Smith: A Memoir* [1883]).

2 Richard Grant White (1821-85; *DAB*), New York poet, essayist, and Shakespearean scholar, wrote an Introduction to *Selections from the Poetry of Robert Browning* (New York, 1883), a volume based in part upon a list of RB's best poems supplied by the poet himself (*BSP*, I, 73*).

3 Coleridge's translation (1800) of Johann Schiller's *The Death of Wallenstein*, V.i.57.

4 Several of the poems in *Ferishtah's Fancies*—most notably "Mihrab Shah" and "A Bean-Stripe: Also Apple-Eating"—deal with the problem of pain and suffering. Ironically, FJF was later to express a strong dislike for the volume (*BSP*, II, 248*).

RB TO FJF, 17 SEPTEMBER 1883

Hôtel Delapierre, Gressoney St. Jean, / Val d'Aosta, Italia. /
Sept. 17. '83.

My dear Furnivall,—let me first of all get rid of a trifle on my mind,—and yet no trifle if it indicated carelessness on my part, as it might seem to do. In my hurry to send off an answer to your letter, I got some stamps from the people of the house,—and, by candle light, the proper *blue* was undistinguishable from the *green* —one fifth of the proper value: I had stamped and despatched my letter, when the mistake was discovered—which *you* have been mulcted for. You will forgive the blunder, which I was sufficiently sorry about.[1]

Your new letter is very affecting—and the portion of it which relates to myself,—well, I don't know whether it pains or gratifies me the more.[2] It is useless to consider—If those little endeavours to please were so successful,—how willingly would one have re-doubled or centripled them! As to the wish of the poor Parents that I should write something on the sad subject—all I can say is,—if such an exceptional experience should happen to me as that I could put the feelings I undoubtedly am full of directly into verse —which should be worthy of the name,—I should hardly require an instigation from the outside to do so: but in the two or three great sorrows of my life it has been the last thing that occurred to me: *incidentally*—I am quite sure—and as I told you—this dreadful accident will have its influence more or less remarkably on what I write. I should hate any mechanical attempt to do what would only acquire worth from being a spontaneous outflow. Understand all this,—indeed, I know you will: but tell the amount of it to the Parents with whom I sympathize from my inmost heart.

My Sister again desires to condole with you in all sincerity. We purpose remaining here for at least another week—after which, as the weather may allow, we shall descend into the lowlands and move towards Venice, where we hope to arrive about the 1st of October. The weather continues surprisingly fine for the place and time of year.

Ever affectionately yours / Robert Browning.
I return the melancholy newspaper account.

MS: HEH. Address: *Inghilterra*. / F. J. Furnivall, Esq. / 3. St. George's Square, / Primrose Hill, / London. N. W. Postmarks: GRESSONEY S JEAN 18 SET 83; [P]ON[T] S. MARTIN 18 SET 83; LONDON NW MA SP 21 83. Note in FJF's hand on envelope: "Teena Smith's / Death." Note in FJF's hand on letter: "On Teena / Rochfort Smith's / death, from her / clothes catching fire." Published: *LRB*, pp. 221-22; *LVC*, 1st Ser., II, 20-23.

1 Note in FJF's hand: "The Post Office didn't notice it.)"

2 Memorandum by FJF: "on Teena's death & her love for Browning" (FJF's copy of *LVC* [King's]). FJF had asked RB to write a tribute to Miss Rochfort-Smith (see RB to FJF, 9 Sept. 1883, n. 1). RB was annoyed when FJF later issued a *Memoir* of her complete with photographs of both himself and RB. Alfred Domett recorded in his diary that RB "did not seem to approve much of Furnivall's having inserted his (B's) photograph into his memoir of 'Tina' (Miss Mary Lilian Rochford [*sic*] Smith), an enthusiastic admirer of his poetry, as he did not know much of the young lady" (p. 291). (The *Memoir* was unsigned and also appeared in the *Cheltenham Ladies College Magazine*, No. 9 [February 1884], pp. 170-80. FJF's personal copy [King's] bears this inscription: "by F.J.F. altered by Miss Beale.") FJF also proposed to issue her photograph to members of the Browning Society so that it could be tipped in their copies of the Society's transactions (*BSP*, I, 96*).

RB TO FJF, 29 SEPTEMBER 1883

Gressoney St. Jean, Val d'Aosta. / Sept. 29. '83.
My dear Furnivall,—first of all, many thanks for your letter—left
unanswered because of the uncertainty of our going or staying
another week: this last we have luckily done, and next Monday
we propose getting under way for Venice—to which place, *poste
restante*, you will please to address any communications with
which you may favour me. Six weeks in this delightful solitude,
with one day only to prevent our leaving the house this same Saturday a fortnight ago! On every morning and afternoon we have
walked right and left never less and often more than five hours a
day—and the good to us both—I hope—certainly to myself—is in
proportion. At Venice we shall be social, however, and I cannot
expect to return with as florid a pair of cheeks as I occasionally
get glimpses of in the glass. I am glad indeed to have the report of
your hard work—it is right and wise to engage in that. My own
things about which you so kindly enquire,—are *not* the "long
Poem," but a continuous set of—shall I call them, Studies?—in
which, at least, you will find "plenty of myself"—with something
to spare, I daresay.[1] Don't say anything about what is all in the
rough, and may continue so. I wrote, of course, to Mr Grant White.
His—or whosoever "Selection"[2] it is—strikes me as confirmatory
of an old opinion that there was no guessing how my poems would
affect people: and as the present sample is altogether from the
smaller pieces, I doubt if it "presents the author at his best, and
nearly all the best of him": if so, I have worked a great deal to very
little purpose. Nothing can be kinder or more indulgent than Mr
White, and I am greatly obliged to him—as I have endeavoured to
let him know.

That was indeed a—*Godsend*, is hardly the appropriate word, to
Dowden,—whom I never cease wishing well to.[3] I wonder if he has
had access to the correspondence of the first Mrs Shelley with—
what was the Bookseller's name, he of Bond Street, Shelley's intimate friend? He put them into my hands,—and a very decided
impression they left with me—the reverse of what I had been prepared for by the biographers of Shelley. Hookham (where was my
memory?) offered them to me unreservedly on the only occasion

of our interview, and they are all-important for a right view of the case as between wife and husband—the latter being, I hold, at that time of his life, half crazy and wholly inexcusable.[4]

So, to Venice,—if the weather allow, for we *walk* the first six hours of the descent,—and there and everywhere remember me

as ever affectionately yours / Robert Browning.

My sister's especially commended kind regards.

MS: HL. Address: *Inghilterra.* / F. J. Furnivall, Esq. / 3. St. George's Square, / Primrose Hill, / London. / N.W. Postmarks: GRESSONEY S. JEAN 30 SET 83 [. . .]; PONT [ST MA]RTIN 30 SET 83; LONDON 7 B[?] OC 3 83. Note in FJF's hand on envelope: "Grant White / Dowden & Shelley." Published: *LRB*, pp. 223-24 (inc.); *LVC*, 1st Ser., II, 24-26 (inc.).

1   The "Prologue" to *Ferishtah's Fancies* was dated 12 Sept. 1883, and most of the poems in the volume were written during RB's stay in Gressoney St. Jean and Venice (DeVane, p. 475). As RB hints in this letter, the character of Ferishtah was a feeble disguise for the poet himself.

2   See RB to FJF, 9 Sept. 1883, n. 2.

3   Edward Dowden (1843-1913; *DNB*), Professor of English Literature, Trinity College, Dublin, found on "a perambulating bookcart in Dublin" Shelley's presentation copy of *A Refutation of Deism* (1814) to his second wife, for which Dowden paid 2d. (*Letters about Shelley Interchanged by Three Friends—Edward Dowden, Richard Garnett and William Michael Rossetti*, ed. R. S. Garnett [1917], p. 84).

4   The profound influence of the poetry of Percy Bysshe Shelley (1792-1822; *DNB*) upon young RB has been amply documented. However, in about 1856 Thomas Hookham, Jr. (1786/87?-1867; *MEB*), bookseller and publisher, showed RB a group of letters written by Shelley's first wife, Harriet Westbrook Shelley, at the time he deserted her, and RB felt that these letters showed Shelley in a most unfavorable light. (The exact year in which RB saw the correspondence has produced disagreement among scholars; see William O. Raymond, *The Infinite Moment and Other Essays in Browning*, 2nd ed. [Toronto, 1965], pp. 234-43. For a detailed account of the conclusions RB reached after talking to Hookham, see *Swinburne Letters*, II, 17-18.) RB admitted to Isa Blagden in 1862 that "I am sadly unsettled in my feelings about Shelley . . ." (*DI*, p. 137). Gradually the unpleasant evidence that RB had privately discovered was slipping into print. William Michael Rossetti dropped a few discreet hints in a memoir of Shelley pubished in 1870; and John Forster's *Walter Savage Landor: A Biography* (1869) contained this curious footnote (II, 537): "It was my intention . . . to have made allusion to the effect produced on Landor by a detailed narrative (I found it among his papers) of all the circumstances of Shelley's first marriage, and its disastrous issue, communicated from a source only too authentic. Later reflection has however convinced me that no good can now be done by reviving a subject so inexpressibly painful." Therefore, when Sir Percy and Lady Shelley asked Edward Dowden in July 1883 to write an authorized biography of Shelley, one of his first undertakings was to search for the document mentioned by Forster and the letters which RB had seen. (See *Letters about Shelley Interchanged by Three Friends*, cited in n. 3 above, *passim.*) Although Lady Shelley destroyed many documents and exerted strong pressure on Dowden not to offer a sympathetic view of Harriet, Dowden did find and publish at least one of the letters which RB had read many years before— addressed by Harriet to Hookham, 7 July 1814 (Dowden, *The Life of Percy Bysshe Shelley* [1886], I, 423). See also Louise S. Boas, *Harriet Shelley: Five Long Years* (1962), and RB to FJF, 15 Oct. 1883, 29 Oct. 1883, 8 Dec. 1885, and 5 Jan. 1886.

RB TO FJF, 9 OCTOBER 1883

Palazzo Giustinian— / —Recanati, / Venice, Oct. 9. '83—but the better address will be simply "Poste restante." My dear Furnivall, we left our Gressoney with abundant regret last Monday,—walked thence for seven continuous hours without a minute's stopping,—and so got to Pont St. Martin: next day brought us to Ivrea and Vicenza—where we stayed for a couple of days,—and on Thursday we reached Venice and all the kindness our friend[1] could heap on us. The weather broke up on the day of our arrival,—our *first* rainy experience for some seven weeks,—but righted itself again and continues admirably fine. October is clearly the best month for visiting Venice—the mornings are fresh, not to say cold,—then follows a clear blue sunny noontide, and the evenings are inaugurated by such sunsets as I believe are only to be seen here—when you float between two conflagrations—that of the sky, reflected in the lagune. There is one miserable barbarism to deplore—the desecration of the beautiful little St. Helena,—two years ago, a wild garden, with thickets of roses round an old picturesque church,—now built over with an iron-foundry, the trees down,—the church blocked up,—and the very outline of the island obliterated by mud-bastions of indescribable ugliness: all this perpetrated in the one jewel-islet nearest to the City, when in the city itself there is space and to spare where ugliness might thrive and welcome, with as little offence as its nature allows,—by the Railway Station, for instance. I love Venice—and correspondingly wish a dynamite explosion to its disgrace with all my heart. The Syndic, here,—Mayor or what comes to the same thing,—boasts (so I am told) that he cares not a whit for the beauty of Venice but aspires to make it "a Liverpool"—as if he or all the devils *could* do that! I am called—and in good time! I suppose that, spite of Venice and the kindness I meet there, I shall return at the end of the month. My sister sends her best regards— You always have those of yours affectionately

Robert Browning.

MS: ABL. Address: *Inghilterra.* / Frederick J. Furnivall, Esq. / 3. St. George's Square, / Primrose Hill, / London. N.W. Postmarks: VENEZIA 9 10-83 6S [. . .]; LONDON NW XX OC 11 83. Note in FJF's hand on envelope: "Venice."
1 Mrs. Bronson.

RB TO FJF, 15 OCTOBER 1883

Palazzo Giustinian-Recanati, / Venice, Oct. 15. '83.

BETTER NOT, my dear Furnivall,—for it is in the lazy blood of the whole people; and telling them of their faults rather saddens than irritates them,—besides doing no sort of good.[1] Everybody who can block up a window, brick over a moulding or other apparently useless ornament,—does so—or, better, disposes of it,—a balcony, well, or such like fixture,—to the Jew antiquity-mongers. It is really an argument against the throwing open museums and galleries to the people on Sundays that here, where the works which glorify such institutions were originally produced, and where similar excellences may be still seen every day,—the inhabitants have the worst taste in the whole world. I believe that remonstrating with the pig-headed authorities here would merely confirm them in their obstinate determination to Liverpoolize Venice. Let them be, poor pigs with the devil in them![2] I wrote a word or two to Dowden:[3] and have no doubt he may get at the letters if he tries; they cannot well have been destroyed.

I never saw that book of Powell's to which you allude, and should refuse to accept a line of it as true—unless I *did* see it,— the author being a person of infamous character,—an unparalleled forger, who only escaped transportation thro' the ill-deserved kindness of his employers,—and who, premeditating a defence of "inborn and ineradicable dishonesty," actually practised forging on every possible occasion,—would send you, for instance, a letter signed "Dickens" or "Thackeray." I heard he had libelled me— who found him out earlier than most of his dupes. Dickens says something about him in the last collection of Letters.[4]

The brilliant weather continues: we arrived eleven days ago, —eleven perfect days have we had,—yet I see that Venice is "drenched with rain"—that is, in the newspaper. I break off— being wanted— but am

ever affectionately yours, / R Browning.

I shall be happy to read the new Seeley book[5]—but at home: do not take the trouble of sending it. While here, I take the opportunity of reading what I cannot so easily get elsewhere.

MS: HL. Address: Inghilterra / Frederick J. Furnivall, Esq / 3. St. George's Square, / Primrose Hill, / London. / N.W. Postmarks: VENEZIA 15 10 83 6S; LONDON NW MA OC 18 83. Note in FJF's hand on envelope: "Venice [illegible word]." Published: *LRB*, pp. 224-25; *LVC*, 1st Ser., II, 17-19.

1 The context suggests that FJF was threatening to launch one of his familiar angry crusades against the desecration of Venice mentioned in RB's previous letter.
2 An allusion to the story of the Gadarene swine; see *Mark* 5:13 and *Matthew* 8:32.
3 RB's letter to Dowden, dated 12 Oct. 1883, is printed in *LRB*, pp. 223-24. See also RB to FJF, 29 Sept. 1883, n. 4.
4 Thomas Powell (1809-87), poet and journalist, lavishly entertained RB and others in his circle in the early 1840s, but by January 1846 RB was denouncing Powell's "unimaginable, impudent, vulgar stupidity" in a letter to Miss Barrett. In July of that year it was learned that Powell had defrauded his employer, Thomas Chapman, of approximately £10,000. RB claimed that Powell affected "to forge, in sport, the signatures of his acquaintances in order to subsequently induce the belief, when his serious forgeries should be discovered, that he was simply a monomaniac on the matter of an irresistible itch at imitating other folks' handwriting" (*LRB*, p. 256). In any event, Powell escaped prosecution for this and subsequent offenses by being committed to a lunatic asylum at Hoxton, and later he escaped to America with a forged letter of credit from Chapman. There he wrote a book entitled *The Living Authors of England* (New York, 1849), revised and published in England two years later as *Pictures of the Authors of Britain*. The book's treatment of RB was sarcastic and patronizing, with an emphasis on RB's poetic obscurity that was damaging to his reputation in America. Dickens was so infuriated by Powell's chapter on him that he sent an account of Powell's shady past to the New York *Tribune*, whereupon Powell unsuccessfully sued Dickens for libel. (Thomas J. Wise, *The Ashley Library* [1922-36], IV, 66-67; *The Letters of Robert Browning and Elizabeth Barrett Barrett 1845-1846*, ed. Elvan Kintner [Cambridge, Mass., 1969], I, 380; Greer, p. 36; Edgar Johnson, *Charles Dickens: His Tragedy and Triumph* [New York, 1952], II, 597, 671.)
5 J. R. Seeley, *The Expansion of England: Two Courses of Lectures*, published by Macmillan.

RB TO FJF, 29 OCTOBER 1883

Venice, Oct. 29., '83.

My dear Furnivall,

Would you believe it?—for I hardly can,—I leave in a couple of days for Athens[1]—where I shall make a short stay enough but still realize an old dream I had thought was likely to remain a dream only. My Sister accompanies me, of course. It will be a great pleasure if I get a word from you and about you directed to me at the *Hotel des Etrangers*, Athens.

The weather continues superb: not a cloud on the blue: I am assured that, some seven years ago, there was *perhaps* such a benediction. We go to Brindisi, thence to Corfù, and so, through the isles, to Piræus.

I had a letter from Dowden saying that he was on the track of those letters and in good hope of catching them,—as, for truth's sake, I hope he may.[2]

Do you see that Robert's Fish-Picture at the Exhibition has obtained a Gold Medal?[3] He is at Paris to superintend the casting in Bronze of his "Dryope";[4] and meanwhile works at another Statue, —good enterprising and laborious fellow!

My Sister sends an energetic message of kindest regards—which accompany mine. Ever affectionately yours   RB.

MS: ABL. Address: *Inghilterra.* / Frederick J. Furnivall, Esq. / 3. St. George's Square, / Primrose Hill, / London. / N.W. Postmarks: VENEZIA 29 10 83 2S; LONDON NW XX OC 31 83. Note in FJF's hand on envelope: "going to / Athens."
1 See RB to FJF, 30 Oct. 1883, n. 2.
2 See RB to FJF, 29 Sept. 1883, n. 4.
3 Pen's painting *A Stall in the Fish-Market, Antwerp* was on display at the International Fisheries Exhibition, London, 13 May-1 Nov. 1883 (*LL*, pp. 77, 170). It had also been exhibited at the Royal Academy in 1879.
4 See RB to FJF, 22 Aug. 1884, n. 4.

RB TO FJF, 30 OCTOBER 1883

Venice, Oct. 30., '83.
"And by-and-by a cloud takes all away!"[1] and in this case, my dear Furnivall, the "glory" has been obscured by a discovery that the arrangements of our friends were hardly compatible with those necessary to ourselves,—so, unwillingly enough, the journey has been given up. Is it ever to be?[2] I make haste to tell you this much, and that, till you hear again, your letters (should you have occasion to write) will reach us here till we give fresh notice.
          Ever affectionately yours / Robert Browning.
Another exquisite day!

MS: Carl H. Pforzheimer Library. Address: *Inghilterra.* / Frederick J. Furnivall, Esq. / 3. St. George's Square, / Primrose Hill, / London. / N.W. Postmarks: VENEZIA 30 10-83; [LONDON] NW [. . .] 83. Note in FJF's hand on envelope: "not going to Greece."
1 Not identified; possibly an inaccurate quotation of Section V of Worsworth's "Ode: Intimations of Immortality from Recollections of Early Childhood" (1807). "Glory" may also be an allusion to "the glory that was Greece / And the grandeur that was Rome," ll. 9-10 of Edgar Allan Poe's "To Helen" (1831).
2 On 8 Nov. 1885 RB wrote to Mrs. FitzGerald: "As for the projected journey [to Athens]—*that* we did well to forego. The first arrangements tempted us—and properly,— but they proved altogether incompatible with the powers of locomotion of our intended companion [Mrs. Bronson]. . . ." (*LL*, p. 173.) RB never visited Greece.

RB TO FJF, 3 DECEMBER 1883

Venice, Dec. 3. '83.

My dear Furnivall,

I have lingered and lingered,—but so far believe now that I am really going at last, that I write to beg you to send whatever needs be to 19. Warwick Crescent,—as I hope to be there in the middle of next week. To-day completes the fourth Calendar month of my absence from England: two of them spent here,—with *one* only rainy day!

I take the word "apparitional" to mean what Mr Erlebach supposes—"the ghost-like gliding of hospital attendants": and no classical allusion at all.[1]

They are going to unveil and display here a monument erected to Goldoni: and the Committee did me the honor to request a word or two for insertion in an Album to which the principal men of letters in Italy have contributed: I made a sonnet which they please to think so well of that they preface the book with it.[2] I cannot stop for the ceremony,—but shall get—and let you have a Proof—surely the Director's Due!

The weather continues wonderful, I shall be glad, however, to see London and my friends again.

Ever yours affectionately / Robert Browning.

My sister sends her kind regards; I write in a hurry, our determination to leave, next Saturday, having only just been taken.

MS: BL. Address: *Inghilterra.* / F. J. Furnivall Esq. / 3. St. George's Square, / Primrose Hill, / London. / N.W. Postmarks: VENEZIA 3 12-83 3S; LONDON NW XX DE 5 83. Note in FJF's hand on envelope: "Goldoni sonnet & 'apparitional." Published: *LRB*, pp. 225-26; *LVC*, 1st Ser., II, 30-31.

1 Alfred Erlebach, an assistant to Sir James A. H. Murray (1837-1915; *DNB*), editor of the *Oxford English Dictionary*, made the following journal entry in June 1884: "Under 'apparitional' there was in the copy as prepared by Dr. Murray a second sense, 'Pertaining to service or attendance, ministering. From the classical sense of "apparition."' This classical sense is given under 'appear' as 'attendance, service, from a special sense of "apparete," to appear at a summons, wait upon, attend.' The only illustrative quotation was from Mrs. Browning's 'Aurora Leigh' [III.1111]. . . . I doubted the probability of the word here meaning anything but 'ghostlike.' Dr. Murray, however, stuck to his opinion. I wrote to Furnivall, asking whether he could get an authentic opinion. He replied that he certainly agreed with Dr. Murray, but would send on my postcard to Browning in Venice. The next communication was the subjoined:—
APPARITIONAL
Erlebach v. Murray and Furnivall.
Judgement for the Plaintiff.

84

(Defendants nowhere).

R.B. Venice. December 3, 1883.

[Here Erlebach quotes a portion of RB's letter.] In accordance with this expression of opinion the sense and quotation were struck out. But when Browning met Dr. Murray afterwards in Edinburgh he expressed some regret that that should have been done. It was only his own opinion, he said. He had never discussed the question with Mrs. Browning, and that might have been the meaning in her mind." ("In the Dictionary Margin: A Sub-Editor's Notes," The Times, 25 Oct. 1929, p. 17; I am indebted to Miss K. M. Elisabeth Murray for this reference.) Years later Dr. Murray made this observation on RB's own use of language: "Browning constantly used words without regard to their proper meaning. He has added greatly to the difficulties of the Dictionary." (K. M. Elisabeth Murray, *Caught in the Web of Words: James A. H. Murray and the 'Oxford English Dictionary'* [New Haven, 1977], p. 235.)

2   RB's sonnet on Carlo Goldoni (1707-93), Italian dramatist, was published by FJF in the *Pall Mall Gazette*, 8 Dec. 1883, p. 2, and *BSP*, I, 98*. The poem is dated Venice, 27 Nov. 1883.

KATHERINE BRONSON TO FJF, 3 DECEMBER [1883]

Palazzo Alvisi / Venice / December 3d

My dear Mr. Furnivall

I enclose you a sonnet wh[ich] Mr Browning has written for an album in honour of Goldoni—wh[ich] is to appear on the occasion of the unveiling of Goldoni's statue here, on the 20th of this month. It seems to me a most spirited little sonnet—& was written as I happen to know in as little time as I am taking to write this brief note.—

With all good wishes believe me

Always yours sincerely / K. deK. Bronson

MS: BL. Note in FJF's hand on letter: "Mrs. Bronson. / B.'s Goldoni poem."

RB TO FJF, 24 DECEMBER 1883

19. Warwick Crescent, W / Dec. 24. '83.

My dear Furnivall,

Thank you much for the "Academy" that comes this morning.[1] I know you will understand the letter which I got my Sister to write yesterday. Your kindness there can be no mistake about—and I feel it as thoroughly as you could desire—but you say quite enough about my poems, and, if your wish to avert the evil eye from them and me, you will report nothing of my doings,—

especially of my intercourse with people, which nowise differs from what it has been pretty nearly for the last half-century. So with Pen,—I am sure you have greatly helped him by calling attention to his works,—especially the sculpture, which excites no great curiosity in England: but a little undue notice will do him harm with his brothers of the brush and modelling-tool,—and they can prevent his *exhibiting:* my dislikers could not hinder my printing, you know.

In case there should occur a gap in your Paper through the excision I trust you will oblige me by making,—see what I will supply to fill up! I observe that Tennyson makes public the lines he wrote for Ld. Dufferin to engrave on Helen's Tower at Clandeboye: there is no harm therefore in giving you my own contribution,[2] similarly requested—though, I imagine or am pretty certain, the request came after that to him.[3] There was no compliment in what I said about the singularly love-inducing Lady.

Ever yours R Browning.

[Enclosure in RB's hand]

Helen's Tower.   Ἐλένῃ ἐπὶ πύργῳ[4]

Who hears of Helen's Tower may dream perchance
   How the Greek Beauty from the Scœan Gate
   Gazed on old friends unanimous in hate,
Death-doomed because of her fair countenance.
Hearts would leap otherwise at thy advance,
   Lady, to whom this Tower is consecrate!
   Like hers, thy face once made all eyes elate,
Yet, unlike hers, was blessed by every glance.
The Tower of Hate is outworn, far and strange;
   A transitory shame of long ago
   It dies into the sand from which it sprang;
But thine, Love's rock-built Tower, shall fear no change:
   God's self laid stable earth's foundation so,
   When all the morning-stars together sang.
Robert Browning.

April 26. '70.

MS: HEH and Newnham College Library. Address: F. J. Furnivall, Esq. / 3. St. George's Square, / Primrose Hill, / *N.W.* Postmark: PADDINGTON 4C DE 24 83. Notes in FJF's hand on envelope: "*Helen's Tower* / given to Newnham / B's own copy."

1 The *Academy*, 24 (22 Dec. 1883), 414, printed four paragraphs (undoubtedly contributed by FJF) about the recent activities of RB and about Pen's *Dryope* in its "Notes and News" column. One of these paragraphs caused a small crisis for George Smith. It read: "We hear that Mr. Browning's publisher has at last resolved to yield in some degree to the appeals that have been made to him so persistently by the press and in private for the last few years for a cheaper edition of some of the poet's works. A new edition of the two volumes of the Selections is to be published, at 3*s.* 6*d.* a volume; and the volumes will be sold separately. Let us hope that a shilling edition of them will follow next year. That is what is needed." In an undated letter to RB (Murray) written shortly after the appearance of this paragraph, Smith declared that a tentative plan to publish the Shilling Selection first would now have to be abandoned because of this premature announcement. "I have no idea," he added, "How the 'Academy' got their information—but from the tone of the paragraph I conjecture that it was written by Mr Furnivall. It would be difficult to say exactly how much that Gentleman's impertinent interference with your works has cost you, but it is no inconsiderable sum." On 1 Jan. 1884 RB replied to Smith (Murray): "I was very vexed,—far beyond what I should hope *you* were,—by the appearance of that paragraph—and all the more that myself was the unwitting prompter of it. Mr Furnivall called on me at Portland Place on the Sunday after I had seen you and had read your letter about the proposed cheaper edition of the 'Selections'—and I mentioned the fact to him as an instance of your readiness to take any step towards a help to the inculcation of my poems whenever you believed it was really in my interest to do so: and he altogether approved and applauded,—adding 'The price of the retail bookseller's will be so much—that quite brings their purchase into the power of everybody.' I could not dream he would at once print the news with the offensive comment,—which could answer no possible good end. Of course, I am all the more hampered by the circumstance that, in spite of his blundering, Mr Furnivall means beyond a doubt to do me all the service he is able: it is the old story of the friendly bear who broke the teeth of the man with the stone he meant should brush away a fly that had settled on his mouth." As a result of FJF's "blundering," Smith did not publish a Shilling Selection until after RB's death.

2 Note in FJF's hand: "given to / Newnham."

3 In 1861 Frederick Temple Hamilton-Temple Blackwood, 1st Marquess of Dufferin and Ava (1826-1902; *DNB*), privately printed a pamphlet entitled *Helen's Tower, Clandeboye*, containing a poem by Tennyson and memorializing a tower erected by Dufferin in Clandeboye, Ireland, in honor of his mother, Helen Selina Sheridan, Countess of Dufferin (1807-67; *DNB*). In 1870 the pamphlet was reissued with the addition of RB's poem "Helen's Tower," dated 26 Apr. 1870. RB's sonnet was printed by FJF in the *Pall Mall Gazette*, 28 Dec. 1883, p. 2, and *BSP*, I, 97*. As FJF's note indicates, he later gave RB's MS of "Helen's Tower" to Newnham College, Cambridge, where it is today. On the verso of the MS FJF wrote this note: "Late in Decr. 1883 I sent Browning a proof of our Brg. Soc. Notes in which I had praised some work of his son's [*Dryope*]. He thought it had better not appear; & when asking me to cut it out, he wrote [here FJF quotes the last paragraph of RB's letter]. This sonnet is the best that Browning ever wrote, & is certainly better than Tennyson's lines on the same subject. / F. J. Furnivall, / 25 May, 1893." Another MS of "Helen's Tower" in RB's hand, also a fair copy, is in the Widener Collection of the Harvard College Library. It has recently been suggested that an alleged offprint of the poem in the Wrenn Collection of the Humanities Research Center, the University of Texas, is a forgery by T. J. Wise

(Clinton Machann, "The Wise-Wrenn Copy of Browning's *Helen's Tower*," *Papers of the Bibliographical Society of America*, 68 [1974], 432-34). The text of the Wrenn copy appears to be based on the text supplied by RB to FJF in 1883 rather than on an 1892 reprint of the poem as Machann asserts.

4 "Helen [approaching] along the tower" (*Iliad*, III.154.) RB's poem is based upon the scene in the *Iliad* in which Helen of Troy looks at the Greek army from the Scœan Gate.

RB TO FJF, 26 DECEMBER 1883

19, Warwick Crescent, / W.* / Dec. 26. '83.

Oh no, my dear Furnivall,—I have not the heart to wish the kind praises *out* now that they are *in*: enough that I did, as in modesty bound, "protest—which, as I take it, is a very gentlemanly" &c &c[1] —and enough, also, that you have disposed of the other allusion,[2] —for which, many thanks.

No, I have written—I believe—at the desire of nobody else,—anything of this kind, at least. I knew and had some particular experience of this Lady many years ago,—how good she could be to a poor Italian boy I recommended to her notice.

All best Christmas wishes to you!

Ever affe[ctionatel]y yours *RB*.

MS: HEH. Address: F. J. Furnivall, Esq. / 3. St. George's Square, / Primrose Hill, / N.W. Postmarks: ST JOHNS WOOD NW AX DE 26 83; [second postmark illegible]. Note in FJF's hand on envelope: "Bibliography."
1 Shakespeare, *Romeo and Juliet*, II.iv.189, slightly misquoted.
2 Note in FJF's hand: "(to the rascal T. Powell)."

RB TO FJF, 11 JANUARY 1884

19, Warwick Crescent, / W.* / Jan. 11, '84.

My dear Furnivall,

The little things have come at last, and here they go begging your acceptance—old Venetian, or rather Bassanese majolica.[1] They will be, at all events, conspicuous in your room—therefore, "When these you see Remember me ["][2]—who am

ever affectionately yours / Robert Browning.

MS: Browning Society of London (reconstituted). Address: Frederick J. Furnivall, Esq. / 3. St. George's Square, / Primrose Hill. / N.W. Note in FJF's hand on envelope: "gives me / Bassanese / Majolica." Published: *NL*, p. 296.

1 The two majolica wall plaques are today owned by the Browning Society of London, which received them as a gift from FJF's granddaughters.
2 Perhaps a paraphrase or inaccurate recollection of Shakespeare, *Hamlet*, I.v.91.

RB TO FJF, 13 JANUARY 1884

19, Warwick Crescent, / W.* / Jan. 13. '84.

⟨My dear⟩ Furnivall,

The paper you are in search of ⟨appea⟩rs in a *Magazine edited* by ⟨La⟩dy Barker, published some years ⟨ag⟩o, and, I suppose, now discontinued. The paper was by her husband, Napier Broome, then abroad, and was a sort of reminscence of men and things he had known.[1]

Ever truly yours / Robert Browning.

MS (not seen): Charles James, Roanoke, Va. Text: *Wilmington Star-News* (North Carolina), 31 May 1970, p. 7B (photograph). Address: F. J. Furnivall, Esq. / 3. St. George's Square, / Primrose Hill, / N.W. Postmarks: LONDO[N W?] 7 JA 1[4?] 84; LONDON NW LA JA 14 84.
1 Alfred Domett recorded in his diary on 9 Dec. 1875 (p. 161): "B.[rowning] spoke of Napier Broome, a gentleman who writing from Port Natal, had sent to a London paper a description of people, interesting it is presumed to the public, whom he had met in England. Among others, he had introduced 'little Swinburne' (as B. called him) recording some of his peculiarities: which had produced some sonnets from Swinburne in the *Examiner* (?) abusing Broome as a 'bug' or some such vermin." The article by Sir Frederick Napier Broome (1842-96; *DNB*), a colonial administrator, appeared under the title "Literature and Art in London at the Present Day" in *Evening Hours*, 2 (1875), 766-75, and Swinburne's indignant poetic reply, "Epitaph on a Slanderer," was published in the *Examiner*, 20 Nov. 1875, pp. 130-34 (reprinted in *The Ballade of Truthful Charles and Other Poems* [privately printed by T. J. Wise, 1910], p. 22). Mary Anne, Lady Barker (1831-91), who married Broome in 1865, edited *Evening Hours* from 1874 to 1877. Since Broome's article refers to both Swinburne and RB, it is not clear which of the two references had aroused the curiosity of FJF.

RB TO FJF, 22 JANUARY 1884

19, Warwick Crescent, / W.* / Jan. 22. '84.

My dear Furnivall,

I saw, to my great delight, in the Paper this morning, the righteous and timely award which Gladstone has done himself honor by bestowing.[1] Afterwards came your letter,—why tell you what you know well enough—that I enjoy your satisfaction which cannot exceed mine?

Affectionately yours / Robert Browning.

MS: HEH. Address: F. J. Furnivall, Esq., / 3. St. George's Square, / Primrose Hill, / N.W. Postmarks: PADDINGTON 5 JA [2]2 84 [...] ; LONDON NW KJ JA 22 84. Note in FJF's hand on envelope: "my Pension."

1 In the Bodleian (MS. Eng. lett. d. 187, fol. 213-14) are two copies of a petition signed by eleven eminent Oxford men, recommending a pension for FJF. (Presumably other copies of the petition were also submitted to the Prime Minister.) FJF had earlier invested his inheritance in Overend and Guerney's Bank, which collapsed in 1867, and was consequently a relatively poor man. On 20 Jan. 1884 Gladstone wrote to FJF (HEH) offering him a Civil List pension of £150 per annum "in acknowledgement of your valuable services to the literature of your country." FJF gratefully accepted the pension and later wrote of it: "I really wanted it, couldn't have made Percy an allowance without it" (FJF to C. H. Pearson, 3 Mar. 1885 [Bodleian MS. lett. d. 187, fol. 208]).

RB TO FJF, 29 JANUARY 1884

19, Warwick Crescent, / W.* / Jan. 29. '84.

My dear Furnivall,

Robert's address is—Maison Lavenue, 1. rue du Départ, Gare Mont-Parnasse, Paris.

What I have to say about the proposed publication of the "Book" causes me great pain, for I feel that my own misapprehension and carelessness are causing you much trouble and perhaps some little pain also: yet you will judge me the more leniently that my hasty inconsideration came of the dislike I cannot but feel at seeming to thwart any action of yours who have done so much to serve my poems and myself. I supposed, when the matter was mooted two years ago, that all wanted was to place a thing, absolutely *unique* of its kind, out of the possibility of loss or destruction—by fire, ignorance or whatever might be the accident,—a copy to be laid up in the archives of your Society, while the original was deposited at Balliol.[1] I never thought of any measure which would, —so to speak—pull up my tree and exhibit the roots to the "Public"—whose sagacity I have had half-a-century's experience of. Before setting to work on the Poem, I examined the "Book" thoroughly; and the result is all that I wish my readers to be acquainted with: it is simply impossible that anybody else—for many a year to come, at least—will devote himself to such a business as a complete study of all the crabbed latin documents which themselves demand a previous series of studies: it would simply prove to be what I say—an useless uprooting of my tree—to the ruin of its branch as well as root. Therefore, pray forgive me if,—in my unwillingness to object to a proposal I ought to have first of all endeavoured to understand in its bearings and consequences,—I cause you inconvenience—which will hardly be commensurate with my regret. You are too good, however, to treat hardly on one who thus comes forward to take the whole blame on himself. I write in great haste—but you ought not to be kept in ignorance of my feeling one moment longer than is necessary.

Ever truly yours / Robert Browning.

MS: HEH. Address: Frederick J. Furnivall, Esq / 3. St. George's Square, / Primrose Hill, / N.W. Postmarks: PADDINGTON W 7 JA 30 84 K; LONDON NW LA JA 30 84. Note in FJF's hand on envelope: "*Book* / of *R. & B.*"

1 In the first Annual Report of the Browning Society (*BSP*, I, iii), issued 7 July 1882, one of the future publications listed is a reproduction of the Old Yellow Book, upon which *The Ring and the Book* was based (see RB to FJF, 20 Feb. 1883, n. 2). A half year later the *Academy* (21 [21 Jan. 1882], 42) announced: "The Browning Society will, we understand, as soon as funds permit, ask Mr. Browning to let it facsimile or print the 'Book' of *The Ring and the Book*. . . ." By 1883 FJF was encouraging American Browningites to raise money for the project (FJF to Hiram Corson, 19 Feb. 1883, above; FJF to Jenkin Lloyd Jones, 11 July 1883 [ABL]), and the Society's Annual Report for 1883 (*BSP*, I, xiii) also recorded donations from several English members. After RB's death T. J. Wise and James Dykes Campbell attempted to revive the undertaking (*Oracle*, p. 85), but the Old Yellow Book was not published until 1908.

R. B. BROWNING TO FJF, 3 FEBRUARY 1884

1. rue du Départ. / Gare Mont Parnasse. / Paris.

My dear Mr Furnivall,

I am very much indebted to you for your kindness in sending me the memoir of Miss Rochfort-Smith.

I have read it with the greatest interest.

Yours very sincerely, / R. Barrett Browning.

Feb. 3. 1884.

MS: HEH. Address: F. J. Furnivall, Esqr. / 3, St. George's Square, / Primrose Hill, / London, N.W. / *Angleterre*. Postmarks: PARIS RUE LITTRE 4E 3 FEVR 84; [LON]DON NW 7U FE 84 [. . .]. Note in FJF's hand on envelope: "*R. Barrett Browning.*"

RB TO FJF, 14 FEBRUARY 1884

19, Warwick Crescent, / W.* / Feb. 14, '84.
My dear Furnivall,

I am backward with a vengeance in wishing you very many and happy returns of the Birthday that happened ten days ago. I was wanting to do some pressing pieces of business (in a little way) and foolishly put off a pleasure for a duty—*foolishly*, because the pleasure was a duty too.

Now, as to your startling proposal about my new book:[1] I think, or am sure, that you are too sanguine,—but I should be wanting in respect to your kindness as well as sagacity if I altogether disregarded it. So I will just say—or rather enquire—what would Messrs. Harper give for twelve consecutive poems in blank verse, preceded by a lyrical prologue and epilogue, forming one poem on a variety of exceedingly serious subjects, connected one with the other, and making together a volume of some 1500 or 2000 lines—very capable of appearing in twelve numbers of their magazine and eventually constituting one work, the whole publication being contingent on its leaving English copyright absolutely in my power? "Tell me *that*, Master Brooke!"[2] and believe me—in spite of the deduction I confidently expect of performance from promise—

Ever truly yours / Robert Browning.

MS: HEH. Address: F. J. Furnivall, Esq. / 3. St. George's Square, / Primrose Hill, / N.W. Postmarks: PADDINGTON W L4 FE 14 84; LOND[ON] NW [. . .] H FE 14 84. Note in FJF's hand on envelope: "Harper's & / new vol. of Poems."

1 As this and the following letter indicate, the "starting proposal" came from an American woman who suggested that *Ferishtah's Fancies* be published in *Harper's Magazine*. There is no record of such a proposal in any of the published histories of the magazine or the house of Harper, or in the *Harper's Magazine* archives in the Manuscript Division of the Library of Congress. The London representative of *Harper's* at this time was William M. Laffan (1848-1909; *DAB*).

2 Master Ford appears in the guise of Master Brook[e] in Shakespeare's *The Merry Wives of Windsor*.

RB TO FJF, 17 FEBRUARY 1884

19, Warwick Crescent, / W.* / Feb. 17, '84.
Oh, *no*—emphatically *ny*, dear Mr Furnivall! As Gladstone said the other night, "You have fallen into the decoy"[1]— I ventured on

tempting you with,—well-knowing what these swollen offers dwindle to when never so gently pricked. Your great kindness claimed of me that I should give a respectful attention to the American Lady's surprising proposal,—but the notion of anybody [']having to see the poem before" &c &c "as they must judge how far it would suit &c"—however "reasonable"—sounds funnily to me who for fifty years have stipulated that my publishers should never read a line of the work they were to publish until it was in *corrected* proofs. I should indeed be going back to "my salad days when I was green in judgment."[2] You incidentally throw a beam of electrical light on a darkling and modest virtue of Smith's, which were it his only one, would suffice to justify my continued dealings with him,—his cheerful acceptance of this condition from the very first—and on the very last of our transactions he good-naturedly remarked "Had you let me read "Jocoseria" I would have printed 500 additional copies at once." NO—such a privilege is well-worth paying-for (if, after all, I *do* pay in any shape) for—what says some poet or other? " 'Tis Liberty that crowns Britannia's Isle, and makes her barren rocks and her bleak mountains smile."[3] Therefore,—pray thank the Lady for her undoubtedly well-intended offer of intervention, and tell her that the rocks and mountains ... but I can versify: "The air one breathes with Smith may be sharper: But—save me from Scirocco's heat in Harper!" All this—absolutely between you and me—you will please to translate into a simple polite thanking and declining of a very flattering proposal.

Yes,—I saw the letter of my unknown advocate in the "Daily News"—a paper I take in regularly. The fussy foolish gentleman who put his little person forward so officiously is laughed at throughout Venice for his pains. The anecdote was even mentioned in the "Times" notice of Rawdon Brown -written, I am told, by Ly. Eastlake: don't give the silliness another word, pray—[4]

Ever truly yours / Robert Browning.

MS: BL. Address: F. J. Furnivall, Esq. / 3. St. George's Square, / Primrose Hill, N.W. Postage stamp not cancelled. Published: *LRB*, pp. 226-27; *LVC*, 2nd Ser., II, 13-16.

1 In a parliamentary debate on 13 Feb., Gladstone declared: "I admit that it was in the nature of a decoy offered to honourable gentlemen, and they took it and cheered it to the echo when I said it did not matter whether the proposal was this or that, provided it was condemnatory" (*Times*, 13 Feb. 1884, p. 9).

2 Shakespeare, *Antony and Cleopatra*, I.v.73-74.

3 Not identified.

4 Rawdon Brown (1803-83; *DNB*), English historian, lived in Venice from 1833 to the
end of his life, doing research in the Venetian archives. According to a letter in *The
Times* (8 Sept. 1883, p. 6)—which is signed "E.E." and is attributed by RB to Elizabeth, Lady Eastlake (1809-93; *DNB*)—"It is long since he paid a visit to England.
Some years ago he prepared to do so, but, stepping to the window, he looked down
on the Grand Canal, all quivering and sparkling with the reflections from the Grand
Bevelacqua Palace opposite, and, turning to his servant with a face of emotion, he
said, 'Toni, unpack my things; I cannot go.' " RB's humorous sonnet based on this
anecdote, dated 28 Nov. 1883, was written at Mrs. Bronson's request and published
in the *Century Magazine*, 27 (February 1884), 640. FJF reprinted it in *BSP* (I, 132*)
with this explanation: "Rawdon Brown's executor, Mr. Cavendish Bentinck, made a
comical fuss in the Papers about the Sonnet, as if Browning had put forth the apoc-
ryphal story in it as Gospel. The *Century* editor was the man in fault: he said that the
Sonnet 'recorded an incident' of Brown's death."

RB TO FJF, 27 MARCH 1884

19, Warwick Crescent, / W.* / March 27. '84.

My dear Furnivall,

I have had many of my songs set to music—that from "James
Lee" was so treated, at the time of publication, by Miss Gabriel.[1]
Mr Lawson,[2] Mr Stanford[3] and others have succeeded very well:
and I have been asked by Sir J. Benedict and Rubenstein[4] to write
songs for them—

I indited a Sonnet for the Fair[5]—too hastily perhaps, but it may
do.

Ever truly yours / Robert Browning

MS: HEH. Address: F. J. Furnivall, Esq. / 3. St. George's Square, / Primrose Hill, /
N.W. Postmarks: PADDINGTON W [. . .] MR 27 84 J; LONDON NW KE MR 27 84.
Note in FJF's hand on envelope: "Words for Music." Note in FJF's hand on letter:
"Ethel Harraden's request for / some words more suited to music, / as B.'s written a
few. / B. doesn't like it, evidently."
In the spring of 1884 (probably March rather than May, as Miss Harraden remembered), FJF visited the Hampstead home of Miss Ethel Harraden (sister of novelist
Beatrice Harraden [1864-1936; *DNB*]), afterwards Mrs. Glover, to suggest that she
compose musical settings for some of RB's poems. Though she admitted that she had
never read any of his works, FJF insisted that she begin composing at once, and he
chatted casually the rest of the evening with her father while she retired to her room
and skimmed through RB's collected works. That same night she composed a setting
for the first stanza of "James Lee's Wife." "And one Sunday afternoon," wrote Miss
Harraden—"a memorable day I shall never forget—Dr. Furnivall took me to see the
great poet, and I had the honour of singing the song to him. He seemed very pleased
with it, and made me very proud by accepting the dedication." (*Furnivall*, pp. 66-67.)
At the Browning Society's third Annual Entertainment, 27 June 1884, Miss Harraden's "The Lost Leader," "Wilt Thou Change Too?" (from "James Lee's Wife"), and
"I Go to Prove My Soul" (from *Paracelsus*) were sung (*BSP*, I, 148*-49*). The latter

two songs (which were published that year by C. Jeffreys) and other compositions by Miss Harraden were also performed at subsequent entertainments of the Browning Society.

1   Mary Ann Virginia Gabriel (1825-77; *DNB*), composer of drawing-room ballads, had provided a musical setting for the initial section of "James Lee's Wife," which was performed at the First Entertainment of the Browning Society, 30 June 1882 (*BSP*, I, 137). During the 1860s there was a rumour that RB would marry her, and she was also involved in his quarrel with Lady Ashburton (*Browning to His American Friends: Letters between the Brownings, the Storys and James Russell Lowell 1841-1890*, ed. Gertrude R. Hudson [1965], pp. 142, 168).

2   Malcolm Lawson (b. 1849), composer and conductor, appeared at the second Annual Entertainment of the Browning Society, 29 June 1883, at which two of his Browning settings were performed, "One Way of Love" and "Is she not pure gold, my mistress?" (*BSP*, I, 140*-41*).

3   Sir Charles Villiers Stanford (1852-1924; *DNB*), composer, conductor, and teacher of music, met RB at Cambridge and saw him frequently thereafter. His setting of "Cavalier Tunes" was performed at three Annual Entertainments of the Browning Society (30 June 1882, 29 June 1883, and 27 June 1884), and his setting of "Prospice" was on the program of the 28 Nov. 1884 Entertainment. (Stanford, *Pages from an Unwritten Diary* [1914], p. 176; Sotheran Catalogue No. 737 [1914], Lot 385; *BSP*, I, 137*, 140*, 152*-53*; II, Appendix.)

4   Sir Julius Benedict (1804-85; *DNB*) and Anton G. Rubinstein (1830-94). RB frequently attended Rubinstein's concerts in London.

5   At FJF's suggestion RB contributed the sonnet "The Names (To Shakespeare)" to the *Shakespearean Show-Book* (1884) for the Shakespearean Show which was held in the Albert Hall, 29-31 May 1884, to raise funds for the Hospital for Women in Fulham Road. The poem—dated 12 Mar. 1884—was reprinted in the *Pall Mall Gazette, BSP* (I, 105*), and many other publications.

RB TO FJF, 25 APRIL 1884

19, Warwick Crescent, / W.* / Apr. 25. '84.

My dear Furnivall,

I don't see that, because a clown's conception of the laws of the Heavenly bodies is grotesque and impossible, that of Newton must be necessarily as absurd,—or that the writer of "La Saisiaz" must see through such horny eyes as those of Caliban: besides, in each case, there is a faculty of reason which should be employed in correcting and adjusting the first impressions of the senses—and, I hope, the two make a very different use of their respective faculties,—one doubts and the other has no doubt at all, "—'sayeth" so and so, as if Prospero could say no otherwise. Then, as to the divergence from Shakespeare's Caliban,—is it so decided?[1] There is no "forgetfulness of his love for music"—since he makes a song and sings it,—nor of his "visions of Heaven," for he speculates on what goes on there,—nor of his resolve to "learn wisdom and seek grace"

—seeing what he falls flat and loveth Setebos, and was a fool to gibe at a Power he had miscalculated. True, "he was a very different being at the end of the Play from what he was at its beginning" —but my Caliban indulges his fancies long before even that beginning. All the same, "fire away!"

I have hardly had a minute, of late, to be quiet in: my son is here, Milsand is here also, and I have been away, as you know, and much engaged in matters of a teasing nature about—well, let me forget them![2] Your young lady was abundantly welcome to the song.[3] I hope to see you on Sunday, of course.

Ever truly yours, / Robert Browning.

MS: HL. Address: F. J. Furnivall, Esq. / 3. St. George's Square, / Primrose Hill, / N.W. Postmarks: PADDINGTON W L2 AP 25 84; LONDON NW KF AP 25 84. Note in FJF's hand on envelope: "my objection / to Caliban." Published: *LRB*, pp. 228-29; *LVC*, 1st Ser., II, 32-34.

1 James Cotter Morison (1831-88; *DNB*), Positivist writer, read a paper on "Caliban upon Setebos" to the Browning Society on 25 Apr. (*BSP*, I, 489-98), and during the ensuing discussion (*BSP*, I, 115*-19*) FJF emphasized the difference between RB's Caliban and Shakespeare's Caliban in *The Tempest* and strongly denounced a passage in *La Saisiaz* as "Calibanism." Memorandum by FJF: "This letter is in answer to one of mine accusing B. of not having done justice to Shakspere's Caliban & having left out all the signs of improvement that Sh. had put into Caliban. I told B. that I meant to pitch into him for it; so he said 'fire away!' Caliban was a Tory at the start of *The Tempest*, but was becoming rational & a Radical at its close." (BL Ashley B.2567.)
2 RB had spent a week in Edinburgh, where he received an honorary degree from the University. (See Rosaline Masson, "Robert Browning in Edinburgh," *Cornhill Magazine*, NS 26 [February 1909], 226-40.)
3 See RB to FJF, 27 Mar. 1884, first note.

RB TO FJF, 20 JUNE 1884

19, Warwick Crescent, / W.* / June 20. '84.

My dear Furnivall,

Certainly you may make that use of the songs and lines which you require. Miss Ethel and Mr Bending are kind indeed,[1] and I am glad my words are found able to be "married" with their notes—as Milton's expression is.[2]

I thank you heartily for the offer of the Ticket for my Sister,[3] —but there is no chance, unfortunately, of her being able to go out of an evening for a long while: her attack has been grave, and though she gets better and stronger every day, she must expect no resumption of her old ways at present. Pen left last week as soon as he was well assured that the main danger was over.

And many thanks to Mr Weld for his references to Motley, and his account of doughty John Haring's deed of valour.[4] It is good to read of and remember, whether I be able to put it into verse or no.

I have only spoken once to Smith about the "Selections": they were doing very well, he said,—but, of course, Country publishers sent back the more expensive edition.[5]

Ever truly yours / Robert Browning.

MS: HEH. Address: Frederick J. Furnivall, Esq. / 3. St. George's Square, / Primrose Hill, / N.W. Postmarks: PADDINGTON W 6 JU 20 84 R; LONDON NW KK JU 20 84. Note in FJF's hand on envelope: "Song, ent[ertainment]."

1   "Miss Ethel" is Ethel Harraden (see RB to FJF, 27 Mar. 1884). Edwin Bending composed "In a Gondola," a duet with violincello obligato, for the Browning Society's Annual Entertainment on 27 June 1884.
2   "And ever against eating Cares, / Lap me in soft *Lydian* Airs, / Married to immortal verse . . ." (Milton, "L'Allegro," ll. 135-37).
3   The ticket for the Annual Entertainment.
4   During the battle of the Diemerdyk (1573) in the Netherlands, "John Haring, of Horn, had planted himself entirely alone upon the dyke, where it was so narrow between the Y on the one side and the Diemer Lake on the other, that two men could hardly stand abreast. Here, armed with sword and shield, he had actually opposed and held in check one thousand of the enemy, during a period long enough to enable his own men, if they had been willing, to rally, and effectively to repel the attack. It was too late, the battle was too far lost to be restored; but still the brave soldier held the post, till, by his devotion, he had enabled all those of his compatriots who still remained in the entrenchments to make good their retreat. He then plunged into the sea, and, untouched by spear or bullet, effected his escape." (John L. Motley, *The Rise of the Dutch Republic* [New York, 1874], II, 441-42.) RB had read the book in 1859 (*DI*, p. 35). Mr. Weld is probably M. R. Weld, M.C.S., of Prince of Wales Road, Dorchester, whose name appears in the Browning Society membership lists and whose verse translation of *Antigone* was published in 1905.
5   A slightly sarcastic allusion to FJF's untimely announcement of the 3/6 selection of RB's poems, an announcement which appeared before Smith, Elder was able to dispose of its stock of an earlier, more expensive selection. See RB to FJF, 24 Dec. 1883, n. 1.

RB TO FJF, 22 AUGUST 1884

Villa Berry, St. Moritz, / Engadine, Switzerland. /
Aug. 22. '84.

My dear Furnivall, I was going to write, when the letter, which I send, reached me: you will know what to do in the matter it mentions.[1] We left London a week ago,—unable to hope of reaching last year's quarters without undergoing quarantine: what the heat was you know: we travelled hither in some forty five hours, and are very comfortably housed in a place where the cold might comfort King John.[2] My Sister who, you remember, was hardly recovered from her illness, bore the transport capitally, and we are both of us walking on the hill-sides after our accustomed fashion. Snow is on all the mountain tops, and the freshness, combined to-day with plenty of sunshine, is restorative indeed. We shall stay here till the embargo is taken off—unless that comes too late. Meanwhile I am correcting the proofs of my poem—"Ferishta's [*sic*] Fancies", I style it instead of the title first hit upon—and the thing will be "out" in Autumn,—probably.[3]

Robert's "Dryope" was too late for the Brussels Exhibition,—which properly (I mean, according to their rules) admitted no work at the time of the Grosvenor's closing: he applied no less for a "délai",—only granted in exceptional cases,—and sent photographs of the Statue to plead for him: the Committee accorded the favour "with unanimity",—in pleasant contrast to the Council of the R.A., and Dryope is on her pedestal at Brussels by this time:[4] all which your friendliness will like to know. In return, you will give me all the news of yourself and your boatings and other delights:[5] such a lake lies before me as I write! but the boats there seem a lazy sort of "land-carracks"—whatever these may be.[6] Goodbye, heartily. My Sister sends her kindest regards.

Ever yours truly / Robert Browning.

MS: HEH. Address: Angleterre. / Frederick J. Furnivall, Esq. / 3. St. George's Square, / Primrose Hill, / London. / N.W. Postmarks: ST MORIZ DORF 23 VIII 84 VI; HAMPSTEAD SO 7 AU 25 84 NW; LONDON N[W] 10 AU 25 84. Note in FJF's hand on envelope: "Ferishta's / Fancies / Prof Pearson. Melbourne / Shaksp. Socy."

1 "As President of the New Shakspere Society, Mr. Browning has received notice from Melbourne that, since May last, two Shakspere Societies have been founded there" (*Academy*, 26 [30 Aug. 1884], 136). FJF's note on the envelope reveals that this message came from Charles H. Pearson (1830-94; *DNB*), English-born historian and politician, who had emigrated to Australia in 1871. In the early 1860s RB knew Pearson and had once consulted him about Pen's university education (William Stebbing, ed., *Charles Henry Pearson . . . Memorials* [1900], p. 171); in the Bodleian there are two letters from RB to Pearson (24 Feb. 1864 and n.d. [1862?]). Pearson was also a Vice-President of the New Shakspere Society and a very close friend of FJF.

2 King John, dying of poisoning, begs "cold comfort" (Shakespeare, *King John*, V.vii.42).

3 *Ferishtah's Fancies* was published on 21 Nov. 1884. I can find no record of an earlier title, though RB did abandon his original titles for the parts (DeVane, p. 475). RB's presentation copy to FJF (Berg) is signed and dated 18 Nov. by RB, with these notes

in FJF's hand: "?this—& not *Jocoseria*, as the *Speaker* says—B's weakest volume";
"All the Songs or Interludes written in one week, after the rest of the Poem, to
lighten it. / R.B. 23 Nov. 1884."

4 Pen Browning's nude bronze statue entitled *Dryope Fascinated by Apollo in the
Form of a Serpent* (photograph in Maisie Ward, *The Tragi-Comedy of Pen Browning*
[New York, 1972], p. 90) was submitted to the Royal Academy, but despite the support of Frederic Leighton it was rejected by the older Academicians, who thought it
coarse. The Grosvenor Gallery (which was usually unwilling to consider works rejected by the R.A.) accepted the *Dryope* for its 1884 exhibition when a tearful RB
personally intervened on his son's behalf. (Gertrude Reese, "Robert Browning and His
Son," *PMLA*, 61 (1946), 796; Charles E. Hallé, *Notes from a Painter's Life* [1909],
pp. 189-90.) The deadline for the Brussels Exhibition was 25 July 1884 (*LL*, p. 183).
On 10 Oct. 1884 RB reported to George Smith (Murray): "You will like to know that
Pen's 'Dryope' is having a hospitable reception at Brussels, and something more, indeed. On sight of the photographs, the Jury granted an exceptional delay, since the
Grosvenor Gallery could not release the Statue till a fortnight after the last day of admission to the Brussels 'Beaux Arts'—and, on its arrival, they gave it the absolutely
best place in the 'Salle de Sculpture'—which contains 178. works: the criticisms in the
newspapers that have reached me, are wholly eulogistic,—and by writers of repute."
See also RB to FJF, 7 Sept. 1885.

5 FJF was on holiday in Yorkshire during August (Edward Bell, *George Bell, Publisher*
[1924], pp. 125-26).

6 The *Oxford English Dictionary* defines a "land-carrack" as "?a coasting vessel" or
"=land-frigate."

RB TO FJF, 28 SEPTEMBER 1884

Villa Berry, St. Moritz., Engadin[e]. / Sept. 28. '84.
My dear Furnivall,

We leave for London next Wednesday—Oct. 1: and count upon
arriving there in a couple of days: so that if you are in Town, and
charitably minded, you will come and "batten on cold bits"[1] with
us this day week, and hear all our news. We had not been here a
fortnight when our kind Hostess[2] was summoned to America, to
her great vexation: imperative as the summons was, she only
obeyed it on condition of our remaining her guests to the end of
our visit's natural term: and we have done so. There was no avoiding the Quarantine established at all the Italian passes till a short
while ago,—and long before then our beloved Mrs Bronson, being
at Kreuznach[3] and similarly shut out apparently from return, de-
termined to go on to Paris and London: our mind was accordingly
made up to forego Venice and return to London when return
needed to be. Two days since, the wonderful friend telegraphed
to us that she should greatly prefer changing her plans, going back
to Venice, and receiving us there,—"if we did not fear the cholera":

the cholera—above all, at Venice where, I believe, it has never yet entered,—does not frighten us at all—but the notion of our friend's making such a sacrifice on our account, was unendurable, and we keep to our determination. There are also many matters which want attending to personally in London: and our seven weeks here have passed so profitably that we must be content without the usual Italian supplement. Nothing could exceed the delightfulness of the weather: I write at this moment (not 9. a.m.) in a blaze of sunshine which I shrink from at the unluckily most convenient table in the room; and so it has been uninterruptedly for the last two weeks:—not a symptom of a cloud in the blue to-day: yet the "season" is over long ago, the hotels are shut up, and the place deserted nearly. We have walked every day, morning and evening —afternoon, I should say—two or three hours each excursion,— the delicious mountain-air surpassing any I was ever privileged to breathe. My Sister is absolutely herself again—and something over: I was hardly in want of such doctoring. Well,—I saw an advertisement, in last week's Saturday Review, of my new Poem[4]—somewhat to my surprise, for there are reasons for keeping back the publication for at least a week or two: my part is done, however —and the last corrected "proofs" are at the Printer's. I can't at all guess how people will like it—but I have managed to say a thing or two that I "fancied" I should like to say.

Since I began this, I have walked on and up the mountain for three hours: the splendor of the day is indescribable. To be sure, you have a fine St. Martin, by all accounts, and so much the better! But you cannot have the air of these altitudes: nor, alas, can I —next week! It would have been pleasant to feel oneself gradually *let down* into the winter, by a two-months' sojourn in Venice.

My Sister sends her kindest regards: *she*, at all events, will witness your great doings in November.[5]

Ever truly yours, / Robert Browning.

MS: ABL. Published: *LRB*, pp. 230-31; *LVC*, 1st Ser., II, 35-39.

1 Shakespeare, *Coriolanus*, IV.v.35.

2 RB's hostess was Mrs. Clara Bloomfield-Moore (1824-99), a wealthy American who was RB's friend and bought several of Pen's paintings (*LL*, pp. 137, 181). Memorandum by FJF: "Mrs Bloomfield Moore, who took rooms for Browning, his sister, & herself, & hired a carriage & horses to drive them out." (BL Ashley B.2567). (See also her article "Robert Browning," *Lippincott's Magazine*, 45 [May 1890], 683-91.)

3 A German spa.
4 In the 20 Sept. 1884 issue of the *Saturday Review*, the Smith, Elder advertisement
   announced *Ferishtah's Fancies* as "in the press."
5 See RB to FJF, 11 Nov. 1884, n. 1.

RB TO FJF, 8 OCTOBER 1884

19, Warwick Crescent, / W.* / Oct. 8. '84.
My dear Furnivall, I am greatly obliged to you. In my haste, I took
the numerals, 1688, up to which time the Dictionary was "En-
larg'd, Corrected and Revis'd"—for the date of the *Second* Edition's printing—MDCCI— Very likely the First Edition was printed
as early as 1692. I have the work, 2 vols folio, and read it right
through when I was a boy,—my Father gave it me many years
after.[1] I had noticed the bit of biography long before I saw a paper
of C. Lamb's—published after his death, I think—in which he gave
the quotation waggishly as "when he pleased he could be as serious
as anybody"![2] Your correction arrived just in time to enable me to
make mine—seeing that the Revise of the Title &c comes by the
same Post.

Ever truly yours / Robert Browning.

MS: HEH. Address: F. J. Furnivall, Esq. / 3. St. George's Square, / Primrose Hill, /
N.W. Postmarks: PADDINGTON W L1 OC 8 84; LONDON NW KE OC 8 84. Note in
FJF's hand on envelope: "Jery. Collier & Shakspere."
1 The following epigraph appears on the verso of the half-title of *Jocoseria*: " 'His genius was jocular, but, when disposed, he could be very serious.'—Article 'Shakespeare,'
   Jeremy Collier's *Historical &c. Dictionary*, 2nd edition, 1701."
2 *The Works of Charles and Mary Lamb*, ed. E. V. Lucas (1903), I, 158; from an article
   which originally appeared in the *Examiner*, 19 Dec. 1813, and was reprinted by Leigh
   Hunt in the *Indicator*, 13 Dec. 1820.

RB TO FJF, 20 OCTOBER 1884

19, Warwick Crescent, / W.* / Oct. 20. '84.
My dear Furnivall,
I have two notes of yours wanting acknowledgement: the first
regards Mr Flügel who does me the honor of wishing to see me,[1]—
and I delayed answering it because of the many matters I had, and
still have, needing attention. Could Mr Flügel look in at the "Athenaeum" on Saturday,—my day for being there? If he would call at

3. o'clock next Saturday, I should be happy to see him. Next,—the questions about "In a Balcony"[2]—all I can reply is that the simile came in quite naturally and without stoppage of the Queen's "passionate feeling"—as I conceived the character, at least: depend on it, I never introduce a simile as an afterthought. The great obstacle, in the Queen's mind, to the possibility of her awakening love, in the case of a young and handsome man, is her consciousness of being neither young nor handsome,—and she seeks for an instance where, in default of these qualities, the desired effect may be produced all the same. And this applies equally, or even more forcibly, to the second instance she gives—when driven to an extremity,—that, though all other attractions fail, men will find them in loving—not youth and beauty—but soul—phantasy— even that poorest one of *rank*—which she *curses* in recognition of its being the very poorest.

Ever truly yours / Robert Browning.

MS: HEH. Address: F. J. Furnivall, Esq / 3. St. George's Square, / Primrose Hill, / N.W. Postmarks: PADDINGTON W 5 OC 20 84 N; LONDON NW KJ OC 20 84. Note in FJF's hand on envelope: "*In a Balcony.*"
1 Ewald Flügel (1863-1914), German-born writer on English literature and philology, was in 1884 preparing his Ph.D. thesis for the University of Leipzig, accepted the following year: *Thomas Carlyles religiöse und sittliche Entwicklung und Weltanschauung* (Leipzig, 1887; English translation, 1891). Flügel had met FJF in 1883 (*Furnivall*, p. 205).
2 The passage in *In a Balcony* which RB here discusses is ll. 503-33. (See also RB to FJF, 11 Nov. 1884, n. 1.)

RB TO FJF, 26 OCTOBER 1884

19, Warwick Crescent, / W.* / Oct. 26. '84.
My dear Furnivall,

I am very sorry to say, I was unable to keep the appointment at the Club with Mr Flügel yesterday. After I made it, I heard by a letter that Mr Williams[1]—having business in London—would at the end of it come here to luncheon, and at once return to Cambridge: I supposed I should easily be at liberty in time for 3. o'clock. But an accident detained him, and the end was that he did not leave till 4: I feared indeed that he would miss the proper train,—as he had to return for his luggage to an out-of-the-way station elsewhere. I can only re-assure you how sorry I was and am, and beg you to explain the matter to Mr Flügel, for whose inconvenience I am full of regret. Will you kindly do this?

I had no doubt that you would understand how the "simile" grew naturally out of the "passion and &c" of that particular woman, who was very peculiarly conditioned and circumstanced: an actress needs to realize that "a woman" is not one particular woman.[2]

I showed you that clever Greek epigram auguring the success of my new poem—with the clever *pun*, you remember. Well, the author,—in a scrap written to let us know that he secured the train after all,—says he inclines to print. I enclose his words—only, the thing would probably suit better the "Academy" than the "Athenaeum".[3] Could you manage it? I will transcribe the Greek as legibly as I am able.

Ever truly yours / Robert Browning.

[*Enclosure in RB's hand*]

A Ferishtah Fancy,
(not by R.B.)

"The best is yet to be."
Ὅσσα τὰ χρῆσθ᾽ ὑμνεῖς · ὅσα καὶ καλλίονα τούτων ·
ΦΕΡΊΣΤΑ μοῦνα λείπεται.

[*Enclosure in J. D. Williams' hand*][4]

⟨. . .⟩

As F. F. is not out, & *my* F.F. remains a happy *fore*cast (unseen by any one but yourself)—could you, would you like to, give it as it stands to the (e.g.) Athenæum Newspaper? of course as by *my* request, but adding neither name nor initials? I ask while it occurs to

Yours very sincerely / ⟨. . .⟩

MS: HEH. Address: F. J. Furnivall, Esq. / 3. St. George's Square, / Primrose Hill, / N.W. Postmarks: PADDINGTON 7 OC 27 84 B; LONDON NW LA OC 27 84. Note in FJF's hand on envelope: "*Flügel* / William's *Ferishtah's* / *Fancy*."

1 The Rev. John D. Williams (1829-1904), Vicar of Bottisham, near Cambridge, had been (1855-78) headmaster and divinity lecturer in Christ's College, Brecon, and, as RB's enclosure indicates, he was an accomplished versifier in both Greek and English. RB's correspondence with him (published in Collins) deals frequently with technical question of poetics.

2 See RB to FJF, 20 Oct. 1883, n. 2, and 11 Nov. 1884, n. 1.
3 The epigram was inserted by FJF in the "Notes and News" column of the *Academy*,
   26 (8 Nov. 1884), 304, with this explanation: "With reference to Mr. Browning's
   forthcoming volume, *Ferishtah's Fancies*, we have received the following epigram
   from a member of the Cambridge Browning Society. The motto is from Mr. Browning's 'Rabbi Ben Ezra'. . . ." The epigram may be translated as "Whatever things you
   utter, however many and however beautiful, the BEST is yet to be." The pun lies in
   the word "BEST"—"ΦΕΡΊΣΤΑ"—which is a close transliteration of "Ferishtah."
4 RB tore out and enclosed the last paragraph of Williams' letter to him.

SARIANNA BROWNING TO FJF, [NOVEMBER 1884]

My dear Mr. Furnivall,

Thank you very much for your kindness in remembering me. I am not quite sure whether it would not cause me more nervousness than pleasure to be present at such a representation, but I am spared the trouble of a decision as I have been suffering for some days, unable to leave the house, from an attack of neuralgia in the face, and though I hope it will pass off, I am sure I shall not be able to go out on Friday evening,—so it only remains to thank you once again for your proferred kindness.

Yours very sincerely, / S. Browning.

MS: HEH. Address: F. J. Furnivall Esq. Note in FJF's hand on address panel: "Miss
Sarianna Browning."
Date: The performance of *In a Balcony* on 28 Nov. 1884 was the only one of the
Browning Society's productions of RB's plays to take place on a Friday evening. How-
ever, as RB's following letter indicates, Sarianna did attend the play after all.

RB TO FJF, 11 NOVEMBER 1884

19, Warwick Crescent, W.* / Nov. 11. '84.

My dear Furnivall,

I will call on Miss Gerstenberg this afternoon with great pleasure.[1]

You have been very helpful about the Greek Epigram,—its insertion will oblige the author, I am sure.

I rejoice that the "settings" are so satisfactory, and have no doubt that the performance of them will be capital. I wish heartily that I could be present, but it would trouble me with Mrs Malaprop's "chameleon blushes".[2] My Sister will report faithfully

104

enough to me,—so will you, for the matter of that.

Ever truly yours / Robert Browning.

MS: HEH. Address: F. J. Furnivall, Esq. / 3. St. George's Square, / Primrose Hill, / N.W. Postmarks: LONDON W 5 NO 11 84; LONDON NW LJ NO 11 84. Note in FJF's hand on envelope: "Nora G. / Entertt."
1 Miss Nora Gerstenberg played the role of the Queen in the Browning Society's production of *In a Balcony* on 28 Nov. 1884 at Princes' Hall, Piccadilly. This was followed by a concert of musical settings of RB's poems. (The program for the Entertainment appears in an appendix to the second volume of *BSP*; for an eyewitness account, see Domett, p. 298.)
2 See RB to FJF, 8 Oct. 1881, n. 1.

RB TO FJF, 29 NOVEMBER 1884

19, Warwick Crescent, / W.* / Nov. 29. '84.

My dear Furnivall,

It is just like you to have sat down and written a letter to me after all the fatigues of your evening! I am sure that it deserved to have been, and really was a brilliant affair, in spite of those disappointments which are inevitable in all such cases. I hear poor Miss G. did not come up to our expectations, and "Prospice" wanted its adequate interpreter:[1] still, my Sister assures me, the result, on the whole, was eminently satisfactory—and I want you to convey my own thanks, really grateful thanks to everybody concerned in this memorable entertainment.

Ever yours most truly / Robert Browning.

MS: HEH. Address: F. J. Furnivall, Esq. / 3. St. George's Square, / Primrose Hill, / N.W. Postmarks: PADDINGTON W 5 NO 29 84 D; [LOND]ON NW KH [N]O 29 84. Note in FJF's hand on envelope: "Entert. of 28 Nov. 1884."
1 According to Frederick Wedmore in the *Academy*, "Miss Gerstenberg, remembering that she is an amateur and young, and not, as the representative of the Queen should be, a professional actress and a veteran, was satisfactory. Her faults at the very worst were negative." (*BSP*, II, 6*.) Mr. W. Main H. Aiken performed C. V. Stanford's setting of "Prospice" as a last-minute stand-in for another singer (*BSP*, II, 7*).

RB TO FJF, 22 DECEMBER 1884

19, Warwick Crescent, / W.* / Dec. 22. '84.

My dear Furnivall,

I don't know by what chance, your kind note and its enquiries get confounded with some letters not demanding immediate notice: pray forgive the inadvertency. I leave the music you mention to the judgement of your ordinary advisers in that matter,—seeing that their exercise of it has hitherto been so satisfactory. I hope the performance at Birmingham[1] was a success: I have heard nothing about it,—there may have been no notice in the papers.

That "Pen"—for whom you intend such favour—came from Paris this day week in very sorry case,—a bad cold upon him, which developed next day into a vile sore-throat: this was promptly attended to, however, and the patient is all but recovered, although he may not leave the house yet. Yes—the heart-symbol is good and significant enough.[2]

I hope we shall soon see you: meantime—and just now, with every proper Christmas wish—remember me always as

Yours cordially / Robert Browning.

MS: HEH. Address: F. J. Furnivall, Esq. / 3. St. George's Square, / Primrose Hill, / N.W. Postmarks: PADDINGTON 5 DE 22 84 E; LOND[ON N]W [. . .] DE 22 84. Note in FJF's hand on envelope: "Music &c. / Pen's sore throat."
1 The Browning Society's production of *In a Balcony* was performed before the Century Club in Birmingham on 16 Dec., with Miss Janet Achurch (1864-1916; *WW*), who had understudied the part, in the role of Constance.
2 The reference is probably to *In a Balcony*. The word *heart* (or *hearts*) appears in the following lines: 61, 76, 329, 337, 405, 581-82, 648, 694, 745, 752, 769, 772, 845, 848.

RB TO FJF, 10 JANUARY [1885]

19, Warwick Crescent, W.* / Jan. 10. '84.
My dear Furnivall, I rely on your goodness too exactingly, I believe—for here is a letter of yours I ought to have acknowledged the receipt of sooner—whereas I said in my heart "He will wait—knowing Pen is here, with other hindrances." Pen is off and away, and I begin with your letter from a pile of less inviting outsides. All I know about the Play is from a paragraph in the "Daily News" extracted from some newspaper which has not reached me: I had a few words from Mr Leonard [*sic*] Barrett to say that he was on the point of bringing it out.[1] As to my seeing Mr Fry,—if he really thinks any good will come from my seeing and talking with him, I shall of course be very willing to help; but I hardly think the visit will repay his trouble.[2] Did you observe what a hand came from

the clouds to corroborate all I ever said about the untoward circumstances which attended the first representation of the play?—I never heard of the existence of Mr May Phelps before I read his letter.[3]

Then,—Henry the Eighth: you know I never credited Shakespeare with more than half or a quarter of the play: I will presently read the whole of it,—with the benefit of a fresh peep through the spectacles of Mr Boyle,—and will have my little speculation about the authorship, which you will take for what it is worth.[4]

No,—I have never received a copy of the Almanac you mention —the Chicago one.[5] Pen left last Tuesday—after finishing the Balliol portrait—satisfactorily, I think.[6] Come and judge—*not* to-morrow, however, unless early—but always with great pleasure

to yours truly / Robert Browning.

MS: HEH. Address: F. J. Furnivall, Esq. / 3. St. George's Square, / Primrose Hill, / N.W. Postmarks: PADDINGTON 5 JA 10 85 [. . .]; LONDON NW KJ JA 10 85. Note in FJF's hand on envelope: "Blot on Scutcheon / Hen. VIII."

1   Lawrence Barrett (1838-91; *DAB*), an American actor, had approached RB during the summer of 1884 for permission to produce *A Blot in the 'Scutcheon* in America. Barrett's production, which involved extensive cuts and alterations in the play (described in the notes to *A Blot in the 'Scutcheon and Other Dramas by Robert Browning*, ed. William J. Rolfe and Heloise E. Hersey [New York, 1887]), opened in Washington, D.C., on 19 Dec. 1884, and toured the United States and Canada until May 1886. From Barrett and friends like Edmund Gosse (Evan Charteris, *The Life and Letters of Sir Edmund Gosse* [1931], pp. 170-71) RB received regular reports of the play's moderate success, which he interpreted as evidence of dramatic merit which had been obscured by Macready's original production in 1843. On 15 Dec. 1884 RB had written to Frank H. Hill (1830-1910; *DNB*), editor of the *Daily News*, to persuade him not to print a disparaging reference to the revival of the play. (Greer, pp. 195-203; *BSP*, II, 43*-44*, 61*-63*, 74*-78*; *LRB*, pp. 234-35, 253-54; Orr, p. 110.)

2   Charles Fry, professional stage-manager of the Irving Dramatic Club, had been persuaded by FJF to produce *A Blot in the 'Scutcheon* for the Browning Society on 30 Apr. and 2 May 1885. According to Fry, "Dr. Furnivall was particularly anxious that Mr. Browning should be consulted about the production, and with this object he kindly gave me an introduction to the poet"; Fry had "many subsequent interviews" with RB about the play. (*Furnivall*, pp. lxvi, 60-61.)

3   During December 1884 and January 1885 the *Daily News* printed an exchange between W. May Phelps—a relative of Samuel Phelps (1804-78; *DNB*), who had taken the chief role in the Macready production of *A Blot*—and a dramatic critic of the *News*. The critic pointed out that Macready was "unable to afford the cost of mounting the piece properly" and that Phelps was ill during rehearsals. The exchange is summarized in *BSP*, II, 25*.

4   Robert Boyle, of St. Petersburg, was the author of a paper entitled "Henry VIII.; an Investigation into the Origin and Authorship of the Play" (*NSST* [1880-86], pp. 443-87), read by FJF at the 16 Jan. 1885 meeting of the New Shakspere Society. In the course of the discussion FJF read the first paragraph of RB's letter of 14 Jan. (p. 119*).

5 "A Robert Browning Calendar, published by the Colgrove Book Co. [of Chicago], is arranged with one poem or group of poems as a subject for each month's study. 'Quotations are given which embody the central thought of the poem, and a few hints added concerning other poems which naturally suggest themselves as following out the line of thought. Sometimes a few bits of information are included to help in the proper understanding of circumstances or setting.' " (*Critic*, NS 3 [10 Jan. 1885], 23.)
6 See RB to FJF, 8 Jan. 1887, n. 1.

RB TO FJF, 14 JANUARY 1885

19, Warwick Crescent, W.* / Jan. 14. '85.

My dear Furnivall,

As you desired, I have read once again "Henry the Eighth": my opinion about the scanty portion of Shakespeare's authorship in it was formed above fifty years ago while ignorant of any evidence external to the text itself: I have little doubt now that Mr Boyle's judgment is right altogether,—that the original play was burnt along with the Globe Theatre, and the present work is a substitution for it—probably with certain reminiscences of "This is Truth". In spite of such huff-and-bullying as Charles Knight's, for example, I see little that transcends the power of Massinger and Fletcher to execute. It is very well to talk of the "tediousness" of the chronicles which have furnished pretty nearly whatever is admirable in the characters of Wolsey and Katherine: as wisely should we depreciate the bone which holds the marrow we enjoy on a toast.[1] The versification is nowhere S's. But I have said my little say for what it is worth.

I received yesterday, by the great kindness of Mr Holyoake, many of the numbers of that strange little Chicago Time-table which contained a reprint of my Poems. This was due to the sympathy of Mr James Charlton, Editor of the Tables, who scrupulously superintended the printing, and stopped the issue when he found himself no longer able to give his attention to it—so anxious was he that the poetry should not be disfigured through carelessness. The series consequently stopped with No. 19. ending with page 190 of vol. III. Now, I cannot recollect how far extends the set which the British Museum authorities were good enough to accept on your recommendation,—but I can now complete it with whatever numbers may be wanting: and if you, at any leisure interval of your labours there, will ascertain how many of these are required, I will furnish them with your ever-kind and ready assistance.[2]

Thank you for the pretty and touching little tribute to you:[3] no doubt many people, with far less reason, are like myself

Yours most truly / Robert Browning.

"Shall I give your best regards" (to my Sister, beside me[)]. "Yes, certainly". (to myself.)

MS: HEH. Address: F. J. Furnivall, Esq. / 3 St. George's Square, / Primrose Hill, / N.W. Postmarks: PADDINGTON W 3 JA 14 85 J; LONDON NW KC JA 14 85. Note in FJF's hand on envelope: *"Henry VIII &c."* Published: *NSST* (1880-86), III, 119* (inc.).

1 A play about Henry VIII entitled *All Is True* was being performed at the Globe Theatre when it burned in 1613. Though the *King Henry the Eighth* (based largely on Holinshed's *Chronicle*) included in the First Folio is inferior to most of Shakespeare's other plays, external evidence suggests that it is his and that it is identical with *All Is Truth*. Charles Knight (1791-1873; *DNB*) had declared in his 1840 edition of *Shakspere's Works* (Histories, II, 398): ". . . there is no play of Shakspere's which has a more decided character of unity—no one from which any passage could be less easily struck out." However, beginning in the mid-nineteenth century a number of Shakspearean scholars suggested that it was a collaborative work in which John Fletcher (1579-1625; *DNB*) and Philip Massinger (1583-1640; *DNB*) had to some degree participated.

2 From December 1872 to October 1874 (with only one brief hiatus) the Official Guide to the Chicago and Alton Railroad printed serially the first complete American edition of RB's works. A Texas railway official, Robert Avery, sent a partial set of the timetables to RB in 1873. While touring the United States in 1884, George J. Holyoake (1817-1906; *DNB*), Secularist writer, met his "old Owenite friend from England" James Charlton (1839-1913; *WWA*), general passenger and ticket agent of the Chicago and Alton, who provided additional parts of the timetable. Holyoake sent them on to RB in November 1884 and January 1885. (*IG*, p. 102; Joseph McCabe, *Life and Letters of George Jacob Holyoake* [1908], II, 120; "Browning Memorial Notes," *Poet-Lore*, 2 [15 Feb. 1890], 110-11; Richard D. Altick, "Robert Browning Rides the Chicago and Alton," *New Colophon*, 3 [1950], 78-81; see also RB to FJF, 10 Apr. 1883.)

3 Miss Mary Grace Walker printed, as a broadside, an adulatory poem about FJF entitled "To F. J. Furnivall . . . New Year, 1885." Miss Walker had contributed "memorial lines" to FJF's *Memoir* of Miss Rochfort-Smith (see RB to FJF, 17 Sept. 1883, n. 2); and in the Huntington Library there are three sonnets by her about RB, with accompanying letters to FJF (dated 12 Feb. 1884 and 22 Feb. 1884).

RB TO FJF, 5 FEBRUARY 1885

19, Warwick Crescent, / W.* / Feb. 5. '85.

My dear Furnivall,

I could not divine—what the Berlin people have so properly

commemorated[1]—that yesterday was your Birthday. Well done of Berlin!—and ill done of me if I ever henceforth forget to congratulate you and myself on its occurrence! All good wishes to you from yours, always gratefully and affectionately

Robert Browning.

MS: HEH. Address: Frederick J. Furnivall, Esq. Phil.D. / 3 St George's Square, / Primrose Hill, / N.W. Postmarks: PADDINGTON W 5 FE 85 D; LONDON NW KJ FE 5 85. Note in FJF's hand on envelope: "my Ph.D." Published: *Furnivall*, facing p. 65 (facsimile).

1   "Mr. F. J. Furnivall being sixty to-day, the Philosophical Faculty of the University of Berlin has paid him the compliment of sending him as a birthday present its degree of Doctor of Philosophy, *honoris causâ*, in witness of the value it sets on his labours in the cause of Early English literature" (*Pall Mall Gazette*, 4 Feb. 1885, p. 9). FJF offered this jocular interpretation of the honor: "... on my 60th birthday, Feb. 4, Berlin sent me an Hon. 'Ph.D.' So I've had to stick Dr. on to my name. It is a joke. Probably due to my having rowd stroke to the Scratch Four in our Maurice Rowing Club last Octr., & won both heats. This tickled people." (FJF to C. H. Pearson, 3 Mar. 1885 [Bodleian MS. lett. d. 187, fol. 208].)

RB TO FJF, 18 FEBRUARY 1885

19, Warwick Crescent, / W.* / Feb. 18. '85.

My dear Furnivall, what am I to say in gratitude for yet another gift—the book with its inscriptions—one so touching? The little Bookcase is nearly full now—perhaps a couple more volumes may squeeze in:[1] if they do,—well! but till that proves impossible for obvious reasons, I am ever

Affectionately yours / Robert Browning.

MS: HEH. Address: Frederick J. Furnivall, Esq. / 3. St. George's Square, / Primrose Hill, / N.W. Postmarks: PADDINGTON W 2 FE 18 85 D; LONDO[N NW . . .] FE 18 85. Note in FJF's hand on envelope: "gift of book."

1   In the carved oak case given to RB on his seventieth birthday (see RB to FJF, 8 May 1882, n. 1), "space was purposely left in the Case for 3 or more volumes of new Poems to take the place of the two 'dummies' sent to fill up," according to FJF's circular of 8 May 1882. As each subsequent volume of poetry by RB was published (in this instance *Ferishtah's Fancies*), FJF would send it to him in a uniform binding. FJF's estimate of the extra space needed, incidentally, was correct: the case eventually held three volumes by RB in addition to the original set, not including *Asolando*, which was published on the day of RB's death. (See *Browning Collections*, Lot 458.)

RB TO FJF, 7 APRIL 1885

19. Warwick Crescent, W. / Apr. 7. '85.

My dear Furnivall,

By a paragraph in the "Daily News", I see ⟨t⟩he amateurs are kindly careful in rehearsing the Play.[1] With the newspaper came the Post, and I got a third consignment of American ⟨n⟩otices,—of the production at Boston, as previously at Washington, Philadelphia, New York & Brooklyn.[2] They are all good natured at least and quite laudatory enough at most,—I send you a sample,—but my reason for remarking on the general tone of them is—that they none of them approve of the alterations and excisions adopted with a view to the play's benefit,—which may confirm your friends in, what I gather is, their intention of keeping the play's integrity if possible. I also got a letter from a thoroughly accomplished judge, Charles Perkins,—the author of the History of Tuscan Sculpture,[3]—and I confide this also to your most particularly private ear and eye that you may learn from an entirely independent source whethe⟨r⟩ the success of the play, be it much or little, has been due to the play's self, such as it is, or the performers, however they are. From *all* the account⟨s⟩ (and I must have received some forty and odd) I gather that, in every case, wherever the play was acted, there was *some* wholly inefficient actor,—and a play, with only four props, cannot well keep from toppling over if one be crazy; whence I conclude that if *your* four be but decently stable, the thing will probably stand firmlier here than there,—where, nevertheless, it has tottered through five trials, you see. Now, please just read and return the *letter*—the slip is not important—and understand that I merely send it that you may stick to your conservatism on my play's behalf.

Ever truly yours / Robert Browning.

Forgive the careless *tearing* to lighten the letter![4]

MS: HEH. Address: Dr. Furnivall, / 3. St. George's Square, / Primrose Hill, / N.W. Postmarks: PADDINGTON W 5 AP 7 85 K; LONDON [NW] KJ AP 7 85. Note in FJF's hand on envelope: "*Blot* in America."

1 See RB to FJF, 10 Jan. 1885, n. 2.
2 *A Blot in the 'Scutcheon*, with Lawrence Barrett in the chief role, was performed in Washington on 19 Dec. 1884; in Philadelphia, 2 and 3 Jan. 1885; in New York, 9, 10, 11, and 14 Feb.; in Brooklyn, 20 Feb.; and in Boston, 16, 18, and 21 Mar. From

there it left on a tour of other sections of the United States and Canada. (Greer, pp. 196-98.) See also RB to FJF, 10 Jan. 1885, n. 1.

3   Charles Callahan Perkins (1823-86; *DAB*), art critic and President of the Handel and Haydn Society, Boston (1850-51, 1875-86), knew RB in Rome in 1859 (*DI*, p. 25). His *Tuscan Sculptors: Their Lives, Works, and Times*, 2 vols. (1864), had brought him a large reputation. Perkins' letter to RB, dated 23 Mar. 1885, is printed in Greer, p. 200.

4   RB tore a strip from the left margin of the sheet, with the result that a few words were partially excised.

RB TO FJF, [30] APRIL 1885

19. Warwick Crescent, W. / Apr. 29. '85.
My dear Furnivall, before I go to bed I must tell you how more than pleased I was with the play this evening: all was done capitally—all that was requisite for getting a fair judgment of the thing: and when I contrast the pains which must have been bestowed in rehearsals &c by these kind and sympathetic amateurs with the carelessness and worse of Macready,—the purist and preeminently capable actor,—I feel very grateful indeed, I am glad I was persuaded by Mr Fry to go: he kept my incognito faithfully:[1] I saw *you* and Mr Campbell,—didn't I just! Well, you were there, and want nothing from me but this assurance that I was highly gratified. So, good night from

Yours truly ever / RB.

MS: HEH. F. J. Furnivall, Esq. / 3 St. George's Square, / Primrose Hill, / N.W. Postmarks: PADDINGTON W 7 MY 1 85 D; LONDON NW [. . .]A MY 1 85. Note in FJF's hand on envelope: "Fry & *Blot.*" Published: *Furnivall*, pp. lxvii-lxviii. Date: First performance of *A Blot in the 'Scutcheon* was on 30 Apr. See also postmarks.

1   Charles Fry, the director, had persuaded RB to attend incognito the performance of *A Blot in the 'Scutcheon* on the evening of 30 Apr. RB was so well concealed behind muslin curtains at the theater that not even FJF was aware of his presence. (*Furnivall,* pp. 61-62; *Oracle,* p. 186.)

RB TO FJF, 7 MAY 1885

19, Warwick Crescent, / W.* / May 7. '85.
Thank you heartily, my dear Furnivall: but don't "bicycle" here or anywhere till you are secure against a tumble: I was sorry indeed to hear of your misadventure that way. Yes, there begins yet another year for me, and however it end or break off, all of it will

find me fast your friend—and find you as friendly to me—I gladly and gratefully believe—being ever yours

Robert Browning.

MS: HEH. Address: Dr. Furnivall, / 3. St. George's Square, / Primrose Hill, / N.W. Postmarks: PADDINGTON W 4 MY 7 85 J; LONDON NW KH MY 7 85. Note in FJF's hand on envelope: "bike, birthday."

RB TO FJF, 11 JULY 1885

19, Warwick Crescent, / W.* / July 11. '85.

My dear Furnivall,

I certainly have not received Professor Kennedy's Edition of the Oedipus,[1]—but is that a reason why you, who are so favoured, should give me yours? You give me, however, so much and so kindly, that one gift more will come not unlike a matter of course.

Ever truly yours / Robert Browning.

MS: HEH. Address: Dr. Furnivall, / 3. St. George's Square, / Primrose Hill, / N.W. Postmarks: PADDINGTON 3 JY 11 85 C; LONDON NW KC JY 11 85. Note in FJF's hand on envelope: "Kennedy's Oedipus."
1 *The Oedipus Tyrannus of Sophocles*, trans. Benjamin H. Kennedy (Cambridge, England, 1885). For RB's subsequent comment on the book's notes, see RB to Williams, 21 Oct. 1887 (Collins, p. 49). Kennedy (1804-99; *DNB*) was Regius Professor of Greek at Cambridge University, 1867-89.

RB TO FJF, 17 JULY 1885

19, Warwick Crescent, / W.* / July 17. '85.

My dear Furnival,

How good you are, and have always been, and doubtlessly will ever be! I accept the gifts with more thanks than I will trouble you with. The "Oedipus"—or at least the notes to it, I shall probably read just as when I tackled the play for the first time: and indeed *that*, and the "Prometheus", were the two plays which I tried my powers upon first of all. Then, the "Lucrece" with *your* notes![1] what a marvel of reproduction!

Ever yours sincerely / Robert Browning.

I am going to hear Miss Alma Murray read this evening:[2] you may perhaps be there.

MS: HEH. Address: Dr. F. J. Furnivall, / 3. St. George's Square, / Primrose Hill, / N.W. Postmarks: PADDINGTON W 4 JY 17 85 P; LONDON NW [. . .]H JY 17 [8]5. Note in FJF's hand on envelope: "books sent by me [?] ."

1 *Shakspere's Lucrece. The First Quarto, 1594. A Facsimile*, with Forewords by FJF [1885]. The British Museum *General Catalogue of Printed Books* assigns 1886 as the year of publication, but this is clearly an error.

2 "At a meeting of the *United Richard Wagner Society (London Branch)* on the 17th July, Miss Alma Murray gave some 'dramatic readings,' one of the pieces being the Prologue to *Pippa passes* ('Day! faster and more fast,' &c.). This was brilliantly rendered and greatly appreciated by the audience, which included Mr. Browning." (*BSP*, II, 88*.) Miss Murray—daughter of the actor Henry Leigh Murray (1820-70; *DNB*) and wife of Alfred Forman (obituary, *Times*, 23 Dec. 1925, p. 7)—achieved her greatest successes on the stage in Shelley's *Cenci* and in performances of RB's plays. RB described her as "the Poetic Actress without a rival." (*Alma Murray*; see also RB to FJF, 12 May 1888, n. 3.)

RB TO FJF, 16 AUGUST 1885

19, Warwick Crescent, / W.* / Aug. 16. '85.

My dear Furnivall,

I have been doubtful, this long while, as to where my Sister and myself should betake us: only recently did we determine that we could do no better than go to the wild place which satisfied us so completely the year before last: this hesitation prevented my writing till now. Whether near or far, as I know you have my concerns at heart, so—believe it,—far or near I gratefully remember the good friend I am fortunate to have: you need no assurance of *that*. I have only to add, therefore, that my abode for some six weeks will be at

(see the foolish person you so sedulously puff
into notoriety!)
Pension Delapierre,
Gressoney St. Jean,
Val d'Aosta,
Italy.

—where a word from you or about you will come cheerily at all times. You are well, and working—I see—and safely bicycling, I hope. My Sister sends her kind regards along with mine. And I am, as always, my dear Furnivall,

Cordially yours / Robert Browning.

We leave on Tuesday, viâ Bâle and Milan,—so, on to Ivrea, and thence, by St. Martino, to Gressoney St. Jean—where we count upon arriving on Friday, if all goes well.

MS: ABL. Address: Dr. Furnivall, / Castleton, / Grosmont, / York. Postmarks: PADDINGTON 7 AU 17 85 B; YORK 6M AU 17 85. Note in FJF's hand on envelope: "going to Gressoney."

RB TO FJF, 7 SEPTEMBER 1885

Hotel Delapierre, Gressoney St. Jean, / Val d'Aosta, Italy. /
Sept. 7, '85.

My dear Furnivall,

I was just going to thank you for your pleasant letter from the Moors when your second arrived: I will begin with the proposal in the latter. Certainly nobody will ever treat of my wife and myself more graciously and partially (if that is desirable at all) than you,— so, by all means, biographize about both of us.[1] For my own part, I will do what I can,—in the talk over the matter, that is to be: I have nothing to keep back, and will answer any question to the best of my power. But in the other case—the little I confidently can profess to *know*, I am forced to be silent about,—and how very little that little is, appears extraordinary to me and may seem almost incredible to anybody else. The personality of my wife was so strong and peculiar that I had no curiosity to go beyond it and concern myself with matters which she was evidently disinclined to communicate. I believe I discovered her birthday—the day, not the date,—three weeks ago, when engaged in some search after missing letters.[2] But I can set right certain errors which appear in the printed notices that I have seen. Any help in that way, which is in my power to give, I will give you readily.

I rejoice that your Yorkshire visit was so successful: you speak of bad or indifferent weather,—ours here has been and continues all we could desire. We are all but alone,—the brief "season" being over, and only a chance traveller turning up for a night's lodging. We take our walks in the old way, two and a half hours before breakfast,—three after it,—in the most beautiful country I know: yesterday the three hours passed without our meeting a single man, woman, or child: one man only was discovered at a distance

115

at the foot of a mountain we had climbed. Yes,—I am writing another poem.[3] It may give you a notion of this place when I tell you that on the 17th of last January an avalanche destroyed two houses close to this Hotel, and a third on the other side of it,—crushing six people at their morning meal,—one child escaping through a couple of beams falling cross-wise over her head. The snow lay four *mètres* deep, so effectually blocking up the hôtel that it was two days before the inhabitants became aware of what had happened. They had provisions enough, but were reduced to melted snow and ice, which kept cows and a mule alive: the Doctor and the Priest were imprisoned in the house, having sought shelter there.

I did not know that Pen's projected trip was so notably recorded in the papers: he leaves Dinant for Venice at the end of this week, takes a studio there, and tries his hand at something different, I hope, from the conventional work. Did I tell you of the success of his "Dryope"[4] at the Paris salon,—where it obtained a *"mention honorable"*—a great distinction for sculpture in the best sculpture-producing country: they proceed grade by grade there, and this is all he could hope for as yet. *Please do not,—in your kindness,—mention this*[5]—which I am glad to have never seen in print—the Academy is unfriendly enough without need of further exasperation!

I suppose we shall stay here till the end of the month. One good storm, with thunder, threatened to break up the genial autumn's beginning (—for it is no more than that,—we have greenness everywhere) but it only deposited snow on the mountain-tops, and left a sky bluer than ever. Goodbye, dear Furnivall,—my sister summons me—taking occasion to send her best regards: I rose at half past five, and am ready for our walk. Do write whenever the happy mood is upon you: your letters are cheery to us both. Don't think I forget to wish your son a triumphant cycling: and believe me always

most truly yours, / Robert Browning.

MS: HL. Address: *Inghilterra.* / Dr. Furnivall, / 3 St. George's Square, / Primrose Hill, / London. N.W. Postmarks: ISSIME 7 SET 85 [. . .]; P[ONT ST] MARTIN 8 SET 85; TORINO FERROVIA 9 9-85 [. . .]; LONDON NW MA SP 11 85. Note in FJF's hand on envelope: "biography." Published: *LRB*, pp. 238-40; *LVC*, 1st Ser., II, 40-44.

1 FJF contributed the articles on EBB and RB to *Celebrities of the Century: Being a Dictionary of Men and Women of the Nineteenth Century*, ed. Lloyd C. Sanders (1887). FJF's summary of EBB's character is as follows: "The notes of Mrs. Browning's poetry are emotion, purity, pathos, intense earnestness, sympathy with every form of suffering, with everything great and good, hatred of everything evil, specially of all oppression. Her want of humour, a few rough and careless rhymes, an occasional forcing of sense and phrase, have made some critics of word and style complain; but students may rely on it, that to know Mrs. Browning as she reveals herself in her works is a liberal education, and to enter into her spirit one of the most ennobling pursuits that a man can undertake" (p. 181). The article on RB concludes with these words: "Browning is the strongest man who has written verse since Milton. His chief topic is the mind and soul of man and woman; the individual is to him above the race. His subjects are mainly taken from far-off times and places; he deals often with sinners and culprits, beings of complex natures, whose motives and self-screenings it delights him to lay bare. His 'notes' are analysis, introspection, vivisection. He is also specially the poet of painting, sculpture, and music. He loves animals; his gift of humour is large, his tenderness and manliness great. He is a Theist to the backbone, a firm believer in the future life; God and the soul are his realities; and stoutly does he battle for his faith. His verse is often difficult from its inability to express his quick variety of thought. His rhymes are sometimes forced. It is as a man, thinker and leader, that he is valued rather than as a technical artist: if once a man gets hold of such poems as *Prospice, Rabbi ben Ezra, Andrea del Sarto,* and *Karshish,* he will bear them with him as treasures to the grave" (p. 183).
2 See RB to FJF, 19 Nov. 1885, n. 1.
3 *Parleyings with Certain People of Importance in Their Day,* published in 1887.
4 See RB to FJF, 22 Aug. 1884, n. 4.
5 As usual, FJF contributed regular reports of RB's activities to the *Academy* during August and September 1885. He complied with RB's request, however, and did not send the news of Pen's award to the *Academy.*

RB TO FJF, 21 SEPTEMBER 1885

Gressoney St. Jean, Val d'Aosta, Italia. / Sept. 21. '85.
My dear Furnivall,

I got your letter duly, and all the papers: those on "wheeling" teem with the glories of your boy, and I share your pride in his prowess—especially as exhibited to our Cousins,[1]—may they triumph less in the discomfiture of the "Genesta"![2] All you tell me interests me thoroughly,—and, in order to get more news and lose none, I write to say that we leave this place, in all likelihood, for Venice at the beginning of next week, when our address will be—"Palazzo Guistiniani—Recanati, San Moise, Venezia."—since we are again to profit by our kind friend's hospitality.[3] Pen must be—I trust—already arrived at Venice,—he was bound to do so last Thursday: but I only heard from him at Milan,—after what he called "a delightful journey". We are actually in some anxiety about the

117

weather here—which is so exceptionally fine that we cannot but fear a sudden break-up, perhaps in snow: we are in the fifth week of residence, and have had *one* rainy afternoon,—a thundery visitation which cleared the air for the next three weeks: you cannot well imagine the effect of day after day breaking on a blue cloudless sky,—the sun's warmth, even at nine-o'clock, requiring to be moderated by the bracing air proper to an altitude of 4495 feet above the sea-level. My Sister and myself are all that, in your kindness, you can wish us to be: and we count upon descending the valley to Pont St. Martin on foot, preferring a seven hours' trudge to mule-back joltings. This lovely place will become more accessible ere very long: next Tuesday (to-morrow) "if fame not Lie"[4] the railway will be open from Torea to Pont St. M.—saving us the two hours' drive—and next April they begin a road from the upper Gressoney to P. St. M.—a work which they engage to perform in some couple of years. Should they do so, I foresee a mushroom growth of Villa, Chalet, Pension, and all that makes a summer retreat generally desirable and particularly (to me) detestable. You lament our loneliness,—so do not we. It was pleasantly intruded upon last week, however, by a young and very agreeable English traveller, who came for two days' stay and remained eight or nine: but one is not sure of such company. I should by no means object to the sound of your "wheels" under my window, but that can hardly be. So, I must shake your hand in fancy, and in very earnest, assure you that I am ever

most truly yours / Robert Browning.

My Sister's best regards must be squeezed in, big as they are.

Monday Eg. Pen has arrived, in high spirits, at Venice—"where he feels as if he had lived for years". He finds plenty of old friends, is about to take a Studio, and will work and enjoy himself, I don't doubt. Again, yours ever

RB.

[*Continued on inside of envelope flap*]

I shall keep the various papers, and return them safely to you.

MS: HEH. Address: *Inghilterra.* / Dr. Furnivall, / 3. St. George's Square, / Primrose Hill, / London. / N.W. Postmarks: [GRE]SSONEY S. JEAN 23 SET 85; PONT S.

MARTIN 23 SET 85; TORINO FERROVIA 24 9-85 9 M; LONDON NW MA SP 26 85. Note in FJF's hand on envelope: "Percy, Penini."
1 In early September Percy Furnivall had participated in major bicycle racing tournaments in Hartford, Conn., and Springfield, Mass., and had won a total of eight first prizes and one second prize. At this time FJF's son was probably the most famous amateur cyclist in England. (*Bicycling World* [Boston], 11 [11 Sept. 1885], 448-49; [18 Sept. 1885], 464-71; William C. K. Albemarle and G. Lacy Hillier, *Cycling*, 2nd ed. [1889], pp. 118-25 *passim.*)
2 On 14 and 16 Sept. 1885 the English yacht Genesta was defeated by the American yacht Puritan in an international match.
3 RB's hostess in Venice was, as usual, Mrs. Bronson. As Henry James explained, "Attached to ca' Alvisi, on the land side, is a somewhat melancholy old section of a Giustiniani palace, which she had annexed to her own premises mainly for the purpose of placing it, in comfortable guise, at the service of her friends" ("Browning in Venice," p. 147).
4 Not identified.

RB TO FJF, 1 NOVEMBER 1885

Venice, Nov. 1, '85.

My dear Furnivall,

Mrs Forman is right in each instance.[1] Colombe, in the 3d Act at the close, "does not mean that she loves Valence"—is not even aware that the seeds of what may grow to Love are already implanted in her by the devotion of Valence—and only expresses, no more warmly than the occasion requires, her appreciation of his conduct and thorough trust in what he shall advise.

She is equally right in her reading of what is meant in the 5th Act when the Duchess is made to listen to—and definitely pronounce upon—that conduct,—forced upon her as the task is by the officiousness and malice of the courtiers: they desire to show that she has put herself in a necessity of returning his love with her own,—though she will be mad to do so,—and her answer is that she sees the urgency of their argument, accepts the situation, and does so really return it. I am very glad that I can justly have confidence in Mrs Forman's sympathy with and understanding of the character of Colombe, as evidenced by her judgment in both cases: I much fear I shall not be able to enjoy her performance in London, however. I am anxious to return thither, on many accounts, but think it will be later in the month by many days than the 16th. I am also very grateful to the other ladies and gentlemen for their interest in the play: may they but succeed in bringing

119

over the audience to their way of thinking and feeling!

Our weather is broken here, but when fine is fine indeed. We are all,—my sister, Pen and myself—eminently well. Talking of theatricals, there is a capital Venetian company playing the Manager's clever comedies,—and Goldoni's every now and then,—to perfection. Zago, the *primo caraterristo*, is superlatively good,—about the most versatile actor I ever saw,—a gondolier, a Canonico, a *ci-devant jeune homme*,—all are rendered to perfection.[2] I supposed so excellent an artist must be of prodigious experience, and find his age to be of about thirty-five years. All the others are good in their degree. I am rejoiced that your boy of the bicycle is back again and flourishing besides. My sister, sitting opposite, sends her kind regards: and they go with the best I have to send,

being ever truly yours, / Robert Browning.

MS: Texas. Address: *Inghilterra*. / Dr. Furnivall, / 3. St. George's Square, / Primrose Hill, / London. N.W. Postmarks: VENEZIA 1 11-85 5S; LONDON NW XX NO 3 85.
1 Alma Murray (Mrs. Forman) played the title role in the Browning Society production of *Colombe's Birthday* at St. George's Hall on 19 Nov. 1885. (See *BSP*, II, 93*-97*.) At the 30 Jan. 1886 meeting FJF acknowledged that his own original view—which he now saw to be mistaken—was that "Colombe had at the beginning fallen in love with Valence" (*BSP*, II, 119*). In a note contributed to the *Academy*, FJF wrote: "Two points of some importance in the interpretation of the character of Colombe on which Miss Murray differed from the stage manager and another authority [FJF] were referred to Mr. Browning; and he has decided both entirely in Miss Murray's favour . . ." ("Notes and News," *Academy*, 28 [7 Nov. 1885], 306).
2 Emilio Zago (1852-1929), Italian character actor, was one of the chief partners in a travelling company formed in 1883. Throughout his career he was known chiefly for his roles in Goldoni's comedies. (*Enciclopedia dello Spettacolo*, IX, 2078.)

RB TO FJF, 17 NOVEMBER 1885

Venice, Nov. 17. '85.

My dear Furnivall,

I find that at last I can get away and go home,—as I hope to do next Monday, arriving thus in London two or three days after. I write at once to apprize you of this,—knowing that your good nature would prompt you to give me an account of the fortunes of "Colombe"—which account, if despatched on Friday, as it needs must be, would reach Venice on Monday, and so fail of reaching myself. Address whatever news,—good or bad,—there may be, to

the London place, and I will read it gratefully the moment I arrive
—probably on Wednesday.

"The London Place": well, your friendliness now must know
that I have been kept thus long here by the business of buying a
Venice Place,—the Manzoni Palazzo, of which you may see an account in the Guide Books:[1] I think, with many or most of them,
that it is the most beautiful house—not the biggest nor most ma-
jestic—in Venice. I buy it solely for Pen who is in love with the
City beyond anything I could expect, and had set his heart on this
particular acquisition before I joined him,—quite unaware that I
had entertained a similar preference for it years ago. Don't think I
mean to give up London till it warns me away—when the hospital-
ities and innumerable delights grow a burthen even as we are assured the grasshopper will eventually do in the case of the stoutest
of us.[2] Pen will have sunshine and beauty about him, and every
help to profit by these: while I and my sister have secured a shelter
when the fogs of life grow too troublesome. We cannot enter into
possession for some months, and Pen returns in our company to
resume work in Paris.

I should have mentioned that I was in the thick of this affair of
a purchase but that the owner was abroad and I needed to first ne-
gotiate with him in person,—and, oh the slips between cups and
lips!—so that I closed mine till the cup's last contents were fairly
inside them.

What sort of weather are you having today? We walked two
hours just now, with abundance of sunshine, a blue sky, and a
bracing wind—pronounced by our servant to be "stupendously
cold." Pen,—who drops in while I write,—sends his best regards,
and congratulations on the successes of your son,[3] which he appre-
ciates as a connoisseur should. My Sister joins me in the hope of
soon a pleasant meeting,—so does Pen,—for he too is only minded
to stay here occasionally,—by no means to detach himself from
the England of us all—and assuredly of

Yours truly ever / Robert Browning.

MS: Yale. Address: *Inghilterra*. / Dr. Furnivall, / 3. St. George's Square, / Primrose
Hill, / London. / N.W. Postmarks: VENEZIA 17 11-85 4S; [LONDON N]W NO 19 85.
Note in FJF's hand on back of envelope: "P. Manzoni 15th centy. / Grand Canal. S. /

from the Piazzetta / on the Lido, past / Salviati's mosaic / manufactory / before you come to the 6th, the iron / bridge leading to the Accademia / delle belle Arti. / P.S. the vendor / of the P.M. afterwards / drew back, as he thought / he could get more for / the Palace. Br. went / to law with him to make / him carry out the contract; / but then, being informed that / the main walls (hidden by / carpets &c when B. saw them) were / crackt, & the foundations shaky, B. / gave it up, paid his own costs, & retired." Published: *LRB*, pp. 241-42; *LVC*, 1st Ser., II, 45-48.

1 Baedeker's *Northern Italy* (1879) described the Palazzo Manzoni as "of the period of the Lombardi (15th cent.), formerly an edifice of great magnificence, and the sole palace which stood in a feudal relation to the republic, now in a dilapidated condition" (p. 274). The 1899 edition of Baedeker added: ". . . now a store" (p. 240). For summaries of RB's unsuccessful attempt to purchase the Palazzo, see FJF's note quoted above; *LL*, pp. 190-91; and "Browning in Venice," pp. 150-51.

2 *Ecclesiastes* 12:5.

3 Note in FJF's hand: "Percy, champion cyclist." See RB to FJF, 21 Sept. 1885, n. 1.

RB TO FJF, [17 NOVEMBER 1885]

Letter the second—My dear Furnivall, pray forgive my stupid oversight in scribbling the letter to you which I have just sent off—without a word of notice of your biographical article:[1] I will only say, in my present hurry to catch the post, that I will send it after giving it my best attention and doing what I can to help in the matter.

Ever yours / *RB*

MS: HEH. Address: *Inghilterra*. / Dr. Furnivall, / 3. St. George's Square, / Primrose Hill, / London. / N.W. Postmarks: VENEZIA 17 11-85 4S; LONDON N[W] XX NO 19 85. Note in FJF's hand on envelope: "biogr. article."

1 See RB to FJF, 7 Sept. 1885, n. 1.

RB TO FJF, 19 NOVEMBER 1885

Venice, Nov. 19. '85.

My dear Furnivall,

You will have received the two letters I wrote on the 17th the one explaining the omission, in the other, of any notice of your biographical paper—which I return by book-post with the present. It is needless to say you are, as ever, only too kind to me—the estimation of my wife I accept altogether. I have not discovered anything considerable that needed correction. It may seem strange that I know so little, and am so uncertain about even that little, of my wife's history, or the date of her birth:[1] it would not, were you or anyone acquainted with the aversion she had to any allusion to a painful past. In my own case, I put in the two omitted "Degrees", because if one only is mentioned the others are supposed to be held cheaply; so, all three or neither, please![2]

Now I want your indulgence,—and surely shall not want it in vain,—for another correction I have made.[3] Your opinions are clearly your own by every right: but you cannot think I would let stand unobjected to the disparaging epithet bestowed on a book,[4] begun—I have always understood—at your own suggestion, and toiled at with abundance of difficulty for some four years, unhelped by anybody; I simply answered every now [and] then a question, without the least notion of its exact bearing and purport.[5] The book at all events had the sanction of the Society of which you are the Head,—and to go out of the way and inflict a punishment on its author seems unjust—quite apart from the merits of the case, which I estimate very differently. I should say thus much if the author of the book were absolutely a stranger to me: how then must I feel when that person is simply the dearest woman friend I can boast of in the world? It has long been a genuine sorrow to me that there should have arisen, from whatever cause, a painful disturbance in the old amicable relation between that friend and the other to whom I am so much beholden—yourself. I have not been careful to go into the question of how this misfortune has been brought about,—such inquiries make too often matters worse: but I have steadily hoped that the difference, whatever may have occasioned it, would yield to time and good natured tolerance on either side. For me, all I can say is that whenever you announce to me that my trouble on this score is at an end—well, don't let me promise rashly! This very evening you and the Society are going to do me a signal honor by the production of my play,—what a success I shall esteem it if you tell me that, over and above the applause if there be any, there was audible the still small voice which conceded this earnestly-craved boon to

Yours ever truly / Robert Browning.

MS: HEH. Address: *Inghilterra.* / Dr. Furnivall, 3. St. George's Square, / Primrose Hill, / London, / N.W. Postmarks: VE[NEZIA] 19 11-85 5S; LONDON NW MM NO 21 85. Note in FJF's hand on envelope: "Mrs. Orr &c."
1 RB's confusion about EBB's birthdate (6 Mar. 1806) drew him into a public disagree-

ment in 1888 with John H. Ingram (1842-1916; *WW*), author of an unauthorized memoir of EBB; their correspondence in the *Athenaeum* during February of that year is reprinted and discussed in *Letters of the Brownings to George Barrett*, ed. Paul Landis and Ronald E. Freeman (Urbana, Ill., 1958), pp. 313-14. See also RB to FJF, 7 Sept. 1885, first paragraph.

2 RB had been awarded honorary degrees by three universities: an LL.D. from Cambridge (1879), a D.C.L. from Oxford (1882), and an LL.D. from Edinburgh (1884). FJF's biographical article mentions only the Oxford degree; in other words, he ignored RB's correction.

3 Note in FJF's hand: "Mrs. Orr's *Browning Handbook.*

4 Alexandra Orr (1828-1903; *DNB*), sister of Sir Frederic Leighton and biographer of RB, was named after the Empress of Russia, her godmother, as her father was court physician at St. Petersburg. In 1857 she married Sutherland Orr, an army officer, who died the following year as a result of privations suffered during the Indian Mutiny. Mrs. Orr first met RB in Paris in the winter of 1855-56, and the two became intimate friends during RB's later years in London. Indeed, there were persistent rumors of a romantic attachment: Thomas Hardy believed "that there was something tender between Mrs. Orr and Browning. 'Why don't they settle it?' said Mrs. Procter." (F. R. G. Duckworth, *Browning: Background and Conflict* [New York, 1932], p. 78.) With RB's encouragement, she wrote a review of *Red Cotton Night-Cap Country* for the *Contemporary Review* (22 [June 1873], 87-106; *NL*, pp. 216-17) and a more general survey of RB's poetry, also for the *Contemporary* (23 [May 1874], 934-65). Mrs. Orr was active from the beginning in the Browning Society, but she infuriated FJF by suggesting in 1883 that the Society's activities should be terminated after five years (*BSP*, I, 83*); FJF's later comment on her proposal was that "it was confidently predicted by folk of little sense when the Society started, that it could not exist for five years" (*BSP*, II, 165*). Though Mrs. Orr had been commissioned by the Browning Society to write an inexpensive *Browning Primer* (a volume originally intended to be written by John T. Nettleship [1841-1902; *DNB*], painter and literary critic [*Academy*, 21 (25 Feb. 1882), 136]), she admitted in the preface to her *Handbook to the Works of Robert Browning* (1885) that "I felt from the first that the spirit of Mr. Browning's work could neither be compressed within the limits, nor adapted to the uses of a primer, as generally understood." FJF's irritated response in the Society's Annual Report for 1885 was as follows: "Mrs. Orr's intended cheap *Browning Primer* has appeared as a six-shilling *Handbook to Browning's Works*; and . . . the Society bought a copy for each of its members. . . . That the work will be of great value to all Browning students is incontestable; but it needs supplementing by a shorter and lighter Primer, more suited to attract outsiders to the study of the Poet's works." (*BSP*, II, iii.) Arthur Symons, when he first read Mrs. Orr's *Handbook*, described it as "a most painstaking & valuable compilation" (Symons to Churchill Osborne, 3 May 1885 [Princeton University Library]), but after discussing it with FJF he called it an "expensive & dull book" (Symons to Osborne, 5 Dec. 1885 [Princeton]). Obviously FJF had expressed some such opinion in his biographical article on RB, but it does not appear in the printed version.

5 RB read both the first and second editions of Mrs. Orr's *Handbook* in proof; in a few instances, such as the section on *La Saisiaz*, RB supplied her with a prose statement of the argument of a poem (Orr to James Dykes Campbell, 27 May, n.y. [BL Add. Ms. 49526]; Orr, "The Religious Opinions of Robert Browning," *Contemporary Review*, 60 [December 1891], 882).

19, Warwick Crescent, / W.* / Nov. 28. '85.

My dear Furnivall,

Out of the eighty four letters I found waiting for me on Wednesday night I looked at yours,—the handwriting my beacon,—first of all. Thank you abundantly for all the notices: the play evidently received every advantage from the zeal as well as ability of the actors—whose kindness I want to acknowledge—though I feel hampered by having to pick and choose among a company every individual of which would appear to have done extremely well in his degree. You must instruct me in this delicate matter: or, what if I write and delegate the business to yourself? I am sure I feel very sincerely grateful to all and everybody for what cannot have been to *amateurs* an occasion for such display as they are usually attracted by. Mrs Forman should have separate recognition, however, and shall—when I can manage it.[1]

I hope you got the Proof:[2] my mind misgives that I *sealed* it, for safety's sake,—not however so as to close the ends and prevent examination,—tying it, into the bargain. I posted it the day I wrote to you.

Of the other matter,[3] I say nothing—no good comes of talking over one's differences of opinion in such a case: time is the only hope—and that a forlorn one. I may just say that no sort of the influence you complain of has ever been brought to bear upon myself—who had no notion that what I fancied was a passing misunderstanding could be so serious, by any means. I was clearly obliged to notice a passage in what was expressly sent to me for notice, or I should have been chargeable with endorsing an opinion I by no means share. I shall trust to your kindness to me,—which, after all, is kindness to yourself—seeing that "gentle words are always gain"[4]—and you can be magnanimous, I am sure,—a virtue which would not exist where there is nothing to be magnanimous about. Lastly, do not make me the sufferer by keeping away from my house,—I had never dreamed there could be any such reason as you give for what I simply thought was occasioned by your having something better to do, as you well might. Come, and see my new purchase in a sufficiently faithful photograph[5]—and gratify my Sister as well as

Yours ever truly / Robert Browning.

MS: HEH. Address: Dr. Furnivall / 3. St. George's Square, / Primrose Hill, / N.W. Postmarks: PADDINGTON W 5 NO 28 85 D; [L]ONDON NW NO 28 85. Note in FJF's hand on envelope: "Performance of one of his Plays / Mrs. Orr."

1 RB's congratulatory letter to Alma Murray, dated 29 Dec. 1885, is printed in *LRB*, pp. 243-44.
2 Lloyd Sanders, editor of *Celebrities of the Century*, wrote to FJF on 27 Nov. (HEH): "Will you kindly return a corrected proof of your articles on Browning and Mrs. Browning? The printers are clamoring for the Bs as they wish to put that letter into pages."
3 Note in FJF's hand: "Mrs. Orr."
4 Tennyson, "Love Thou Thy Land," l. 23.
5 See RB to FJF, 17 Nov. 1885, n. 1.

RB TO FJF, 29 NOVEMBER 1885

19, Warwick Crescent, / W.* / Nov. 29. '85.

My dear Furnivall, I am sorry indeed about the mischance of the Proof: it *will* come, I suppose, ruinously stamped meâ culpa. If you trust me with another, I will repeat the little that was needed for the other, and return it without delay.

Ever yours truly / Robert Browning.

MS: HEH. Address: Dr. Furnivall, / 3. St. George's Square, / Primrose Hill, / N.W. Postmarks: [. . .]ON SW [. . .] NO 30 [. . .]; LONDON NW OA NO 30 85. Notes in FJF's hand on envelope: "Nov. 30 '85 / proof lost in post."

RB TO FJF, 8 DECEMBER 1885

19, Warwick Crescent, / W.* / Dec. 8. '85.

My dear Furnivall,

You are, as always, very good in wishing to invest me with new honors,—but the acceptance of this last is impossible:[1] it would be tantamount to a profession of belief that what the B. Society has done so helpfully in my case,—mine, who stood in need of it, —should now be repeated in the case of Shelley who, for years, has tasked the ingenuity of his admirers to leave no scrap of his writing nor incident of his life without its illustration by every kind of direct or cross light,—*not*—I very much suspect—to the advantage of either. For myself—I painfully contrast my notions of Shelley the man and Shelley—well, even the poet,—with what they were sixty years ago, when I only had his works, for a certainty, and took his character on trust.[2]

Moreover I am frightened, just a moment after reading your proposal, by learning that I was last night "unanimously elected Honorary President of the University of Edinburgh in the room of Lord Reay"—see the Times of to-day. No hint of such an intention had reached me,—what is expected of such a President I have no notion,—and, if anything more is required than the thanks for the honour, that honour will be assuredly declined.[3]

I shall not say a word about my feeling in your case; you know it.

Remember we expect you and your son next Sunday. I returned (at 2. p.m) from Cambridge: the playing was admirably done.[4]

Ever yours / Robert Browning.

MS: Smith College Library. Address: Dr. Furnivall, / 3. St. George's Square, / Primrose Hill, / N.W. Postmarks: PADDINGTON W 3 DE 8 85 D; LONDON W [. . .]C DE 8 85. Note in FJF's hand on envelope: "*Shelley Socy. / Edinburgh &c.*" Published: *LRB*, pp. 242-43; *LVC*, 1st Ser., II, 49-51.

1 RB declined the presidency of the Shelley Society which FJF, with characteristic enthusiasm and haste, had decided to form only two days earlier. According to Edward Dowden, "The Presidency of the new Shelley Society was designed for Browning, and in case of his refusal, for me; but both Browning and myself would have discouraged the formation of the Society. . . ." (*The Shelley Society's Papers* [1888-91], p. 4*; Dowden, *Fragments of Old Letters, E.D. to E.D.W.*, 2nd ser. [1914], p. 158.) William Michael Rossetti (1829-1919; *DNB*) became chairman of the Society's Committee, but no president was elected.

2 See RB to FJF, 29 Sept. 1883, n. 4.

3 "Edinburgh, Dec. 7.—Tonight at a meeting of the associated societies of the University of Edinburgh it was unanimously agreed to elect Mr. Robert Browning honorary president in room of Lord Reay" (*Times*, 8 Dec. 1885, p. 6). The five Associated Societies periodically elected as Honorary President a distinguished individual who was expected to deliver a Presidential Address. RB assumed the office during the 1886-87 academic year, though there is no evidence that he ever gave an address. The Honorary President at this time was Donald James McKay, 11th Baron Reay (1839-1921; *DNB*), whose name is mistakenly transcribed in *LRB* as "Lord Bury."

4 A production in Greek of Aeschylus' *Eumenides* opened at the Theatre Royal, Cambridge, on 1 Dec. The one female role, that of Pallas Athene, was taken by Miss J. E. Case, formerly of Girton College; all other parts were played by Cambridge men. The music was by Sir Charles Villiers Stanford. After the performance, according to Stanford, RB's "last word to me was a request to use my influence to let him see the 'Cyclops' of Euripedes before he died." (*Times*, 2 Dec. 1885, p. 6; Stanford, *Pages from an Unwritten Diary* [1914], p. 234.)

RB TO FJF, 5 JANUARY 1886

19, Warwick Crescent, / W.* / Jan. 5. '86.
My dear Furnivall,

I return K's kind letter;[1] I don't like you to think I fail to see
how much he, and the friends of the "previous appeals", are desirous of helping on the books: but Smith, without being "God",
is the publisher who has just brought out a cheap collection of
my poems, and would not unreasonably object to the wind being
taken out of his sails immediately by a still cheaper edition than
his own which goes off very well. K. "believes the new venture
would not interfere at all with the disposal of the present one":
if he can convince Smith of *that*, the arrangement will be easy, of
course.

I formed my opinion upon Shelley's behaviour to his wife from
her own letters to their friend, H. the Bookseller of Bond St.,—I
don't suppose they have been published:[2] and I was confirmed in
it by the papers of Peacock, in Fraser's Magazine,—on which no
controversy has been raised by any admirer of Shelley that I know
of;[3] "alas, 'tis pity—and pity 'tis, tis true."[4] Let me purge the memory by a pleasant hope, for the future, that you will enjoy the happiest of new years and continue to believe me

Yours truly ever / Robert Browning.
I had a really charming little reply to my congratulatory letter,
from Mrs Forman.[5]

MS: HEH. Address: Dr. Furnivall, / 3 St. George's Square, / Primrose Hill, / N.W.
Postmarks: LONDON W 5 JA 5 86; LONDON N[W] L JA [. . .] 86. Note in FJF's
hand on envelope: "cheap Selection / Shelley & Harriet."
1 "K" is William G. Kingsland (1848-1933), proofreader for the *Army and Volunteer
Gazette* (London) and an adoring disciple of RB who was active in the Browning Society (*Oracle*, pp. 87-91). Kingsland had written to FJF on 2 Jan. (HEH): "I thought
I would just call your attention to a suggestion I intended to offer you at our last
meeting, and that is whether the Browning Society (through its publishers) could not
get Mr. Browning's consent to issue a 'cheap selection' (say 6d or 1s.) from his short
poems—*each poem prefaced with some remarks illustrative or explanatory of its subject*. You see *the PEOPLE*, whom we want to get interested in Browning, do not care
to spend even 7s 6d on the 2 vols of 'Selections'—more especially as they have been
told they cannot understand him. Now as some of us have been lecturing to Societies
composed largely of the working people, if we could call their attention to a *CHEAP*
selection, with 'prefatory notes,' it would put them in the way of eventually getting
the *present selections*, & would not interfere at all with *their* sale—rather the contrary. At any rate, I offer the suggestion for what it is worth." Kingsland was embarrassed to learn that FJF had passed on his letter to RB and sent an apology at

128

once to the poet. RB's reply to Kingsland, dated 6 Jan. (printed in Kingsland, *Robert Browning: Chief Poet of the Age*, 2nd ed. [1890], pp. 35-36), repeats essentially what he had told FJF the day before, though the tone of irritation is less pronounced.

2   See RB to FJF, 29 Sept. 1883, n. 4.

3   The memoir of Shelley by Thomas Love Peacock (1785-1866; *DNB*) appeared in *Fraser's Magazine* of June 1858, January 1860, March 1860, and March 1862.

4   "That he is mad, 'tis true: 'tis true 'tis pity; / And pity 'tis 'tis true . . ." (Shakespeare, *Hamlet*, II.ii.97-98).

5   See RB to FJF, 28 Sept. 1885, n. 1.

RB TO FJF, 30 JANUARY 1886

19, Warwick Crescent, / W.* / Jan. 30. '86.

My dear Furnivall,

Some months ago, Mr William Sharp applied to me for leave to put into a proposed Collection of Sonnets[1] several by my wife and two by myself: I broke a rule imposed on me by the Publisher, and gave the consent required. Here comes the book, and the first glance at my Sonnet (about "Liberty," you remember) shows me that friendly editorship substitutes therein "purchase" for "purpose"—making thorough nonsense of the passage: two lines after, "gaily" is turned into "gladly". Whether this is a sample of the general exactitude, I shall not spend another minute in ascertaining: but I do think its too bad that such carelessness should be exercised, when all that one requires is that what has been begged as a favour may not fare at a friend's hands as if it fell into those of Austin, Courthope,[2] and their like, who forge what they cannot find. I have written to Mr Sharp: but I should much like *one word* sent to the "Academy" to simply say that the error is none of mine. Can you do this for me,—you who have done so abundantly? You don't look me up, as you engaged—yet Sundays remain Sundays, and 1 o'clock strikes duly.

Ever truly yours / Robert Browning.

MS: HEH. Address: Dr. Furnivall, / 3. St. George's Square, / Primrose Hill, / N.W. Postmarks: PADDINGTON W X JA 30 86 D; LONDON NW KL JA 30 86. Note in FJF's hand on envelope: "Mr. Sharp's mistakes / in reprint of poems."

1   *Sonnets of This Century*, ed. with a Critical Introduction on the Sonnet by William Sharp (1886). The Browning sonnets included were RB's "Helen's Tower" and "An Answer" (the latter, which RB describes as being on "Liberty," was subsequently entitled "Why I Am a Liberal") and EBB's "The Soul's Expression" and Nos. 14, 17, 22, and 43 of *Sonnets from the Portuguese*. Sharp (1855-1905; *DNB*), Scottish poet and journalist who also wrote under the pseudonym "Fiona Macleod," knew RB

slightly and in 1890 published the first book-length biography of him. Sharp read a paper on "Browning and the Arts" to the Browning Society on 3 June 1882 (*BSP*, I, 34*-40*).

2 Alfred Austin (1855-1913; *DNB*), afterwards Poet Laureate, was bitterly satirized by RB in "Of Pacchiarotto, and How He Worked in Distemper" (1876). William John Courthope (1842-1917; *DNB*), poet and critic, was co-editor with Austin of the *National Review* from 1883 to 1887.

RB TO FJF, 1 FEBRUARY 1886

19, Warwick Crescent, / W.* / Feb. 1. '86

My dear Furnivall,

I get this morning such a penitent letter from Mr. Sharp—with such assurances that he will do all in his power to set things right by printing a leaflet,[1] &c that I shall beg you to be so kind as to take no notice of my request—now rendered unnecessary. He was careless certainly, but will take better care for the future.

Ever yours truly / Robert Browning.

MS: HEH. Address: Dr. Furnivall, / 3. St. George's Square, / Primrose Hill, / N.W. Postmarks: PADDINGTON W 12 FE 1 86 D; LONDON NW KD FE 1 86. Note in FJF's hand on envelope: "Mr. Sharp."

1 The errors enumerated by RB in his previous letter were corrected in subsequent printings of the volume. In a postcard to James Dykes Campbell, postmarked 1 Feb. 1886, Sharp wrote: "I much regret to find that (mainly owing to an attack of neuralgia in the eyes during proof correcting) I have omitted to correct two printer's errors in the second of Browning's sonnets. . . . Mr Browning is naturally put out about it—but fortunately it can be so far remedied—firstly by errata-slips sent out with the vols, & later on the edition-de-luxe of the book (to be completely reset) to be issued 6 months or so hence." (Typescript in BL Add. MS. 49526.)

RB TO FJF, 11 APRIL 1886

19, Warwick Crescent, / W. / Apr. 11. '86.

My dear Furnivall,

Pray let me sit in the stalls beside you, not elsewhere:[1] my sister will be glad to accompany me, and so will Pen if—as I expect—he will be in London at that time. We three will be safe under your caring.

Ever truly yours / Robert Browning.

Copy (in FJF's hand): HEH. Note in FJF's hand on letter: "given to F. S. Ellis [bookseller and author, 1830-1901; *DNB*], for a charmer."

1 On 7 May 1886, at the Grand Theatre, Islington, FJF's newly-formed Shelley Society
   sponsored a performance of *The Cenci* with Alma Murray and Hermann Vezin in the
   chief roles. As an honored guest, RB sat next to James Russell Lowell; George Meredith and other literary notables were also present. The following day RB wrote to
   Miss Murray: "I must say,—what many have already said, perhaps more energetically,
   —how much impressed I was by your admirable impersonation of that most difficult
   of all characters to impersonate: after such a display of passion and pathos, what is impossible for you—the Poetic Actress without a rival?" (*Alma Murray*,
   p. 11; see also the *Note-Book of the Shelley Society* [1888], pp. 50-80, and a pamphlet entitled *Alma Murray: Portrait of Beatrice Cenci, with Critical Notice Containing Four Letters from Robert Browning* [1891]). According to a letter from FJF
   published in the *Pall Mall Gazette* during May 1886, "Mr. Browning, when young,
   naturally and just because he was himself a poet and dramatist, sent his copy of the
   original edition of *The Cenci* to [Edmund] Kean, and askt him to put it on the stage"
   (*Note-Book of the Shelley Society*, p. 101). In a letter to Sir Henry Taylor, 28 Dec.
   1886, FJF offered this account of the *Cenci* performance: "One strong reason for my
   decision to have the *Cenci* performed, was, that Shelley wisht to have his play acted.
   The fulfillment of that wish seems to me a duty on the part of Shelley honourers
   now. Moreover, the drama is confessedly the greatest in modern drama, & ought to
   be treated as an acting play. When I wrote to Miss A. Murray (Mrs. A. Forman) to
   ask her to act Beatrice, she answered that it had been the dream of her life to play
   the part,—she had read the 5th. Act in public, to the Wagner Society—& had only the
   night before been scheming with her husband how she could get the Play on to the
   stage." (Bodleian MS. Eng. lett. d. 16, fol. 352.)

RB TO FJF, 30 APRIL 1886

19, Warwick Crescent, / W.* / Apr. 30. '86.

My dear Furnivall,

I am really confused at the quite unexpected allocution at end
of the "Prolog"[1] (as I can't help writing the word, since you set me
the example)—and but that the writing is so really fine, I should
want it, so far at least, broken up: how good everybody is to me in
these late years—also following your example! No,—the "and" is
necessarily retained if the word "Beatrice" is to be pronounced as
a trisyllable,—not so, if as in Italy, with the final *e* accented. This,
the proper way, was used by Byron (he directs it to be so used in a
note to the 1st Canto of the "Prophecy of Dante:)[2] and it is curious that Shelley chose the English mode—as is certain from the occurrence of such lines as "I knew not aught that Beatrice designed"
—"No, Beatrice; have courage, my sweet girl!"[3] and others. The
"Prolog" *is* very decidedly fine, I think.

Ever yours / Robert Browning

Robert returns next Tuesday and will be with us: I am increasingly
interested in the performance.

MS: John Todhunter Collection, MS 202/1/1, fols. 325-26, University of Reading Library. Address: Dr. Furnivall, / 3. St. George's Square, / Primrose Hill, / S.W. Postmarks: PADDINGTON W AP 30 86 [. . .]; LONDON NW [. . .] AP 30 86.

1 At the *Cenci* performance Leonard Outram recited a rhymed prologue by Dr. John Todhunter (1839-1916; *WW*), Irish poet and playwright, which alluded to RB's birthday (*Note-Book of the Shelley Society* [1888], p. 58).

2 Byron's note reads: "The reader is requested to adopt the Italian pronunciation of Beatrice, sounding all the syllables."

3 *The Cenci*, II.i.159; II.i.80.

RB TO FJF, 12 MAY 1886

19, Warwick Crescent. / W.* / May 12. '86.

My dear Furnivall,

Congratulations, first and foremost, on your victory,[1] of Monday—and your smart letter in the Pall Mall, the day before:[2] in each case the "scull" has been well employed, and whether better employed in "rŏwing" or "rōwing" is a moot point. Next, I am heartily glad if my little word of appreciation gave any pleasure to the lady we are so much indebted to.[3] You see the charge of inflicting boundless *ennui* on the audience is insisted on in the "World":[4] "It shall to the barber's with the critic's beard: he's for a jig or &c. or he sleeps"[5]—I daresay. Lastly—the omitted word,— which I never noticed,—must almost certainly be "surely" as Mr Symons suspects: *some* word is *out, that* is too evident.[6] By the way,—you spoke of making use of my Essay for the Society, and also of the little poem: if you can do any good with the "Cenciaja" it is at your service, of course.[7]

I am amused at the objection taken by some of the critics to the Eve-like simplicity of Pen's peasant-girl,[8] who before going on to saintliness (which the Church still withholds from her) was satisfied with the proverbially next step to it—cleanliness. If they knew anything of Joan's habits even when advanced in her saintly career, they would remember she was no prude by any means: her favoured young cavalier, the Duc d'Alençon,[9] mentions that he had frequently seen her undress, and that "aliquando videbat ejus mammas quae pulchrae erant"[10]—in his very words.

Ever truly yours, / Robert Browning.

MS: Yale. Address: Dr. Furnivall / 3. St. George's Square, / Primrose Hill, N.W. Postmarks: PADDINGTON W 6 MY 12 86 D; LONDON NW KK MY 12 86. Note in FJF's hand on envelope: *"Cenci, / Penn's Joan of Arc."* Published: *LRB*, p. 247; *LVC*, 1st Ser., II, 54-56.

1 Note in FJF's hand: "1st Sculling-Fours Race [Putney to Hammersmith] in Maurice Rowing Club. I was 3. [in the winning boat] behind Percy Ward."

2 In response to an unfavorable review by the *Pall Mall Gazette* (8 May 1886, p. 4) of the Shelley Society's production of *The Cenci* (see RB to FJF, 11 Apr. 1886, n. 1), FJF had written an extremely intemperate letter (*PMG*, 10 May 1886, p. 4) in which he described the anonymous reviewer as a liar and "base beast" no longer fit for the society of "honourable men and women."

3 Note in FJF's hand: "? Alma Murray." RB's congratulatory letter—dated 8 May 1886 —to Miss Alma Murray, who had played the role of Beatrice Cenci in the Shelley Society production (see RB to FJF, 11 Apr. 1886, n. 1), is printed in the *Note-Book of the Shelley Society*, p. 105.

4 "W.A." described *The Cenci* as an "impossible play," tedious and boring, but confessed that "to me there was one vivid personal pleasure and a solace, in the proceedings of Friday last. It was to see the author of *In a Balcony, A Blot in the 'Scutcheon,* and *Colombe's Birthday* seated in the stalls, a victim among victims." ("The Theatre," *The World: A Journal for Men and Women,* 12 May 1886, p. 17.)

5 Shakespeare, *Hamlet*, II.ii. [521-23].

6 I cannot identify the poem in question. Arthur Symons was at this time writing his *Introduction to the Study of Browning* (see RB to FJF, 5 Oct. 1886, n. 1).

7 RB's poem "Cenciaja," its title a pun on *The Cenci,* appeared in the *Pacchiarotto* volume (1876). In the first Annual Report of the Shelley Society, 26 Jan. 1887 (*The Shelley Society's Papers* [1888-91], p. 11*), the following title was announced for publication by the Society in 1887: "Robert Browning's *Essays and Poems on Shelley.* (Reprinted by permission of the Author.) With a Portrait of Browning and Forewords by Dr. F. J. Furnivall." Like many of the Society's projected publications, this one did not materialize, but in 1888 the Shelley Society reprinted RB's *Essay on Shelley,* edited by W. Tyas Harden.

8 Pen's painting *Joan of Arc and the Kingfisher,* which portrayed a nude Jeanne d'Arc (1411-31) about to bathe in a river, was exhibited at the Grosvenor Gallery in the spring of 1886. RB's anger at the prudishness of Pen's critics inspired a passage in the "Furini" section of *Parleyings* (1887) which indirectly attacked John Calcott Horsley (1817-1903; *DNB*), treasurer of the Royal Academy (1882-97) and leader of an antinudity campaign in the English art world (William C. DeVane, *Browning's Parleyings: The Autobiography of a Mind* [New Haven, 1927], pp. 183-84, 211).

9 Jean Duc d'Alençon testified to Jeanne d'Arc's good character in a deposition at one of a series of official enquiries into the conduct of her trial, Paris, 1455-56.

10 "Sometimes he had seen her breasts, which were beautiful."

RB TO FJF, 25 MAY 1886

19, Warwick Crescent, / W.* May 25. '86.

My dear Furnivall,

You are quite at liberty to make the use you mention of "Pauline"—taking care that it is no infraction of the copyright,—as indeed it can hardly be.[1] Don't give me a single copy "for my friends"—but keep them for the more than friendly subscribers to the Society.

I don't understand what Mrs Dall can mean by saying that "Sordello" has been "re-written": I did certainly at one time intend to rewrite much of it,—but changed my mind,—and the edition which I reprinted was the same in all respects as its predecessor—only with an elucidatory heading to each page, and some few alterations, presumably for the better, in the text—such as occur in most of my works: I cannot remember a single instance of any importance that is "rewritten"—and I only suppose that Mrs Dall has taken project for performance, and set down as "done" what was for a while intended to be done.[2]

Well cycled you and your worthy son both![3] All congratulations from

Yours truly ever / Robert Browning.

MS: BL. Address: Dr. Furnivall, / 3. St. George's Square, / Primrose Hill, / N.W. Postmarks: PADDINGTON O 3 MY 25 86; LONDON NW K O MY 25 86. (Insufficient postage marked on envelope.) Published: *LRB*, p. 248; *LVC*, 2nd Ser., II, 28-29.

1   A facsimile reprint of *Pauline* (1833), RB's first published poem, was issued by the Browning Society late in 1886. The printing of the facsimile was supervised by Thomas J. Wise (1859-1937; *DNB*), the notorious book-collector, who shortly thereafter used the skills acquired in this undertaking to produce a series of bibliographic forgeries (*Oracle*, pp. 79-86).

2   A pamphlet by Mrs. Caroline Dall, *Sordello: A History and a Poem* (Boston, 1886), was reviewed by J. T. Nettleship in *BSP*, II, 146*-47*, where RB probably saw Nettleship's allusion to the alleged revision of *Sordello*. RB unsuccessfuly attempted a major reworking of the poem in 1845, but when he reissued it in 1863 it was rewritten only slightly.

3   On 18 Apr. 1886 Percy Furnivall narrowly missed winning the Surrey Cup in a race at Kennington Oval Track (*Bicycling World* [Boston], 13 [7 May 1886], 17).

RB TO FJF, 28 MAY 1886
_____

19, Warwick Crescent, / W.* / May 28. '86.

My dear Furnivall,

I shall, of course, be happy to see both your friends on Sunday, and to give them the book:[1] will they be good enough to so time their visit as to let me leave at 1. o-clock? For I have, unluckily, to take luncheon at a distance a little later—unusual as it is for me to be absent from home so early on a Sunday.

Ever truly yours / Robert Browning.

MS: Wellesley College Library. Address: Dr. Furnivall, / 3. St. George's Square, /

Primrose Hill, / N.W. Postmarks: PADDINGTON 5 MY 28 86 [. . .]; LONDON NW KK MY 28 86. (1*d.* postage due.)
1 The two friends may have been Walter B. Slater (see RB to FJF, 5 Mar. 1888, n. 2) and Thomas J. Wise, who were at this time making arrangements for the facsimile of *Pauline* (*Oracle*, pp. 81-83; "Literary Societies," *Academy*, 29 [5 June 1886], 397; see RB to FJF, 25 May 1886, n. 1).

RB TO FJF, 20 JULY 1886

19, Warwick Crescent, / W.* / July 20. '86.

My dear Furnivall,

In the Royalist rhymes entitled "Vanity of Vanities, or Sir Harry Vane's Picture"—wherein Vane is charged with being a Jesuit— occur these lines

"'Tis said they will give him a Cardinal's hat:
They sooner will give him an old nun's twat!"

The ballad is partly quoted in the Appendix to Forster's Life of Vane, but the above lines are left out—I remember them, however, and the word struck me as a distinctive part of a nun's attire that might fitly pair off with the cowl appropriated to a monk.[1] To "twattle" was used for "tattle" sometimes—as in Croxhall's Fables, where the birds that object to carrying the tortoise who is to hold a stick in his mouth, do so because "he will be twattling"—and let it go thereby.[2]

Ever truly yours, / Robert Browning.

MS: ABL. Address: Dr. Furnivall, / 3. St. George's Square, / Primrose Hill, / N.W. Postmarks: PADDINGTON W 4 JY 20 86 D; LONDON NW KH JY 20 86. Published: *LRB*, pp. 251-52; *LVC*, 1st Ser., II, 59-60.
1 RB is defending his use of the word "twats" in *Pippa Passes* (IV.ii.95-98): "Then, owls and bats, / Cowls and twats, / Monks and nuns, in a cloister's moods / Adjourn to the oak-stump pantry!" The poem which RB cites as his authority appeared in *Rump: or An exact collection of the choycest poems relating to the late times. By the most eminent wits, from anno 1639. to anno 1661.* (1662; first edition, 1660) and was, as RB indicates, partially reprinted in an appendix to John Forster's *Sir Henry Vane the Younger* (1840). RB's explanation was quoted in *Select Poems of Robert Browning*, ed. William J. Rolfe and Heloise E. Hersey (New York, 1886), prompting H. W. Fay to write a letter to the *Academy* (33 [16 June 1888], 415) about RB's "distressing blunder." "Twat" actually denotes the female genitals. RB's embarrassing mistake was duly recorded in the *Oxford English Dictionary*, probably by FJF.
2 This story does not appear in the popular English translation (1722) of Aesop's *Fables* by Samuel Croxall (d. 1752; *DNB*), a translation which RB's mother read aloud to him (Orr, p. 26).

135

RB TO FJF, 21 JULY 1886

July 21. '86.

My dear Furnivall,

I enclose, as desired, a letter which you will deal with as you please.[1] The writer, a stranger to me, said he was going to lecture upon my poems, and wanted to know where he could find any information about them,—so, I referred him to the Handbook[2] and the Society's transactions. Whereupon he writes again,—after the unnecessary fashion of his kind,—wants me to give him a book—Tennyson having done so, &c &c. All these things are significant enough of a man's capability to treat of what he begins by casting about for somebody to teach *him*.

Ever truly yours / R Browning.

MS: ABL. Address: Dr. Furnivall, / 3. St. George's Square, / Primrose Hill, / N.W. Postmarks: PADDINGTON 4 JY 21 86 P; LONDON NW KH JY 21 86.

1 Note in FJF's hand: "from the Rev. J. R. Vernon / St. Andrew's Rectory, Bridgwater—a pre- / sumptuous flunky [?]." The address of the Rev. John Richard Vernon was actually St. Audrie's Rectory, Bridgwater; he was the author of several religious tracts (*Crockford's Clerical Directory*). RB's letter to Vernon, dated 28 July 1886, is in the Pforzheimer Library (Misc. 1751).

2 Mrs. Orr's *Handbook to the Works of Robert Browning* (1885).

RB TO FJF, 11 AUGUST 1886

19, Warwick Crescent, / W.* / Aug. 11, '86.

My dear Furnivall,

I should have been glad to see you before we left town—though the distance from it will not be far this time: we go to the "Hand Hotel, Llangollen".[1] My Sister is quite well, nearly quite strong: but we could not venture to go as far away from home as in years past. Our stay will be as the weather may prescribe. All health, and safe cycling to you, with our united best regards!

Ever truly yours / Robert Browning.

MS: HEH. Address: Dr. Furnivall, / 3. St. George's Square, / Primrose Hill, / N.W. Postmarks: PADDINGTON W 4 AU 11 86 J; LONDON NW KH AU 11 86.

1 The 1890 edition of Baedeker's *Handbook to Great Britain* (p. 304) speaks of the Hand Hotel as "an old and comfortable house, close to the Dee," with a "harper in the hall."

RB TO FJF, 6 SEPTEMBER 1886

Hand Hotel, Llangollen, N. Wales. / Sept. 6. '86.

My dear Furnivall,

I had thought to say something before this of our stay here, and the good effect it continues to have on my Sister's health—but the object of this letter is different indeed. I should be sorry if you heard incidentally from another than myself that my friend Milsand died two days ago—on the 4th, at his place, Villers la Faye, in the Côte d'Or. We had been long aware of his declining health; and the last letter, of Aug. 28, spoke of increasing bodily weakness,—"the head remaining strong." We were unprepared for what has followed so fast—and which we are apprised of by a telegram this morning.

It is due to your kindness to say this much.

Ever truly yours / Robert Browning.

MS: ABL. Address: F. J. Furnivall, Esq. / 3. St. George's Square, / Primrose Hill, / London. / N.W. Postmarks: LLANGOLLEN E 6 SP 86; LONDON NW C7 SP 7 86. Note in FJF's hand on envelope: "Milsand's death." Published: *LRB*, p. 254; *LVC*, 1st Ser., II, 61-62.

RB TO FJF, 12 SEPTEMBER 1886

Hand Hotel, Llangollen, Sept. 12, '86.

My dear Furnivall,

Often enough, or too much, you have said kind things of me, done kind things to me, and if I have not in every case straightway told you how I was impressed by your kindness it has been through a confidence that you would understand easily how, while feeling much, one seems to need little speaking. This time, however, you have so thrilled me through with gratitude for your notice of Milsand that I am as willing as able to thank you from my heart. You did all I could wish in the way of sobriety and succinctness as well as adequate recognition and handsome appreciation— adequate for the "public"—who will never know what only an intimate of thirty-five years knows and never will attempt to put into words. Your notice was so excellently devised, you see, that *The Times* at once transferred it to its columns,[1] so giving it all the circulation desirable. I sent it to Mad[am]e Milsand, and others will of course see what they would have probably missed. I do not "inform" you that Milsand liked you greatly, little as was the intercourse between you permitted by circumstances—your own penetration and sympathy must have divined that.

Truest thanks once again and always from

Yours affectionately, / Robert Browning.

Text: *LRB*, p. 255. Published: *LVC*, 1st Ser., II, 63-64.
1 FJF's unsigned obituary of Milsand (*Academy*, 30 [11 Sept. 1886], 169), which made use of information supplied in RB's letter to FJF of 6 Sept. 1886 and emphasized Milsand's association with RB, was summarized in *The Times*, 10 Sept. 1886, p. 3.

RB TO FJF, 5 OCTOBER 1886

Hand Hotel, Llangollen. / Oct. 5. '86.

My dear Furnivall,

I make haste to say by the early Post that Messrs. Cassell are in no danger of finding such a churl in me as they seem to think might possibly be the case: I receive by this same Post a set of Proofs of Mr Symons' "Introduction,"—which I will open and inspect presently,—and a letter from the Publishers to the same effect as yours. Will you kindly give them, on my part, the full authorization they require? I remember very well that Messrs. Cassell are scrupulous and honorable,—having had a pleasant little "proof" of that kind once on a time.[1]

I believe we shall continue to profit by the exceptionally fine weather for another fortnight. Thank you for the newspaper which records your triumphs, in which I am sure I sympathize.[2] My Sister (quite her old self again) sends her kindest regards along with mine, who am

Yours truly ever / Robert Browning.

MS: HEH. Address: Dr. Furnivall, / 3. St. George's Square, / Primrose Hill, / London. N.W. Postmarks: LLANGOLLEN B 5 OC 86; LONDON NW J5 OC 5 86. Note in FJF's hand on envelope: "Consent to Symons' book." Note in FJF's hand on letter: "to be returned to / F.J.F."
1 Arthur Symons' *Introduction to the Study of Browning* was published by Cassell in the autumn of 1886 and distributed to every member of the Browning Society.
2 On 18 Sept. FJF was a member of the winning crew in the second Sculling Four race held in Europe, and on the same day his son Percy had won two more bicycling competitions: the Surrey ten-mile Challenge Cup and the one-mile Challenge Trophy.

RB TO FJF, 7 OCTOBER 1886

Llangollen, Oct. 7. '86.

My dear Furnivall,

By this Post, I return the "Proofs" to Messrs. Cassell,—having read them carefully and set right the very little that was wrong in the printing. I enclosed in the parcel, a letter of acknowledgement to Mr Symons.[1] I tell him truly that I hardly know how to praise his book without praising myself—but I try to convey some sense of the great gratification he has given me—however my poetry may come short of what his generosity endeavours to find there.

Oh, yes—I subscribe cheerfully to the new boat[2]—"et vogue la galère!" Only, let me owe it you till you please to call for it, in about a fortnight's time—when I hope to be at home again. We have done so well here that I was unwilling to cut our stay short. I am hurrying to catch our early Post—but am none the less

Ever yours / Robert Browning.

MS: HEH. Address: Dr. Furnivall, / 3. St. George's Square, / Primrose Hill, / Highgate, / London. / N.W. Postmarks: LLANGOLLEN B 7 OC 86; LONDON NW J5 OC 7 86. Note in FJF's hand on envelope: "Biography proofs / A. Symons."

1 RB wrote to Symons: "How can I manage to thank—much more praise—what, in its generosity and appreciation, makes the poorest recognition 'come too near the praising of myself'? It does indeed strike me as wonderful that you should have given such patient attention to all these poems, and (if I dare say farther) so thoroughly entered into—at any rate—the spirit in which they were written, and the purpose they helped to serve." (Symons, "Some Browning Reminiscences," *North American Review*, 204 [October 1916], 603.) RB's letter to Cassell & Co., dated 7 Oct. 1886, is in the Free Library of Philadelphia.

2 FJF, who militantly championed the superiority of sculling over rowing, sent out a printed appeal (dated 8 Oct. 1886) for subscriptions for a Sculling Eight to be used by the Maurice Rowing Club (of the Working Men's College). At the end of the appeal RB was listed as having already subscribed £1.

RB TO FJF, 9 DECEMBER 1886

19, Warwick Crescent, / W.* / Dec. 9. '86.

My dear Furnivall,

I do want you to understand what my feeling is about the Play,[1] and why I find it impossible to be present at it. Nothing is farther from my thoughts than any sort of disrespect to the performers— and, as for the Society, you know how thoroughly grateful I am, how sensible of its immense help to my works. But I am really too doubtful of the power of "Strafford" to make itself effective unless with such another as Macready: Mrs Forman will do all humanly possible for her part—but unluckily it is not the principal one: she knows how I believe in her power whenever that power is fully available. I shall hear all about the performance from more trustworthy critics than those who, I seem to notice, think themselves bound to stick to the old and safe saying about my plays *"They did not succeed*: what matters how or why it happened?" Witness the gentleman—, or rather, don't witness anything! If there should be a success after all, I will gladly attend any repetition of the piece, as I suppose might be managed. Now, don't tell the actors that I mistrust them—the fact being that I mistrust my own play.

[2]Ever truly yours / Robert Browning.
My poem is gone to press a week ago.[3]

MS: HEH. Address: Dr. Furnivall, / 3 St. George's Square, / Primrose Hill, / N.W. Postmarks: PADDINGTON 4 DE 9 86 F; LOND[ON NW] KH DE 8 8[6]. Note in FJF's hand on envelope: "performance of *Strafford*. / signature cut off."

1   The Browning Society planned to sponsor a production of *Strafford* at the Strand Theatre in November 1886, with Alma Murray and Leonard Outram (d. 1901) in the lead roles, but in October Outram had ignited FJF's explosive temper by attempting to raise a subscription for himself from Browning Society members without authorization from FJF. FJF immediately dismissed Outram as both actor and director of the play and began writing angry circulars and letters to the press about Outram's "scandalous attempt to get money from our Members under cover of my name." A nasty public exchange of insults ensued, with the result that in February 1888 FJF was found guilty in a libel suit brought against him by Outram. Hence in early December 1886 it was obvious to RB that the *Strafford* production was likely to be a disaster, especially when he learned a few days later (see RB to FJF, 13 Dec. 1886) that Miss Murray had also dropped out. Despite RB's suggestion that the play be again postponed, FJF stubbornly insisted upon its performance on 21 Dec. under these unhappy circumstances. (*Oracle*, pp. 40-48.)

2   The remainder of the letter is excised and transcribed in FJF's hand, with this explanatory note: "(cut off for Mrs. J. A. H. Gordon. 2 Nov. 1891)."

3   *Parleyings with Certain People of Importance in Their Day* was published by Smith, Elder on 28 Jan. 1887. FJF's presentation copy from RB (Berg) has this inscription: "Dr. Furnivall / from his gratefully ever / Robert Browning. / Jan. 28. '87."

RB TO FJF, 13 DECEMBER 1886

19, Warwick Crescent / W.* / Dec. 13, '86.
My dear Furnivall,

I return Alma Murray's letter with great regret that she should have been obliged to write it:[1] tell her how sensible I am of her good will in the matter, and how thoroughly she is justified in not attempting an impossibility.

Do not you think this is a very proper occasion for postponing the representation?[2] You see the judicious remarks of the Critic in this morning's *Daily News*: not a doubt as to whether the bankrupt management of that day did what was requisite for the success of the piece,—whether the wretched acting of the inferior people might not have done harm, (a stone-deaf Charles, a silly, simpering Carlisle, &c.)—and whether the management "that dressed the Scots Commissioners in kilts" might not refuse (as it did) "one rag for the new piece,"—The only conclusion to draw is—that a play which did not obtain the enthusiastic praise of the critics, *then*, cannot deserve a better fate *now*, under quite other conditions.[3] I would strongly advise that you run no such risk, but let a thing which has so long lain dormant, sleep a little longer. Of course I do not know what the engagements are, and whether it is not too late to recede: but surely with the loss of Alma M. goes the last chance of a gratifying result.

In haste, but ever truly yours,

Robt. Browning.

MS: BL. Published: *LRB*, p. 259; *LVC*, 1st Ser., II, 65-67.

1 Miss Murray wrote FJF on 12 Dec. (Symington Collection F724x, Rutgers University Library) that she would have to give up the role of Lady Carlisle in *Strafford*: "My Doctor says if I persist in going on with her it is quite likely that I should not be able to appear on the 21st and moreover get myself seriously laid up. For the last week or two one of my nervous troubles has been a swelling of the lips & eyes, which comes on in the night & yesterday I was so disfigured that I had to spend the whole of the day at my Doctor's house so that he could paint my face every five minutes & make me presentable enough to appear at Drury Lane at night. This is the third time it has been so bad during the last fortnight & I am getting frightened. . . . I am suffering very much today from the strong remedies used. . . . I cannot tell you how grieved I am, specially as Mr Browning is to be present. I have clung to it until the last moment hoping to be able to pull through till the 21st but yesterday my Doctor finished me off & was peremptory about my getting immediate rest of mind & body." According to Dr. Todhunter, "Miss Webster, who replaced Miss Alma Murray at a very brief notice, gave a respectable, if not altogether satisfactory rendering of the part" (*BSP*, II, 152).

2 Note in FJF's hand: "NO!"

3 RB felt strongly that the first production of *Strafford* by Macready in 1837 was unsuccessful because of inept management and acting. For the unhappy details of that production, see *The Diaries of William Charles Macready, 1833-1851*, ed. William Toynbee (1912), I, 380-93 *passim*.

RB TO FJF, 16 DECEMBER 1886

19, Warwick Crescent, / W.* / Dec. 16. '86.

My dear Furnivall,

Your slip in the address caused the card belonging to Mrs Forman to come here! I enclose it—and indeed ought to have done
so sooner, but was much engaged—and not very well, into the bargain.

Your notion that nobody is missed,—or seriously missed,—in
a Company of Actors any more than of Cabinet ministers,—has
much to recommend it. I shall be curious to learn the result, and
if the thing *does*, after all, go decently,—the more merit in the
propellers of it. You must tell me all about it—"a passionate and
weighty nuntius".[1]

Ever truly yours / Robert Browning.

MS: HEH. Address: Dr. Furnivall, / 3. St. George's Square, / Primrose Hill, / N.W.
Postmarks: PADDINGTON W 4 DE 16 86; LONDON NW KH DE 16 86. Note in
FJF's hand on envelope: "coming performance of one of / B's plays."
1 Messenger or announcement of news.

RB TO FJF, 20 DECEMBER 1886

19, Warwick Crescent, / W.* / Dec. 20. '86.

My dear Furnivall,

The question whether I could attend the Dress-Rehearsal to-
morrow is unluckily put an end to by the ordinance of the Doctor,
who will permit me nothing of the kind just now. I am very unwell
—and have been forced to give up all engagements last week, and
even this on which we enter. It all comes of an English winter—
which I shall try and escape, if may be, another year, if I reach it.
You must tell me what happens,—and perhaps things may turn out
better than one has a right to expect.

Ever truly yours / Robert Browning.

MS: HEH. Address: Dr. Furnivall, / 3. St. George's Square, / Primrose Hill, / N.W.
Postmarks: PADDINGTON W A7 DE 20 86; LONDON NW LA DE 20 86. Note in
FJF's hand on envelope: "can't be at / Dress Rehearsal."

RB TO FJF, 8 JANUARY 1887

19, Warwick Crescent, / W.* / Jan. 8. '87.

My dear Furnivall,

I was on the point of writing to enquire about you—not having seen nor heard since your benevolent drop-in on the "Strafford" evening. I had fancies of a tumble from the tricycle,—on frozen snow: of the sculling who could think? I am very sorry to hear that you have been suffering from the ugly complication you confess to: my best wishes go to your recovery.

I am unable to send a photograph of Pen's picture,—and there is no getting one from the fixture at Balliol: there are surely likenesses enough in the States, by the sun *ad vivum*, [not] to need one from Pen's portrait.[1]

I have just heard (last evening) that my Poem will appear "towards the end of the month"—as the "Athenaeum" has it this morning.[2] It is all printed off and ready—but advance-sheets are required in America. It consists of a number of confabulations with certain people dead and gone, but once more or less notable, —whose personalities serve to strike out some sort of spark from myself—all in rhyme, as you know,—the prologue and epilogue being in a lyrical measure.[3]

Pen has been here for a fortnight—and goes away on Monday— he will be away to-morrow morning, or I would try to give him the pleasure of seeing you, if you could lunch here.

If not too late,—how can it be?—take best New Year's wishes from yours

truly ever / Robert Browning.

MS: HEH. Address. Dr. Furnivall, / 3. St. George's Square, / Primrose Hill, / N.W. Postmarks: PADDINGTON 5 JA 8 87; LONDON NW KJ JA 8 87. Note in FJF's hand on envelope: "Penn's portrait of B. / Parleyings."

1 Pen's portrait of his father in an academic gown hangs today in Balliol College. On 27 Dec. 1886, William J. Rolfe (1827-1910; *DAB*) had written to FJF (HEH) asking him to secure a photograph of the painting for reproduction in *A Blot in the 'Scutcheon and Other Dramas by Robert Browning* (New York, 1887), which Rolfe and Miss Heloise E. Hersey were then editing. They did in fact use an engraving of a different portrait of RB in their volume.

2 See RB to FJF, 9 Dec. 1886, n. 3.

3 The historical personages with whom RB "parleys" in the poem are Bernard de Mandeville (1670?-1733; *DNB*), Daniel Bartoli (1608-85), Christopher Smart (1722-71; *DNB*), George Bubb Doddington (1691-1762; *DNB*), Francis Furini (1600-49), Gerard de Lairesse (1641-1711), and Charles Avison (1710?-70; *DNB*).

RB TO FJF, 2 MARCH 1887

19, Warwick Crescent, / W.* / March 2. '87.

Dear Furnivall,

Thank you much for your ingenious paper and kind commentings.[1]

You read at the Museum.[2] When you have an opportunity, I should be glad if you would discover whether it possesses a copy of the "Song to David", published as a small paper-bound book nearly sixty years ago. It professed to be the Poem in a greater state of correctness and completeness than had hitherto been attainable, and was accompanied by a few notes. I bought this at the time, and received the impression I still retain. But unluckily I lent the copy, some years afterwards, to a friend now dead—who never restored it. I once saw the portion given by Chalmers—for but a few minutes—and was struck by more than one gross blunder whether of the Editor's committing or by the Printer's carelessness.[3]

I should be happy indeed if I could retrieve a loss I have felt for a full half century or very nearly. Any how, *that* edition has the trust-worthy text: what if your Society reprinted it?

Ever truly yours / Robert Browning

MS: HEH. Address: Dr. Furnivall, / 3. St. George's Square, / Primrose Hill, / N.W. Postmarks: PADDINGTON 4 MR 2 87 [. . .]; LONDON NW KH MR 2 87. Note in FJF's hand on envelope: *"Smart's Song to David."*

1 FJF read a paper entitled "A Grammatical Analysis of *O Lyric Love* [*The Ring and the Book*, I.1391-1416]" to the Browning Society on 25 Feb. 1887 (*BSP*, II, 165-68).

2 The British Museum Reading Room.

3 The "Song of David" by Christopher Smart (1722-71; *DNB*) was written, according to tradition, by inscribing it with a key on the wainscot of a madhouse. The poem was privately issued in 1763 but was not included in the posthumous collection of Smart's poems (1791). An edition with explanatory notes was published by Rodwell and Martin in 1819; this was reprinted in 1827 with minor changes. It was evidently this latter edition which RB read, though (as the following letter shows) he was startled to learn from FJF that the 1827 volume was a second edition, since it bore the same Advertisement as the first edition. RB also saw another reprint of the "Song" in Chambers' *Cyclopaedia* (1844). RB was deeply impressed by Smart's poem and treated it at length in *Parleyings*. (William C. DeVane, *Browning's Parleyings: The Autobiography of a Mind* [New Haven, 1927], pp. 102-05; *LRB*, p. 374.)

RB TO FJF, 4 MARCH 1887

19, Warwick Crescent, / W.* / March 4, '87.

My dear Furnivall,

Don't trouble yourself about Smart on my account—unnecessarily, since, after nearly fifty years, I remember the whole pretty well. I think it was the reprint in Chambers that I saw,—not in Chalmers,—indeed I am sure of it—although I discovered it there on an occasion that would excuse much mistiness in my memory. Depend on it, no goody-goody writer ever conceived or executed the stanzas I could repeat—as I did—with all the effect I supposed would follow—to people of authority enough—Tennyson, the present Bishop of London[1]—and—last year to Wendell Holmes,[2] who had asked me innocently at Oxford "whether I knew the wonderful poem." Weak passages there undoubtedly are,—but the strong ones are decisive as to Smart's power and right of place. You heard what Rossetti thought and said,—I was not aware of it.[3]

I am surprised at an Edition appearing so early as in 1819: that which I bought professed to be just out some years later.

"Human"[4]—so as to be *ready*, at the first summons to general service, to drop down &c. The *readiness* implied as a necessary quality of the humanity.[5]

Ever yours, / Robert Browning.

MS: HL. Address: Dr. Furnivall, / 3. St. George's Square, / Primrose Hill, N. Postmarks: PADDINGTON 4 MR 4 87 [. .]; LOND[ON NW . . .] 4 MR [87 . . .]. Notes in FJF's hand on envelope: "Smart, poet. / O Lyric Love!" Published: *LRB*, p. 262; *LVC*, 1st Ser., II, 68-70.

1 Frederick Temple (1821-1902; *DNB*), Bishop of London, 1885-96; afterwards Archbishop of Canterbury, 1896-1902.

2 Oliver Wendell Holmes (1809-94; *DAB*), American poet and essayist, who met RB in London in 1886.

3 Dante Gabriel Rossetti (1828-82; *DNB*) was quoted as saying that the "Song to David" was "the only *accomplished* poem of the last century" (*Athenaeum*, 19 Feb. 1887, p. 248).

4 Note in FJF's hand: "O Lyric Love."

5 *The Ring and the Book*, I.1396. (See RB to FJF, 2 Mar. 1887, n. 1.) FJF paraphrased (rather clumsily) RB's explanation in *BSP*, II, 166.

RB TO FJF, 27 JUNE 1887

29, DE VERE GARDENS. / W.* / June 27. '87.

My dear Furnivall,

I am glad to hear that "this—(the proposal that you should become in word as well as deed President of your Society)—"this took you quite aback"—as a push forward to the proper place was calculated to do: indeed you have all along really "presided," and any interloper would cut a poor figure in your visionary stead.[1] Continue, I beseech you, to play the "fire-brand",—which warms one in cold weather,—and "agnostic" who pleasantly reminds those who need it that they don't know everything,—and, above all, continue to be the good friend and kind helpmate of

Yours truly ever / Robert Browning.

I am installed in the new place,[2] you are to observe: come and see us all—Pen being here for a short time.

MS: HEH. Published: *Furnivall*, p. lxix (inc.).

1 At the Annual Meeting of the Browning Society on 24 June 1887, FJF was appointed President (*BSP*, II, xx), an office that had remained vacant until that time. In fact, as RB suggests, FJF had always been the guiding hand behind the activities of the society, since he was chairman of the Committee and presided at many of the meetings.
2 RB had just moved from 19 Warwick Crescent, where he had lived since 1862. The departure from Warwick Crescent was achieved only with some difficulty, as RB had failed to give his landlord proper notice (*IG*, pp. 114-15). See RB to FJF, 15 Aug. 1882, n. 6.

RB TO FJF, 21 AUGUST 1887

Villa Berry, St. Moritz, S.[witzerland] / Aug. 21. '87.

What do you think, dear Cyclist? We are "snowed up" this morning,—cannot leave our house to go to the Hotel opposite, close by, where we get our meals! Such is Alpine treatment of travellers! Our amends is in the magnificence of the mountain, and its firs black against the universal white-spread. The natives assure us that this little summer-interlude only heralds a particularly fine September,—and so it may—let us hope, for both my Sister and myself have greatly benefited by our month's stay in these altitudes. So you, for your part, have managed to enhance the enjoyment of your holiday by an overset, damaged wrist, and so following! When

I read in a newspaper that an adventurous somebody had chosen to skate down a steep incline and break his neck,—I thought of Dr. Furnivall literally riding his hobby to death, and ruining the Browning Society—a climax only equalled by one I had from the mouth of my old piano-forte master, Abel:[1] said he "Yes, I am in love,—it destroys my appetite, interferes with my sleep,—and considerably breaks in upon my practising." But to brighter matters: I had not been here a week before I was altogether my old self with perhaps an addition,—quite well: and my sister, who needed rest and change far more than I, profited conspicuously. We had three perfect weeks of blue sky and living air,—last Sunday the weather broke up, but mended next day,—some days ago we were surprised by an earthquake,—so those say who felt it past mistake, and they are in such a number that one cannot doubt it, I suppose. Today comes exactly such a snow-storm as I happened to read of this morning in the Iliad, the only book I brought with me: but Homer expressly makes it fall on a $\eta\mu\alpha\tau\iota \; X\epsilon\iota\mu\epsilon\rho\acute{\iota}\omega$[2]—a winter's day,—while we are in mid-August. I shall stay, I hope, a week or two or three longer. Oh, for your subject—the young lady[3] stripping for humanity's sake—or rather that of the Blue-ribbon Cause:[4] really it is not versifiable—sufficient to the deed is the prose description thereof. Besides, since she could swim a mile with ease,—the reward of the feat was surely in itself during the hot weather of last month: "Accoutred as she was *not*, plunging in, She watered, so to speak, the boatman's gin—" I had a genial and considerate letter from Lytton respecting my application (on your suggestion) about Mr. Brown. He says that Mr Hollingshead knows all there is to teach about the Knebworth Asylum—and Mr H is away in America: when he returns, &c. Meanwhile he in turn suggests an application to the Literary Fund,—which he thinks might give some £80 (a treasure to the poor fellow!)—and he engages, if I write to apply, to back me up energetically: altogether a really kind answer to my request.[5] What do you say? But I ought to have written to you before this: the days glide away uneventfully (NEARLY) and I breathe in the pleasant idleness at every pore. I have no few acquaintances here,—nay, some old friends: but my intimates are the firs on the hillside, and the myriad butterflies all about it—every bright wing of them under the snow today,—which

147

ought not to have been for a fortnight yet. Moral: flutter-out your own life while you can, and don't crush it with "wheels"! My sister sends a cordial greeting, and I am ever affectionately yours,

Robert Browning.

MS: HL. Published: *LRB*, pp. 267-68 (inc.); *LVC*, 1st Ser., II, 71-74 (inc.)

1 Johann Leopold Abel (1795-1871), German-born pianist and composer of a distinguished musical family, travelled to America in 1819 because of his health, and in 1820 he arrived in London to become a music teacher (*Grove's Dictionary of Music and Musicians*; John S. Sainsbury, *A Dictionary of Musicians from the Earliest Times* [1825]).

2 *Iliad*, XII.279.

3 Note in FJF's hand: "(A fisherman agreed to take the [temperance] pledge if the lady who prest him to do it would strip like Godiva. She swam to him.)"

4 A temperance crusade known as the Blue Ribbon Gospel Temperance Mission was being conducted in London during the summer of 1887 by William Noble. FJF himself was a teetotaler.

5 Edward Robert Bulwer Lytton, 1st Earl of Lytton (1831-91; *DNB*), statesman and poet who wrote under the pseudonym "Owen Meredith," and an old friend of the Brownings, had written to RB on 23 July 1887 about a needy writer, Henry Brown, author of *The Sonnets of Shakespeare Solved* (1870). RB was attempting to secure for Brown a grant from the Guild of Literature and Art—founded by Charles Dickens and Lytton's father, Sir Edward Bulwer-Lytton (1803-73; *DNB*)—to enable him to pursue his Shakespearean studies. John Hollingshead (1827-1904; *WW*) was, according to Lytton, one of the Guild's executors, and therefore responsible for administering the Guild's land and houses at Knebworth, the Lytton country estate. (*Letters from Owen Meredith . . . to Robert and Elizabeth Barrett Browning*, ed. A. B. and J. L. Harlan, Jr. [Waco, Tex., 1936], pp. 235-38.) Hood (*LRB*, p. 375) asserts that Brown "wrote to, and probably saw, Browning, who asked Dr. Furnivall to take up his case. Applications for a money grant were made to the Government, to the trustees of the Royal Literary Fund, etc., but without success." RB's letter indicates, however, that it was FJF who had initiated the inquiries. T. J. Wise was evidently also involved in the negotiations (postcard, RB to Wise, postmarked 22 July 1887 [BL Ashley A.2530]).

RB TO FJF, 30 AUGUST 1887

Villa Berry, St. Moritz, Switzd. / Aug. 30. '87.
My dear Furnivall,—you forget that I know nothing of Brown or of his Book: all I take for granted is that he is poor, meritorious in his endeavours, whatever may be the worth of his attainment,—on the strength of which knowledge I will at once write and press his claims if you will be kind enough to state them succinctly—his age, condition, experiences in life, literary labours, and the fruit of it all such as it is—which *you* can do, and I cannot by any means. Let me have such a summary of work done, and I will let Lytton have it "with what flourishes I may"; Lytton, the intended backer-up

of my petition being altogether as ignorant on the subject as I. If we simply prayed "Give Brown a sum of money" we should "sue to be despised."[1]

I did not think of the mere feat of the lady when I wrote,—is it so wonderful? I think I could have managed it once on a time, but I gave up swimming because of a peculiar affection of the throat,— real strangulation,—if the salt-water got into it: and I rather aimed at long continuance in the sea than going far away from shore: Pen could have performed the feat with ease.[2] But I thought your approbation went to the fact that Miss MacNaughten stripped and swam to win over a sottish fellow to leave his bestiality—and I hold that if he were unamenable to the ordinary reasons why he should cease to make a beast of himself, his life was not worth saving at any price—and I, for my part, would have refused "accoutred as I was, to plunge in"—unless "I bade him follow"—sure that he would go to the bottom. Such a fellow, after exacting such a sacrifice, would be sure to get drunk the next day on the strength of his having made a fool of her.

Our weather is glorious—I shall probably move-off in a week to Ragatz, BUT—Here is an interruption, a visitor—"but none in the affection I bear to &"[3] (—old style, wanting to us moderns!)

Kind genial paper, that you sent me!

Ever yours / Robert Browning.

MS: ABL. Address: *Angleterre.* / Dr. Furnivall, / Little Alne, / Henley in Arden. / viâ London. Postmarks: ST MORIZ DORF 30 VIII 87-8; BIRMINGHAM 298 SP 2 87. Published: *LRB*, pp. 268-69; *LVC*, 1st Ser., II, 75-77.
1 Shakespeare, *Othello*, II.iii.276.
2 According to William Lyon Phelps (who discussed the subject with Pen Browning in 1904), "Late in life he [RB] was very fond of swimming, though he did not learn early. The son taught him how to swim at Pornic, in Brittany, and he was venturesome for a man well on in years. He learned with great eagerness, and swam far out with boyish delight. The poet alludes to this in the prologue to *Fifine at the Fair.*" (Phelps, *Autobiography with Letters* [New York, 1939], p. 451.)
3 Not identified.

RB TO FJF, 12 FEBRUARY 1888

29, De Vere Gardens, W. Feb. 12. '88.

My dear Furnivall,

I was sorry indeed to find, on getting home, that you had just left. I miscalculated the distance, and supposed I could return much earlier. I had more than one thing I was wanting to say. My sister tells me your reason for not coming to luncheon was that you fancied we might be inconvenienced by making the hour *two* instead of *one*. Nothing of the kind! Do believe in our utter indifference in the matter, so you but apprise us by a word beforehand. I have a letter of yours which came when I was far from well, and when I got better there was an accumulation of minor worryings, which I found in the way both of work and pleasure. Do manage to come soon and have a talk as in the days of old—for they seem "'old" already!

I was looking over the account of that paper concerning my treatment of the Jews.[1] It was remarked that I mistook a Rabbi for a High Priest! This comes of forgetting that one writes dramatically. The speaker, Baldinucci,[2] is a typically ignorant Tuscan, and makes the gross mistake already noted in Arbuthnot's *Martinus Scriblerus*—of whom it is said, at the very beginning: "Those who had never seen a Jesuit took him for one, while others thought him rather to be some High Priest of the Jews."[3] Somebody objected to a Jewish burying-ground being in the neighbourhood of any habitation,[4] but Baldinucci tells the story, and describes the locality as he knew it—and I follow him, of course.

I shall not comment on the disgraceful issue of the Trial,[5] the grotesque perversion of equity, whatever may be the ruling of law —or rather, the lawyers. I have always had a supreme contempt for the profession, and the lawyers in my poems get the benefit thereof.[6] I believe you have the thorough sympathy of everybody worth caring for, and as for your adversary—pity it is that you ever wasted a word on him. He was just the fellow to make money out of a kick, the beggar!

This is a sad case of the poor man whose letter you enclose; my unlucky absence from the Club prevented my attempting to help. Could there be a second application? I would try and make up for the past.[7]

Ever, my dear Furnivall, / Yours most cordially, / Robert Browning.

Text: *LRB*, pp. 286-87. Envelope: ABL. Address: Dr. Furnivall, / 3. St. George's Square, / Primrose Hill, N. W. Postmarks: LONDON W 7 FE 13 88 65; LONDON NW

L A FE 13 88. Note in FJF's hand on envelope: "Baldinucci / Libel action against me." Published: *LVC*, 2nd Ser., II, 60-63.

1 On 25 Nov. 1887 Percy A. Barnett (1858-1941), Professor of English at Firth University College, Sheffield (obituary, *Times*, 28 Oct. 1941, p. 7), delivered a paper to the Browning Society on "Browning's Jews and Shakespeare's Jew" (*BSP*, II, 207-20). The charge of factual error in "Filippo Baldinucci on the Privilege of Burial" was made during the discussion afterwards (*BSP*, II, 222*) by Dr. Edward Berdoe (1833-1916), a Browning cultist who later wrote several books on the poet (*Oracle*, pp. 60-66).

2 RB's poem was based on an episode in the life of Lodovici Buti, a Florentine painter, that is described in Filippo Baldinucci's *Notizie de' Professori del Disegno* (Florence, 1681-1728), X, 35-41. Though RB drew upon Baldinucci's book as a source of historical information in several poems, he had a low opinion of Baldinucci and attacked his prudery in *Parleyings*. (DeVane, pp. 412-13.)

3 The sentence which RB slightly misquotes appears in the Introduction to the *Memoirs of Martinus Scriblerus* (1741) by John Arbuthnot (1667-1735; *DNB*).

4 The observation was made by Barnett in his paper (*BSP*, II, 214).

5 For the background of Outram's libel suit against FJF, see RB to FJF, 9 Dec. 1886, n. 1. At the trial on 2 Feb. 1888, the jury found FJF guilty and awarded Outram £100; with costs added to this figure, FJF was made liable for more than £300 altogether. FJF's friends had to raise the money through public and private appeals, and James Dykes Campbell reported on 6 Feb. that RB was taking a strong interest in the case: "Of course he is very sympathetic and he & Miss [Sarianna] Browning desire to be associated in any scheme which may be planned." RB apparently contributed £10 to the Furnivall Fund. Nevertheless, to other correspondents RB wryly passed unfavorable judgment upon FJF's indiscreet behavior. (*Oracle*, pp. 44-48).

6 The best-known example of RB's satirical portrayal of lawyers is in Books VIII, IX, and XII of *The Ring and the Book*. FJF himself had been a conveyancer.

7 This perhaps refers to an unsuccessful application of membership to the Athenaeum Club, but I cannot identify the person involved.

RB TO FJF, 17 FEBRUARY 1888

29, De Vere Gardens, W. Feb. 17. '88.

Dear Furnivall,

Very glad to hear we shall have you on Sunday week.

As for the "Trial," everybody I have seen takes the right view of the subject.

The "Correspondent"[1] may complete his answer to objections by mentioning that, in *Holy Cross Day*, Ben Ezra is not supposed to acknowledge Christ as the Messiah because he resorts to the obvious argument "even on your own showing, and accepting for the moment the authority of your accepted Lawgiver, you are condemned by His precepts—let alone ours."

I shall do my best to be present at the Play.[2] I wish Pen would accompany me, and bring his wife. Excellent news of her, three days ago.[3]

Yours truly ever, / Robert Browning.

Text: *LRB*, pp. 287-88. Published: *LVC*, 1st Ser., II, 78-79.
1 In his paper Professor Barnett had cited a number of factual errors in RB's poetic treatment of Jews (*BSP*, I, 214), and in the Browning Society's "Notes and Queries" column shortly thereafter (*BSP*, II, 227*) an anonymous correspondent defended RB against one of these accusations.
2 The Browning Society sponsored a production of *A Blot in the 'Scutcheon*, with Alma Murray as Mildred Tresham, at the Olympic Theatre on 15 Mar. 1888. Miss Murray's acting was acclaimed by reviewers, but the play itself received few favorable notices. (See *BSP*, II, 250*-55*.)
3 In September 1887 Pen married Fannie Coddington, a wealthy American. At this time they were on an extended visit to the United States, where Fannie was convalescing following a miscarriage (*LRB*, p. 284).

RB TO FJF, 5 MARCH 1888

29, DE VERE GARDENS. / W.* / March 5. '88.

My dear Furnivall,

The letter of Mrs Forman greatly interests me,—how otherwise? It is a powerful incentive,—if I wanted one,—to try hard and do my very best, if the power to write a Tragedy be still in me,—or ever was, I should have premised: and this whether for the stage or no.[1]

I apply to you, at present, on this account: Mr. Slater, when he offered me a Box at the Olympic was good enough to say that if I required any Tickets for friends he would send me some.[2] I have a great unwillingness to be obtrusive, but if I can be spared three tickets, it will greatly oblige me. I would ask the favour directly of Mr S. were it not that I have mislaid the letter which contained his address.

I wish Pen—and his wife—could be present, but they will be in the middle of their voyage homewards when the performance takes place.[3]

Ever truly yours, / Robert Browning.

MS: Texas. Address: Dr. Furnivall, / 3. St. George's Square, / Primrose Hill, / N.W. Postmarks: LONDON [. . .] 4 MR 5 88 3; [L]OND[ON . . .]. Note in FJF's hand on envelope: "Keep this."
1 RB, in a letter to Miss Murray on 16 Mar. 1888 praising her recent performance in *A Blot in the 'Scutcheon*, wrote: "Such treatment as yours to a play much maltreated so many years ago, goes near to reviving in its author something of the old impulse once strong in him to try afresh in that direction" (*Alma Murray*, p. 15). RB had not written any plays since *In a Balcony*, which appeared in *Men and Women* (1855). Shortly before his death RB confided to Mrs. Bronson that his ambition was "to write a tragedy better than anything I have done yet. I think of it constantly." (Katherine Bronson, "Browning in Asolo," *Century Magazine*, 59 [April 1900], 930.)

2 Walter B. Slater (1862?-1944) was the third Honorary Secretary of the Browning Society (*Oracle*, pp. 14-15). RB wrote to Slater on 8 Mar. 1888 (ABL) thanking him for
the tickets to the Society's production of *A Blot in the 'Scutcheon.*
3 See RB to FJF, 17 Feb. 1888, n. 3.

RB TO FJF, 22 JANUARY 1889

29, DE VERE GARDENS. / W.* / Jan. 22. '89.

My dear Furnivall,

I let myself seem very ungrateful,—it can hardly be otherwise,
—but this comes of my intimately knowing that I am *not*. I was
much obliged by the present of your reprints, and forbore to say
so because I was on the point of sending you my Vol IX.,—still
lying here unsent.[1] Perhaps the best way *now* will be to wait till
the end of the week when Vol X. will accompany it. Do forgive
these delays—caused by no sort of idleness, but the need of getting rid of a quantity of letter-answering which, done with or half-
done with, induces me to shut up desk and forget pen and ink for
a time.

Thank the kind Professor very warmly for his message to me: I
shall try and inform myself about his biography of the Abbé: the
photograph is a pleasant object in my room.[2] Will somebody else
be a pleasant one some Sunday afternoon, I wonder, before rowing
and cycling engross him altogether in the not far distant Spring
time?

Ever truly yours / Robert Browning.

MS: HEH. Address: Dr. Furnivall, / 3. St. George's Square, / Primrose Hill. / N.W.
Postmarks: LONDON W 3 JA 22 89 3; LONDON NW LC JA 22 89. Note in FJF's
hand on envelope: "Abbé Vogler foto."
1 The sixteen volumes of RB's *Poetical Works* (1888-89) were being issued by Smith,
Elder at monthly intervals. In the first volume of FJF's set is the following inscription by RB: "Dr. Furnivall / With Robert Browning's / most grateful regards. / Dec.
16. '88." Below this inscription FJF wrote: "Sunday evg at R.B.'s house, / 29 De
Vere Gardens, Kensington.)" A similar note in FJF's hand appears in the third volume. (Maggs catalogue, 29 Apr. 1921, Lot 58.)
2 "The biographer of *Abt Vogler*, Prof. [Karl] von Schafhäutl [1803-90] of Munich
has sent Dr. Furnivall a good photograph of [Eduard] Zeller's [1814-1908] charming
portrait of Abbé Vogler at 63. It is being processed at Vienna for the Society, and will
be issued in 8vo. for vol. ii. of our *Papers*, and in post 8vo. to slip into Browning's
Works." (*BSP*, II, 311*.) RB's poem "Abt Vogler"—about the musician Abbé Georg
Joseph Vogler (1749-1814)—was first published in *Dramatis Personae* (1864).

RB TO FJF, 23 FEBRUARY 1889

29, De Vere Gardens, W. Feb. 23. '89.

My dear Furnivall,

By really an unpardonable oversight, I forgot to reply to your question of the day before yesterday, a multiplicity of matters having diverted my attention from it.

The meaning of the passages[1] is much as you say—entirely so, indeed. "Neither body nor mind is born to attain perfect strength or perfect health at its first stage of existence respectively, in each case, by the want of and desire for the thing as yet out of reach, they get raised towards it, and are educated by the process—as would not happen were the body strong all at once—or the soul at once perfect in apprehension.

"Wishing what I write may be read by their light"—*viz.* of Shakespeare, Dekker, Heywood and the others mentioned in the preface to *Vittoria Accorambona* by Webster.[2]

Ever, in haste as in leisure,

Yours truly / R. Browning.

Text: *LRB*, p. 301. Published: *LVC*, 1st Ser., II, 88-89.

1 *Parleyings with Certain People of Importance in Their Day*, "With Bernard de Mandeville," Sections II-III. FJF's discussion of this passage at the Browning Society meeting of 22 Feb. 1889 is recorded in *BSP*, II, 324-26*.

2 The following query was printed in the Browning Society's transactions:

   I dare say you can inform me where the following quotation from the *Dedication to Luria* is and what it means; but if not, may I trouble you kindly to put it among our Queries.

   " 'Wishing what I write may be read by his light,' a phrase originally addressed by not the least worthy of his contemporaries, to Shakespeare."

FJF's reply: "The phrase askt about is John Webster's, from the last paragraph of his address "To the Reader" before his *White Devil, or Vittoria Corombona*, 1612 . . ." (*BSP*, II, 320*). John Webster (1580?-1625?; *DNB*), Thomas Dekker (1570?-1632?; *DNB*), and Thomas Heywood (d. 1641; *DNB*) were all dramatists.

RB TO FJF, 2 MARCH 1889

29, De Vere Gardens, W. Mar. 2. '89.

My dear Furnivall,

I should prosaically state the meaning[1] thus: I do not ask a full disclosure of Truth, which would be a concession contrary to the law of things, which applies equally to the body and the soul, that it is only by striving to attain strength (in the one case) and truth (in the other) that body and soul do so—the effort (common to both) being productive, in each instance, of the necesssary initiation into all the satisfactions which result from partial success; absolute success being only attainable for the body in full manhood —for the soul, in its full apprehension of Truth—which will be, not *here*, at all events.

The sense is much the same whether you place a comma after "effort," or leave it out as I have done. "Effort whereby," or general effort, the result of mind's striving to urge the body to get strong all at once.

And now, I have to beg you to do me a very serious favour. Read this letter and the accompanying summary of the writer's husband's services.[2] I should be happy to help the poor fellow in the way he wants were I able, but I am not. I cannot apply either to Gladstone or Buckle[3] just now for very certain reasons, nor to Bright[4] either.

Can you contrive simply to bring the matter under Gladstone's notice, he being the person the parties evidently most count upon —I fear, hopelessly? He has not the power now, if he had—as he probably may have—the will; but I can only do, or attempt to do, what is prescribed by the letter. Only, something I am anxious to do, and I want a more efficacious hand than mine to make the effort. I know you will help me if you can. Mr. Barnett Smith wrote many good-natured notices of me in *The Times*, and other newspapers—which, at least as early advertisements, did good to my books, I have no doubt. At all events forgive my troubling you and believe me,

Ever truly yours, / Robert Browning.

I was much pleased by Mr. Robertson's article.[5] There is another —an essay in a book of which I never heard till the other day, *Cross Lights* by I don't know what person, which highly interested me.[6]

Text: *LRB*, pp. 301-02. Envelope: ABL. Address: Dr. Furnivall, / 3. St. George's Square, / Primrose Hill, / N.W. Postmarks: LONDON W 2 MR 4 89 6; LONDON NW LF MR 4 89. Note in FJF's hand on envelope: "B. de Mandeville. Barnett Smith— Secty. / Envelope—Monday." Published: *LVC*, 1st Ser., II, 90-93.

1 Again, the reference is to *Parleyings*, "With Bernard de Mandeville," Section II. RB's explanation is quoted by FJF (without attribution) in *BSP*, II, 326*.

2 In 1889 George Barnett Smith (1841-1901; *DNB*), literary journalist, was forced by lung disease to retire from London to Bournemouth, where he remained an invalid

the rest of his life. In 1891 he received a Civil List pension. Smith became acquainted with RB after writing a memoir of EBB for the *Encyclopaedia Britannica* in 1876, and for a number of years he was favored with advance proofs of RB's books from the poet. His wife's maiden name was Julia Timmis.

3   George E. Buckle (1854-1935; *DNB*), editor of *The Times*.

4   John Bright (1811-89; *DNB*), Liberal statesman and orator, who died on 27 Mar. of this year.

5   A paper on *La Saisiaz* by the Rev. William Robertson (1853-90), a clergyman of the Church of Scotland, was delivered at the Browning Society meeting of 25 Jan. 1889. Robertson judged the poem severely by literary standards but praised its distinctively Christian viewpoint. (The paper is printed in *BSP*, II, 312-22, and in Robertson's *Essays and Sermons* [1892], pp. 20-59; the latter volume contains a memoir of Robertson.)

6   An essay entitled "Wordsworth's Successor" (pp. 59-90), in the anonymous volume *Cross Lights* (1888), praised RB's writings as "instinct with the same spirit of kindly wisdom that fashioned the best of Wordsworth's utterances" (p. 68) and emphasized that his optimism is tempered by a realistic acceptance of an imperfect world. The preface to *Cross Lights* reveals that its last chapter was reprinted from the June 1886 issue of *Macmillan's Magazine*, and the *Wellesley Index to Victorian Periodicals* attributes the article in question to Harry B. Simpson (1861-1940; *WW*), a barrister; presumably Simpson was the author of the entire book.

RB TO FJF, [5 MARCH 1889]

29, De Vere Gardens, / W.*

Gratias ago tibi, amici. Manibusque pedibusque (ut aiunt) descendo in tuam sententiam. *RB.*

MS (postcard): HEH. Address: Dr. Furnivall, / 3. St. George's Square, / Primrose Hill, N.W. Postmark: [LO]NDON W 2 MR 5 89 12.
Translation: "I thank you, O friend. With my hands and feet (as they say) I concur with your opinion."

RB TO FJF, 10 MARCH 1889

29, DE VERE GARDENS. / W.* / March 10. '89.

My dear Furnivall,

Have you not some—or considerable—influence with the Editor of the "Academy"? A young Poet of my acquaintance,[1] author of some exceptionally good poems which were published some time ago, but may easily have escaped your notice,—this gentleman is desirous of being engaged occasionally as a critic of the subjects with which he has sympathy—Poetry and Fiction in generally [*sic*] .

Can you help in the matter? A simple trial would answer every purpose: and Mr Thompson's address is—1. Talgarth Road, W.

If I trouble you—blame your own kindness which encourages me,—how can it else?—to speak on a matter which much interests me[.]

Ever truly yours / Robert Browning.

MS: HEH. Address: Dr. Furnivall, / 3. St. George's Square, / Primrose Hill, / N.W. Postmarks: LONDON NW 3 MR 15 89 47; LONDON NW [. . .] MR 15 89. Notes in FJF's hand on envelope: "Thompson. / young poet."

1 Francis Thompson (1859-1907; *DNB*), poet and essayist, "The Hound of Heaven" being his best-known poem. An impoverished drug addict, Thompson had attempted suicide the previous year but at this time was supporting himself by writing for Wilfred Meynell's periodical, *Merry England*, where his poems "The Passion of Mary," "Dream Tryst," and "Not Even in Dream" had appeared during 1888. Thompson did not contribute to the *Academy* until 1896. A few months before his death RB wrote to Meynell that Thompson's prose and verse were "indeed remarkable" (Everard Meynell, *The Life of Francis Thompson* [1913], p. 120). For Thompson's estimate of RB, see his article "Robert Browning," *Academy*, 51 (8 May 1897), 499-500.

RB TO FJF, 27 MARCH 1889

29, De Vere Gardens, W. Mar. 27. '89.

My dear Furnivall,

1st question—you answer rightly—except perhaps that the lady, a passionate Italian, means "Whether I shall find a new lover and bestow on him all you despise, and even more—forgetting all else; or whether I shall not rather bethink myself of taking a thorough revenge on you—that is for after consideration: you are not 'out of the wood yet' "!

2nd. St. Mark's is constructed out of various objects originally intended to illustrate some other cult than that which, by the superior power of the Christian symbol, has exclusively appropriated earth's homage.[1]

Ever truly yours / Robert Browning.

Text: *LRB*, p. 304. Published: *LVC*, 1st Ser., II, 94-95.

1 Both paragraphs of this letter refer to alleged obscurities in RB's poetry which FJF had discussed at the Browning Society meeting of 22 Feb. 1889 (*BSP*, II, 327*). The first paragraph offers a paraphrase of "Another Way of Love"; the second explicates these lines in *Sordello*: ". . . till their Dome / From earth's reputed consummations razed / A seal, the all-transmuting Triad blazed / Above" (V.648-51).

RB TO FJF, 3 MAY 1889

29, DE VERE GARDENS. / W.* / May 3. '89.

My dear Furnivall,

I am greatly obliged to Mr Jones[1] for his kindness and wish I could avail myself of it without damaging my character irreparably —so constantly do I refuse to go—I should rather say—be taken to plays acted in by friends of mine: I have not entered a theatre this long while, and am only saved from embarrassment when I meet an actor of my acquaintance by his knowledge of the fact. Do say all this, which is mere truth, with as little indulgence to my folly as you please, but much sense of obligation to those who, like Mr Jones, are so good as to wish to overcome it.

Here are the two last volumes for your acceptance.

Ever truly yours / Robert Browning.

MS: HEH. Address: Dr. Furnivall, / 3. St. George's Square, / Primrose Hill, / N.W. Postmarks: LONDON W 3 MY 4 89 52; LONDON NW LC MY 4 89. Note in FJF's hand on envelope: "declines H. A. Jones's offer / for 1st night of his play."
1 *Wealth* by Henry Arthur Jones (1851-1929; *DNB*) opened at the Haymarket Theatre on 27 Apr. 1889. Jones had been introduced to RB in 1886 by FJF (*Furnivall*, p. 88).

RB TO FJF, 4 MAY 1889

29 De Vere Gardens, W., May 4. '89.

My dear Furnivall,

My own reading of the passage is, and always has been, as follows: 'To be, or not to be,'—*that* is the question:—*videlicet*,—whether 'tis nobler in the mind to suffer, &c., or, in other words, to endure the conditions of this life,—'*to be*';—or to violently resist these,—make war against the sea of troubles which are inseparable from life, and by opposing these, in the only way possible, 'end them'—which means '*to die*'—that being tantamount to sleeping—safely removed from them all: but *are* they all so surely escaped from? 'To *sleep*' may involve the subjection to dreams—of what nature, who can say? The obscurity arises from the modern editors making that a question of itself, which is only the restatement of a question already in existence. There should be no mark of interrogation after 'opposing end them'—a full stop or colon at most.

Ever truly yours, / Robert Browning.

Text: *NSST* (1887-92), pp. 48*-49*.
This letter responds to a question raised by FJF at the 10 May 1889 meeting of the New Shakspere Society (*NSST* [1887-92], p. 48*):

DR. F. J. FURNIVALL then asked the meeting to consider a point to which his attention had recently been called—the construction of the passage in *Hamlet*, III.i.56-60:—

"To be, or not to be; that is the question
Whether 'tis nobler in the mind to suffer
The slings and arrows of outrageous fortune,
Or to take arms against a sea of troubles,
And by opposing, end them."

The question was, did the passage, "Whether 'tis nobler," &c., down to "end them" stand in apposition to, and expand the words "To be, or not to be," or was it an introductory adverb-clause to it, as if the sense was, "Independently of the point, whether it is nobler to suffer ills here, or resist them, *the* question is, is there a future life?"

In the former case the question was one of Life or Death *here*, of Suicide or not: was it nobler to suffer our ills, or to fight them and end them,—that is, lose one's life either by an adversary's hand or one's own? In the latter case, it became a question of *Future* Life or not: irrespective of whether it was nobler to suffer or fight evils in this world *the one* question was, is there life after death or not?

DR. FURNIVALL had submitted the point to the President of the Society, as well as to several eminent scholars. MR. ROBERT BROWNING in reply, wrote as follows:—[Here the letter is quoted.]

RB TO FJF, 5 MAY 1889

29 De Vere Gardens, W., May 5. '89.

My dear Furnivall,

Certainly if you think the trifle is worth citing, it is at the service of the scrap-collector.

You say, 'men constantly *do* conquer their troubles by resolutely fighting against them'—Ay,—but the typically irresolute Hamlet entertains no notion that such conquest is possible, or he would undertake it. He is not 'pigeon-livered'—would 'drink up esil, eat a crocodile,' and so on,—but sees no cure for the 'pangs of despised love,' 'scorns taken from the unworthy'—and the like 'slings and arrows of outrageous fortune,' whose 'buffets' the quite resolute Horatio would easily dispose of; as he says admiringly and perhaps envyingly.

What a glorious morning is this!

Ever yours, / R.B.

Text: *NSST* (1887-92), p. 49*.

RB TO FJF, [EARLY JUNE 1889]

⟨. . .⟩

Is not the key to the meaning of the poem in its title—νυμφόλη-πτος [caught or entranst by a Nymph], not γυναικεραστής [a woman-lover]?[1] An allegory, that is, of an impossible ideal object of love, accepted conventionally as such by a man who, all the while, cannot quite blind himself to the demonstrable fact that the possessor of knowledge and purity obtained without the natural consequences of obtaining them by achievement—not inheritance,—such a being is imaginary, not real, a nymph and no woman: and only such an one would be ignorant of and surprised at the results of a lover's endeavour to emulate the qualities which the beloved is entitled to consider as pre-existent to earthly experience, and independent of its inevitable results.

I had no particular woman in my mind; certainly never intended to personify wisdom, philosophy, or any other abstraction; and the orb, raying colour out of whiteness, was altogether a fancy of my own. The "seven-spirits" are in the Apocalypse, also in Coleridge and Byron: a common image.[2]

The short summary in Mrs. Orr's handbook seems satisfactory enough.

⟨. . .⟩

Text: *BSP*, II, 338*.

1 At the Browning Society meeting of 31 May 1889, two papers on "Numpholeptos" were read by Dr. Berdoe and Mrs. Ethel Glazebrook (d. 1926), wife of a Harrow master and organizer of various literary study circles (obituary, *Times*, 21 May 1926, p. 11). "After a vote of thanks to the writers of the two papers, a discussion followed, in which such opposite views were expressed, that no agreement could be come to; and it was concluded that the Chairman [FJF] should ask Mr. Browning whether his poem was an allegory only, or meant to represent any type of woman present or past. This has accordingly been done; and as the author's own interpretation follows, the

printing of the discussion becomes needless." (*BSP*, II, 338*.) (The translations in square brackets appear in the printed text and were presumably not supplied by RB.) DeVane's comment is that "Browning's explanation is perhaps not so clear as the poem itself" (p. 405), for both DeVane and Betty Miller (*Robert Browning: A Portrait* [1952], p. 260) identify the cold nymph of the poem with EBB.

2   For a discussion of RB's recurrent use of the image of a rainbow or prism (which he apparently borrowed from Shelley), see William O. Raymond, *The Infinite Moment and Other Essays in Robert Browning*, 2nd ed. (Toronto, 1965), pp. 193-213. The references to the seven angels or spirits appear in l. 19 of "Numpholeptos"; *Revelation* 15:1, 15:7, and 17:1; Coleridge, "Religious Musings" (1803 version), l. 80; and Byron "Heaven and Earth," I.40.

RB TO FJF, 16 JULY 1889

29, De Vere Gardens, / W.* / July 16. '89.

My dear Furnivall,

Yes, it is sad to think, as Keats says, that "Honey can't be got without hard money,"[1] and literary honey, of whatever the sort, any more than the bee's product: but Smith sells "Collections," and pays me for the right of doing so, while he cannot hinder the Americans for taking them and paying nothing at all: so that you cannot wonder if he is disinclined to allow the payers-of-nothing *there* to compete with his publications *here*, and pay nothing into the bargain:[2] so, "curse nobody but grin and bear it!"[3]

As to my own utterance after receiving unexpectedly an outrage,—why, like all impulsive actions, once the impulse over, I believe I might preferably have left the thing to its proper contempt: but there was something too shocking in a man,—whom I never saw in my life, whom my wife never even heard of, "feeling relieved at her death, he must say": and I too said what I must. The people who tell you "his opinion was really on the woman-question" talk nonsense: he might have uttered any amount of impertinance, without getting a word out of me: but "to be relieved at the *death* which would stop the work, thank God!"—[4]

How Editor and Publisher could let this passage remain in the letter which a pen-scratch would have left unobjectionable, passes my power of understanding. It is noticeable that the passage is immediately preceded by a sign (. . .) that something considered *really* objectionable has been omitted: this might pass!

I have your XVth volume, but the XVIth will follow so soon now that I may send them in one packet.[5]

Ever truly yours / RB.

The answers to the Examination paper are perfect: "lasagne" are the long broad ribbon-like strings of maccheroni.[6]

MS: BL. Published: *LRB*, pp. 312-13; *LVC*, 1st Ser., II, 96-98.

1 John Keats, "Robin Hood," ll. 47-48.
2 Note in FJF's hand: "Answer to my cursing Geo. Smith for stopping Prof. Alexander's *Introduction to B.* coming into England on acct. of its printing some Poems. I ordered 200 copies for the [Browning] Socy., but we can't have em. F." (See also *BSP*, II, xxxiv.) Since British copyright law did not permit the distribution of William J. Alexander's *An Introduction to the Poetry of Robert Browning* (Boston, 1889), in England, FJF reprinted a large portion of the book (not including, of course, the poems by RB) in the Society's transactions (*BSP*, III, 1-25).
3 Anonymous proverb.
4 Note in FJF's hand: "B.s Sonnet against E. FitzGerald for his 'thank God, no more *Aurora Leighs*' & on Mrs. B.'s death." After reading a recently published FitzGerald letter—"Mrs. Browning's Death is rather a relief to me, I must say: no more Aurora Leighs, thank God!" (*Letters and Literary Remains of Edward FitzGerald*, ed. W. Aldis Wright [1889], I, 280-81)—RB had written an angry poetic reply entitled "To Edward FitzGerald" which was published in the *Athenaeum*, 13 July 1889, p. 64. RB's extraordinarily abusive poem, dated 8 July 1889, concluded: "Kicking you seems the common lot of curs— / While more appropriate greeting lends you grace: / Surely to spit there glorifies your face— / Spitting—from lips once sanctified by Hers." RB had actually attempted to withdraw the poem before publication, but the editor of the *Athenaeum* deliberately ignored his telegram (*LRB*, p. 378).
5 See RB to FJF, 22 Jan. 1889, n, 1.
6 The "Notes and Queries" section of the Browning Society's transactions (*BSP*, II, 348*-49*) had included a jocular "Senior Examination Paper on Robert Browning's Poems (the 2 Vols. of Selections, 1882). By the Late F. J. Church, M.A., New Coll., Oxford, Barrister-at-Law." The correct answers to the twenty-one questions were supplied by a member of the Society, Mrs. Alexander Ireland (1843-93), who, however, confessed: "We do not know what *'lasagne'* was, but it does not *sound* nice, eaten in 'slippery ropes,' and no doubt dangled from the hand into the mouth, as Leporello ate his *maccaroni* on the stage in *Don Giovanni*" (*BSP*, II, 348*). A footnote (probably by FJF) quotes RB's definition: "We have Mr. Browning's word for it that 'the long broad ribbon-like strings of maccheroni,' go by this name."

RB TO FJF, 28 AUGUST 1889

29, DE VERE GARDENS. / W.* / Aug. 28. '89.

My dear Furnivall,

I must not go away without a word to bid you goodbye, besides thanking you for your letter and advice—followed by me duly for the most part. The corrections will be made, no doubt.[1]

We start to-morrow for Bale, Milan, Vicenza, and Asolo—where we stay for a month or more—then, go on to Venice.[2] The addresses will be—*Asolo, Veneto, Italy*—and *Palazzo Rezzonico, Venice, Italy*. I hope to be back in London much earlier than I was last year—in November perhaps. Do be kind (but you always are so) and write to me sometimes: I hope you are enjoying yourself—so, by your account of your doings, seemed to be the case. What a hideous scribble!—but I put my heart into the last good wish for you. My Sister's kind regards go with mine.

Ever truly yours / Robert Browning.

MS: HEH. Address: Dr. Furnivall, / Freeford House, / Tamworth Road, / Lichfield. Postmarks: LONDON W 7 AU 29 89 64; LICHFIELD B AU 29 89. Note in FJF's hand on envelope: "off to Asolo &c."

1 One of RB's last acts before leaving London was to submit to his publisher a list of corrections for the sixteen-volume *Poetical Works of Robert Browning*. Some, but not all, of these changes were made in a new edition issued early in 1890. (Philip Kelley and William S. Peterson, "Browning's Final Revisions," *Browning Institute Studies*, 1 [1973], 95-98.)

2 RB's visit to Asolo, with Mrs. Bronson as hostess, was an unusually happy one, and many of the poems of *Asolando* were written there. (See Bronson, "Browning in Asolo," *Century Magazine*, 59 [April 1900], 920-31.) In Venice, however, he caught a severe bronchial cold and died on 12 Dec. in Pen's home, the Palazzo Rezzonico. His body was returned to London and buried in Poets' Corner of Westminster Abbey on the last day of the year.

APPENDIX A

Browning and the New Shakspere Society

INTRODUCTORY NOTE†

To a correspondent who was planning to organize a Shakespeare reading-party, F. J. Furnivall wrote on 6 April 1879: "When a man makes up his mind to get fellows to take up a subject like Shakspere, he's sure to succeed if he puts steam & tact into his effort." That the industrious Furnivall put steam into the founding of the New Shakspere Society in 1873, no one would deny; but the tact was less in evidence, for the Society was in fact embroiled in controversies throughout its short history. One of these is worth recounting here in some detail, because though both Furnivall and Browning were principals, the episode is reflected only indirectly in their correspondence. There can be no doubt that Browning's distressing involvement in one of Furnivall's public quarrels made him even more cautious and wary in his subsequent relationship with Furnivall.

The original Shakespeare Society (1840-53) had devoted its energies primarily to antiquarian scholarship. Furnivall's Society, by contrast, was from the beginning preoccupied with metrical and verbal statistical tests which would establish the order of composition of Shakespeare's plays. For Furnivall, counting run-on lines was not an end in itself: he believed that by arranging the Shakespearean canon in proper sequence one could see the playwright's personal and artistic growth, and thus one might at last discover the elusive personality of Shakespeare.

†This Introductory Note is based primarily upon unpublished correspondence in the Folger Shakespeare Library (cited in the text) and the following printed sources: Oscar Maurer, "Swinburne vs. Furnivall," *University of Texas Studies in English*, 31 (1952), 86-96; and S. Schoenbaum, *Shakespeare's Lives* (Oxford, 1970), *passim*.

165

The scholar upon whom Furnivall depended most heavily to devise the proper metrical tests was Frederick Gard Fleay, headmaster of Skipton Grammar School. Fleay was a pedant lacking any literary sensitivity but obsessed with quantification, and almost immediately Furnivall began sharply criticizing Fleay's papers in private and at the Society meetings. As early as 3 March 1874 Edwin Abbott had to dissuade Fleay from resigning, with the explanation that "Furnivall is the best fellow in the world equally devoid of selfishness—and *tact*." Furnivall also urged him not to resign: "On the whole question, pray understand that I'm in entire good humor with you & every one else," he wrote on 23 March. However, tensions between the two men continued to grow, indignant letters flew back and forth ("I'm altogether bewildered by the in's & out's of the voluminous correspondence," Abbott wrote to Fleay on 7 May), and by 27 April Furnivall was declaring to Fleay, ". . . we feel that you're the most stimulating Shaksp. fellow we've ever come across—a regular hedgehog as to no. of prickles—& you must be fought or submitted to."

Beginning in May 1874 Furnivall and Fleay agreed to communicate with each other only through Abbott, and because Fleay was deeply offended by Furnivall's frequent impromptu remarks at the Society meetings, a Revision Committee was established to supervise the printing of the record of discussions. (This Committee's main responsibility, it appears, was to delete from the record Furnivall's more pungent observations.) But Fleay stopped contributing papers to the Society (after having supplied six to the first seven monthly meetings), and Furnivall, in a letter to C. M. Ingleby (22 September 1874), described his antagonist as "a lying sneak & cad. The shuffling, evasions, & effrontery of the man during the last 4 months are almost beyond belief."

Fleay resigned from the Society's Committee in July 1874 (though he reappears briefly in this narrative in a letter written to Browning on 5 February 1881, printed below), but Furnivall soon found a more formidable opponent in the person of Algernon Swinburne, whose alcoholism seems to have offended Furnivall's teetotaling sensibilities. In a letter to Ingleby (18 November 1876), discussing the membership of the New Shakspere Society, Furnivall declared: "The only Shaksp. Englishmen we haven't [as members], are Swinburne: we feared his coming drunk to the meetings. . . ." Later, discussing Swinburne's published attacks upon the New Shakspere Society, Furnivall wrote (to Ingleby, 17 June 1880) that "Pigsbrook's [his Anglo-Saxon translation of Swinburne's name] vol. is probably so bad because it was done on his recovery from the often-renewed & at last nearly fatal attack of drunken diarrhea. . . ." Swinburne, for his part, cherished a similarly intense hatred of Furnivall and his Society, which he satirized as "Fartiwell & Co." and the "Shitpeare Society" in scatalogical verses privately distributed among his friends.

Swinburne's public pronouncements on the Society were less indecent but not less vehement. Between 1875 and 1879 Swinburne and Furnivall exchanged abusive articles and letters in several periodicals, the former attacking the metrical tests of the "Sham Shakespeareans" and the latter assaulting the poet's critical judgment. Meanwhile Furnivall's indignation was growing ever more violent: as he was later to write to Ingleby (18 March 1881), "When men attack me, I am free to use weapons in defence that I should never use in attack." When he learned in 1879 that Swinburne was planning to reprint his anti-Furnivall essays in *A Study of Shakespeare*, and that the volume would be dedicated to James O. Halliwell-Phillipps, a prominent member of the New Shakspere Society—Furnivall's pent-up wrath suddenly descended upon the head of that hapless gentleman.

Halliwell-Phillipps had devoted a long life to the discovery and publication of documents relating to Shakespeare. Indeed, he was the most distinguished Shakespearean antiquary of the nineteenth century, though his early career had been clouded by allegations (evidently true) that he had stolen manuscripts from the library of Trinity College, Cambridge. Furnivall's relationship with Halliwell-Phillipps, according to his own testimony (in a letter to Ingleby, 22 July 1880), had always been uneasy:

You'll admit that he [Halliwell-Phillipps] is no gentleman. No one can pretend that he is one. He acted like a cad in accepting Pigsbrook's dedication of those reprints of the little beast's abuse of the N. Sh. Soc. & me, when he knew well what they were. I gave him 2 warnings that if he did it, I'd cut him, —& so I have.
As to his work, I've acknowledged its value. . . . [In the *Leopold Shakspere*

(1879) Furnivall had damned with faint praise the scholarship of Halliwell-Phillipps, whom he called "Woodenhead."] I *do* think he's one of the *commonest* & *meanest* minds that I've ever come across among students of Shakspere. He is also a sneak. But his redeeming point is his work at S.'s life, & illustrations of S. Still, when he sets up his stupidity to sneer at our methods; &, to get praise from Pigsbrook, & gratify his (H.P.'s) vanity thereby, joins in insulting us, I say he deserves kicking. And when he crosses me I shall try to use my foot.

If he thrashes me, well & good, I shall deserve it for having associated with him. Every other day in his house I said to myself 'if you mean to keep your manliness & gentlemanliness, you've no business here'; & I ought to have come away the day after I got down: but like a fool I stopt on, —& I have had my proper reward. My wife always warned me against the connection; & after Aldis Wright's telling (in 1868?) me about that Trinity MS, I kept out of H.P.'s way: then in -75, I think, the Sh. work led me to give up my resolve not to see H.-P.

Halliwell-Phillipps' view of Furnivall at this stage in the quarrel is summarized in his letter of 3 December 1879 to Ingleby:

You mention Furnivall's want of temper about this matter. I have all along wished to be as friendly as possible with him & with the NSS. saving a desire not to be guilty of countenancing the Founder's Prospectus, which I regard as silly and mischievous—but now I have fallen under His Royal Highness's displeasure in this way. Swinburne offered to dedicate his new book to me, & of course I could not refuse so high a compliment. F. hears of this, & because said book contains some animadversions on the N.S.S. displeasing to said F., said F. writes to me to say that he will drop my acquaintance if I don't withdraw the dedn. In the whole course of my literary experience I never knew such dictatorial insolence. . . . F. himself [has] lately put in my hands a printed paper containing a most disgraceful attack on Swinburne's personal character. . . . It is a great pity, for he [Furnivall] is clever, very ready, extremely active & has undoubted enthusiasm, but that is no excuse for his kicking everyone all round the shop.

Furnivall struck back at both Swinburne and Halliwell-Phillipps in his "Forewords" to a facsimile reprint of the Second Quarto *Hamlet* (1880), where he described them as "the two leading members of the firm of Pigsbrook & Co." and, with malicious glee, rang changes on the pig metaphor. What happened thereafter—and how an unwilling Browning became ever more drawn into the controversy—is told in the following letters. This extraordinary episode had a profound effect upon Browning's subsequent relationship with Furnivall; Browning's later unwillingness to be connected in any way with the Browning Society's activities is attributable not only to his modesty but also to his fear that Furnivall might once again make a spectacle of himself and others as he had done in the New Shakspere Society.

The episode also had unforeseen consequences for Shakespearean scholarship. On 14 February 1880 Halliwell-Phillipps announced to Ingleby that because of Furnivall's attacks upon his character, he intended to publish little more: "It is a pity, for my inedited collections on the life & the history of the stage are enormously valuable & include so much that no one could now obtain for love or money. If they are lost for ever to the Shakespeare student, he has only to thank the insolence of F.J.F. for the result." Halliwell-Phillipps, despite this threat, did publish a few more documents, but on 11 June 1880 he revealed to Ingleby that "I am amusing myself just now by destroying nearly all my mineur MS. collections on the plays, not wanting them after my death to be travestied[,] used & misrepresented by an insolent lunatic."

ᕧ

J. O. HALLIWELL-PHILLIPPS TO RB, 26 JANUARY 1881

Hollingbury Copse, / Brighton. / 26 Jany., 1881.

Sir,

A few weeks ago there appeared in the Preface to a Facsimile of the second edition of Hamlet some coarse & impertinent language in reference to a work of mine on that tragedy. In that Preface I am described as a "leading member of the firm of Pigsbrook & Co."; some of my observations are denounced as "porcine vagaries,"—& others as being promulgated "on the prongs of a dung-fork." Not being versed in the phraseology of Billingsgate, I am at a loss to understand the application of these words, but anyhow you will acknowledge that they cannot belong to the language accepted by gentlemen in literary or any other controversy.

This language, not appearing in the work of an obscure individual, but in a Preface conspicuously announced on the title-page as written by the "Founder & Director of the New Shakspere Society,"—& the indefensible nature of that language of studied insult precluding communication with its writer—I considered myself entitled to ask the Committee of that Society, in a note of the 14th Inst., if such offensive vulgarities had even their tacit sanction. The Committee, in their reply, dated the 22nd Inst., inform me that they "do not consider the matter referred to as falling within their jurisdiction, the quartos in question not being published by the Society."

In other words, the Committee are of opinion that their officer is at liberty, in any work not absolutely issued by the New Shakspere Society, to publicly announce himself as the Director of that Society, & under the credit of that title to print what he likes without involving the Committee in the responsibility of his repulsive discourtesies. This convenient isolation puts one in mind of an anecdote, current in Shakespeare's time, of the only person in a church who was not moved to tears by a pathetic sermon, & who excused his want of sympathy by the observation that he belonged to another parish.

The position assumed by the Committee cannot, however, be sustained. If it could be, a commanding officer might use his own official title to give weight to scurrilous attacks on a member of his regiment, & escape remonstrance merely because he happened to be off duty at the time of their publication.

The Committee being thus indifferent to the ungentlemanly manner in which I have been treated, the obvious course would have been to have appealed to a general meeting of the Society, but here a difficulty arises, there being no provisions under which such a meeting can be summoned, there being no constitution, no laws, no regulations, & no power whatever vested in any of the members—there being, in fact, no Society at all. What is called the New Shakspere Society is really a mere book-club supported by annual subscriptions, & conducted by an irreversible self-elected Committee. The members of this Committee, however, are obviously even more responsible for the character of observations published in the name of their Director than if they derived their functions by a recognized election from the votes of the subscribers.

Under these circumstances, the entire power being vested in yourself, as President, & in the Committee, you will, I feel sure, excuse my asking if you will not insist upon the Director's withdrawal of the above-quoted disreputable language used by him in a work published in his acknowledged position as your Director. The offence is greatly aggravated by its being entirely unprovoked. Neither in my essay on Hamlet before mentioned, nor in any of my Shakespearean publications, now extending over a period of forty years, is there an unkind word respecting your Director or any one else.

I am, Sir,

Your obedt. Servt. / J. O. Halliwell-Phillipps

To Robert Browning, Esq. / President of / the New Shakspere Society

MS: Folger. Published: *A Letter from Mr. J. O. Halliwell-Phillipps to the Members of the New Shakspere Society, with a Copy of Correspondence on the Extraordinary Language Used Under the Apparent Sanction of That Society* (Brighton, 1881), pp. 3-4.
For a discussion of the general background of this quarrel between FJF and Halliwell-Phillipps, see the Introductory Note, above. James Orchard Halliwell-Phillipps (1820-89; *DNB*) was one of Victorian England's best-known Shakespearean scholars.

RB TO J.O. HALLIWELL-PHILLIPPS, 27 JANUARY 1881

19 Warwick Crescent, W. / Jan. 27, '81.

Dear Sir,

I am sorry indeed to receive your letter of yesterday's date, and doubly sorry that there should have been occasion for your writing it. I never saw the Preface in question, and altogether fail to understand the meaning or relevancy of the language you quote from it. My position with respect to the Society is purely honorary, as I stipulated before accepting it, nor have I been able hitherto to attend any one of its meetings: and should I ever do so, my first impulse will be to invoke the spirit of "gentle Shakespeare" that no wrong be done in his name to a member of the brotherhood of students combining to do him suit and service.

Pray believe me, Dear Sir,

Yours very respectfully, / Robert Browning.

J. O. Halliwell-Phillipps Esq.

MS: University of Edinburgh Library. Published: *Letter . . . to Members of the New Shakspere Society*, p. 5.

J. O. HALLIWELL-PHILLIPPS TO RB, 31 JANUARY 1881

Hollingbury Copse, Brighton, / 31st January, 1881.

Dear Sir,

The receipt of your note of the 27th Instant has occasioned me not a little embarrassment. As you are conspicuously advertised as President of the New Shakspere Society in a prospectus now being extensively circulated by the Society, it never occurred to me that the dignity was merely nominal. The public can know nothing of this, and hence your eminent name is made use of to give weight to an influence to which the Society is not entitled. The duties attached to the office of Vice-President being, no doubt equally impalpable, the Members nowhere, and the Committee attenuated, the governing body of the Society resolves itself into what is nearly, if not quite, a case of "dearly beloved Roger and I."

Every person of good feeling will sympathise in your wish that the gentle spirit of Shakespeare should prevail in the New Shakspere Society; but, unless gentleness be permitted to degenerate into submission to any kind of indignity, the generic invocation you suggest will hardly be appropriate to a case where the offence proceeds from an individual source. There has been no provocation from my side; and although this fact may appear to outsiders to be singularly incompatible with the nature of the onslaught to which I have been subjected, the latter will be regarded by others as the outcome, in an exaggerated form, of the indecorous slang which for some years past has thrown ridicule on Shakespearean criticism. In plain-speaking lies the only chance of suppressing what has become an intolerable bore to quiet-loving students. In one of the publications of the Society there is something far more objectionable even than slang, in the advocacy of extreme political opinions and the admission of scandalously jocular references to the Bible, while in another place there is the scandal of the plays of our national dramatist being allotted out into the unfitnature group, the tempter-yielding group, the lust-group, the cursing-group, the under-burden-falling group, the false-love group, —all this miserable nonsense appearing under the directorship of the New Shakspere Society.

It is this official connexion with these inconvenient eccentricities that is the gist of the mischief. I should never have dreamt of taking serious notice of anything the Director might choose to say respecting myself, so long as it was uttered strictly in his individual capacity. There is no harm in anyone forming a book-club, calling it a Society, making himself the Director, and coaxing Prince Leopold[1] and other distinguished personages to support his position by joining the most wonderful list of Vice-Presidents ever seen outside the announcement of a cottage-garden flower-show. This is a matter that chiefly affects the individuals whose names are thus grotesquely paraded, and, *so far*, it is no manner of consequence whether the Director makes the Society or the Society makes the Director, the same effect being produced from either cause. But when the public are blinded to the real nature of the Society, and dazzled by the apparently elective and sympathetic influence conferred on the Director, then there arises a very serious objection when that influence is sued for the dissemination of personal antipathies.

As to the offensive language of which I have specially complained, it cannot be palliated by any extent of friendly advocation. It is a resuscitation of the coarseness of Swift without his humour. Only fancy the editor of one newspaper accusing the editor of another of writing his leaders with the prongs of a dung-fork inked in a pigsbrook! Fortunately no such journal can be discovered, at least in this country, or if one did appear that indulged in such ribaldry, we should have to engage a detective to search the low pot-houses for a copy. One would have thought that the Committee, instead of moving a technical objection, would have been anxious to have repudiated even an indirect association with the use of the reeking imagery derived from mixens and pigstyes. Perhaps, however, my appeal was heard solely by the "I," unassisted even by the counsels of "dearly-beloved Roger."

I had hoped to have been spared the necessity of publishing this correspondence by the decisive action of either yourself or the Committee in a case so detrimental to the best interests of all concerned in the pursuit of Shakespearean studies. You will, however, see that under the circumstances I have in self-defence no other alternative.

173

I am, Dear Sir, / Yours very respectfully, /
J. O. Halliwell-Phillipps
To Robert Browning Esq. / President of the New Shakspere
Society

MS: Folger. Address: Robert Browning Esqr. / No. 19. Warwick Crescent / London. /
W. Postmarks: BRIGHTON 7 FE 1 81 E; LONDON W B7 FE 2 1881. Published: *Letter . . . to Members of the New Shakspere Society*, pp. 5-7.
1 (1853-84; *DNB*), fourth son of Queen Victoria.

F. G. FLEAY TO RB, 5 FEBRUARY 1881

33, Avondale Square / London. S.E.* / 5 Feb 1881
Sir

An utter stranger to you has possibly no right to address you
on the subject of the correspondence between Mr. Halliwell-
Phillipps & your self just published: but I can not see the name
of one whom I have 25 years since publicly described as "a dramatist surpast by none & equalled by scarcely any since the time of
Shakespeare" thus dragged in the dirt by an unfortunate connexion with a society that sanctions such proceedings as those referred
to by Mr. Phillipps without protesting against their continuance.

I am fully aware of your *honorary* position: but you are advertised to the public as "President" not as "Honorary President" &
if you allow the issue of a single advertisement with the unqual-
ified title of President attached to your name after the publication
of this correspondence with Mr Phillipps you will undoubtedly
incur the responsibility of sanctioning the proceedings of the Society. It would be a deplorable result if the revival of Shakespearean criticism should culminate in the sanctioning of opprobrious
insult offered to a most ardent student of our greatest dramatist
& that this sanction should emanate from Shakespeare's greatest
living representative.

I am Sir / Yours most sincerely / F. G. Fleay
R. Browning Esq

MS: ABL.
Frederick Gard Fleay (1831-1909; *DNB*), Shakespearean scholar, had earlier carried
on a prolonged quarrel with FJF in the New Shakspere Society (see Introductory
Note, above).

RB TO F. G. FLEAY, 6 FEBRUARY 1881

19. Warwick Crescent, / Feb. 6. '81.

Dear Sir,

I beg to acknowledge the kindness and courtesy of your letter, and will pass at once to the single point that can possibly be at issue between us—"the responsibility incurred by the President (why not the Committee?) of sanctioning the proceedings of the Society." Does a publication by a member of the Society come under that category, when it is altogether independent and unsanctioned in any way? This is not the case of a Review,—which is supposed in some sort to authorize the various contributions it furnishes with a name and character: the writer avows himself and may therefore be directly dealt with; and as he receives no shelter from the Society he surely may expect no interference on its part. I repeat my true sorrow that language which I scarcely understand and by no means I have any sympathy with should be applied to a scholar and a gentleman; but the assailant is at all events no anonymous skulker behind an editorial "we," and the assailed party has already taken advantage of that circumstance to retaliate—fairly enough.

Believe me, Dear Sir, / Yours very sincerely /
Robert Browning.

MS: Folger. Note in unidentified hand on letter: "To Fleay."

A. C. SWINBURNE TO J. O. HALLIWELL-PHILLIPPS 6 FEBRUARY 1881

THE PINES, / PUTNEY HILL, / S.W.* / Feb. 6th 1881

My dear Sir

I am much obliged by your gift of a pamphlet[1] which will be only too long remembered with astonishment by those who have not before known anything of the Founder and Director of the Sham Shakespeare Society at the incredible insolence of that incomparable blackguard, & by all admirers of Mr. Browning's genius with far greater & more unspeakable amazement & regret that he should for one moment longer permit his name to be polluted

175

by association with one which it is degrading for a gentleman to pronounce, to transcribe, or to remember.

I send you herewith a small volume of poems[2] just published, in the assurance that they will be kindly received as evidence at least of my gratitude as a student of the divine poet whose name such dunghill dogs[3] as this unmentionable Founder would defile if they knew how to spell it.

Believe me / Ever sincerely yours / A. C. Swinburne

MS: University of Edinburgh Library. Published: *Swinburne Letters*, IV, 190.

1 *A Letter from Mr. J. O. Halliwell-Phillipps* ... , in which Halliwell-Phillipps had printed the correspondence between himself and RB. In a letter to Mrs. FitzGerald on 5 Feb., RB offered the following comment on the pamphlet: "A few days ago Mr Halliwell-Phillips [*sic*] must needs call on me to take the Director of the Shakespeare Society to task for some abuse of him in a publication of the Director's—not in any way warranted by the Society: I at once told him I was sorry but could do nothing in the case: whereupon last evening I got a portentous 'publication of the correspondence'—including my own modest bit of sorrow and explanation. Had I guessed this consequence would come of my politeness I should have either said more or nothing whatever. Still, there are compensations in plenty when the post brings such a charming letter from Swinburne as it did at the same time. He is a noble heart, I am sure, spite of some early eccentricities and perversenesses." (*LL*, p. 111.)

2 Swinburne's *Studies in Song*.

3 "Such dunghill curs" (Shakespeare, *Henry IV*, Part II, V.iii.108).

A. B. GROSART[1] *TO A. C. SWINBURNE*
15 FEBRUARY 1881

Brooklyn House / Blackburn Lanc[a]shire /
15th Feby 1881.

My dear Mr Swinburne

I could spit in the face of that contemptible creature Furnivall. On receipt of his vulgar and outrageous pamphlet[2] I sent to withdraw my name from the Subscribers List of the New Sh. Society. Since, I have heard from Dr Aldis Wright of Cambridge, Dr Ingleby, Timmins, Ebsworth[3] & others, *who had done the same*. I can't tell you how filled with rage I was; & yet it is too good a tribute to pay to so mosquito-brained a creature. But I regard myself as insulted and wronged by your insult and wrong. Do you know Robert Browning? I am as sure as I live that he is sick of Furnivall; & it would be a glorious collapse to the New *Shexpur* S's "Founder" if by hook or crook you could get some one to put it to him if he will continue as President of the Society to give his (virtual) sanction to such infamous attacks on a brother-poet (yourself). I quite expect a large seccession of members.

I'm grieved for poor old Halliwell-Phillipps; but I'm simply *maddened* for you. F's pamphlet shouldn't have been a second *before* me until it was ignonimously *behind* me, had I not required it to influence friends to withdraw from his Society.

Ever yrs cordially / Alex. B. Grosart

A. C. Swinburne Esq

[. . .]

MS: Berg.

1 Alexander Balloch Grosart (1827-99; *DNB*), Presbyterian minister and scholar.

2 FJF had issued a pamphlet, entitled *The "Co." of Pigsbrook & Co.* and dated 8 Feb. 1881, which is too long to quote here in its entirety. It is an extraordinarily abusive document, attacking Halliwell-Phillipps for—among other things—writing to RB: "And how much more manly it would have been in him to stand up and fight his own battle, than to go whining to our President, like a little sneak at school, 'Please, Sir, Furnivall's been rappin' my knuckles. I never done nothin' to him. You punish him.' Just fancy you or me, or any fellow who's ever pulled in a racing-eight, going to the President of the *Antiquaries*, and saying, 'Here's Mr. Hell.-P., *F.S.A.*, been sneering at me! Please stop him.' Wouldn't it have been a joke?" *Pigsbrook* was FJF's cruel translation of Swinburne's name into Anglo-Saxon; Swinburne retaliated by Latinizing FJF's name as *Brothelsdyke*.

3 William Aldis Wright (1831-1914; *DNB*); Clement Mansfield Ingleby (1823-86; *DNB*); Samuel Timmins (1826-1902; *WW*), editor of a two-text *Hamlet* (1860); Joseph Woodfall Ebsworth (1824-1908; *DNB*). All were prominent members of the New Shakspere Society.

RB TO C. M. INGLEBY, 16 FEBRUARY 1881

19. Warwick Crescent, W. / Feb. 16, '81.

Dear Sir,

I much regret that I can only return, to your obliging letter of yesterday, the same answer as that which I have given to other gentlemen who have honoured me with similar communications. While thoroughly depreciating the use of such language as is complained of, I cannot see that the Society is responsible for a publication altogether independent of and unauthorized by it; and which, being prefaced by the name of the author, in no way evades reprisal. Perhaps I am unduly prepossessed by the contrast between the fairness of at least this part of the procedure with the ordinary management of a literary—which is nine cases out of ten a personal

—attack: the aggressor seeks no shelter behind the shield of some big Ajax[1] of a Review. It is curious (if I understand anything of the quarrel) that Mr Furnival considers himself the aggrieved party on a ground very like that on which you base your complaint: certain papers in which he has been roughly handled are dedicated to,—and, he presumes, sanctioned by,—Mr Halliwell-Phillips—whom he accordingly involves in the offence—with somewhat more justice apparently than you would involve the Society in one which never was committed under its patronage. Besides to call a man "pig" gives me no such precise notion of the evil qualities imputed thereby, as to style him a "drunken clown"[2]—which I attach a very definite meaning to. What a pity that there should be a revival of the old terms of controversity in favour with the scholars and theologians two centuries ago! Friend—if he must call friend "pig" —should imitate Horace rather than Salmasius or Scaliger[3]—"me pinguem et nitidum bene curatâ cute vises, *cùm ridere voles*, Epicure de grege *porcum*."[4]

Believe me, Dear Sir, yours very obediently

Robert Browning.

MS: Folger.

1 A Greek warrior at Troy known for strength rather than intelligence.
2 In *The "Co." of Pigsbrook & Co.* (p. 2) FJF had called Swinburne a "drunken clown," adding a footnote: "This epithet having been applied by that author to me, a thirty years' teetotaller in the pages of *The Athenaeum*, I felt, and still feel, justified in using it of him, to whom it was, in literal truth, once applicable, as everyone knows."
3 Claudius Salmasius (1588-1653) and Joseph Scaliger (1540-1609), French philological scholars.
4 "As for me, when you want a laugh, you will find me in fine fettle, fat and sleek, a hog from Epicurus' herd" (Horace, *Epistles*, I.iv.15-16).

A. C. SWINBURNE TO NORMAN MacCOLL[1]
16 FEBRUARY 1881

February 16th, 1881.

To the Editor of the Athenæum,

Within the last day or two my attention has been called to the appearance of a pamphlet which I have not seen, and which had it been sent to me as others from the same quarter have previously been sent, would likewise have been at once consigned without a single reading to the obvious destination of all such papers—the waste-basket or the fire. Its appearance may easily be accounted for by those who are aware of the fact that the writer has been publicly assured under my hand that he must not hope and need not fear to draw down upon himself any kind of answer or notice on my part by any excess of insolence or any malignity of libel; having carefully secured himself against any possible contingency of the kind by the use of such tactics as those attributed to the cuttle fish.

Terms of flattery or professions of friendship are the only weapons of offence by means of which a person of this kind can possibly injure or seriously insult his most abhorred superiors, and from the risk of any such outrage in this instance I am happy to feel myself perfectly and infallibly secure. If the poets or the princes on whom he fawns in public or in print can afford to forgive the dishonour done them by his adulation, I may well afford to overlook the honour done me by this abuse.

A. C. Swinburne.

Text: Bonchurch Edition of Swinburne's *Complete Works*, ed. Edmund Gosse and T. J. Wise (1927) XX, 549. Published: *Swinburne Letters*, IV, 192-93.
1   Norman MacColl (1843-1904; *DNB*), editor of the *Athenaeum*, 1871-1900.

NORMAN MacCOLL TO A. C. SWINBURNE
18 FEBRUARY 1881

Athenaeum Office, / February 18th, 1881.
My dear Mr. Swinburne,

I am very reluctant to refuse any request of yours, but do you think it would be advisable to publish the letter you have sent me? You have already said you would not take notice of further attacks of his, and is it worth while to repeat the statement? I am afraid its publication would infallibly draw from Furnivall another abusive letter which it would be difficult for me altogether to refuse, as he would say I had allowed him to be attacked. I had a great deal of unpleasantness on the last occasion[1] because I struck out some sentences in Furnivall's letters which seemed to me altogether outrageous, and which I declined to print, and I confess I do not desire to act the part of Bowdler again. I should not of course draw back if I thought the renewal of the controversy would be for your interests, but I am strongly of opinion that vulgar abuse is best met by silence.

Yours very sincerely, / N. MacColl.

Text: Bonchurch Edition of Swinburne's *Complete Works*, XX, 550.

1 FJF and Swinburne had exchanged angry letters in the *Athenaeum* during March-April 1877.

A. C. SWINBURNE TO A. B. GROSART
18 FEBRUARY 1881

THE PINES, / PUTNEY HILL, / S.W.* / Feb. 18. 81.

My dear Dr. Grosart

I would very readily consent that a dozen such effusions as that of Mr. Flunkivall Brothelsbank (*Lat.* Fornicis—or Furni? vallum) should appear weekly or monthly in attack or abuse of me, on the condition that they brought me such thoroughly cheering and cordial assurances of goodwill from men whom I honour & esteem as this emission of virulent drivel has been the unconscious instrument of doing.

Before your letter, came one from Mr. Halliwell-Phillipps, equally gratifying for me to receive & equally creditable to the writer's kindness & sense of right.

With regard to Mr. Browning, with whom I have long been on friendly & civil terms of slight social acquaintance,[1] nothing could possibly vex me so much as the idea that any one—most especially any friend of mine—should suggest to him to take a step out of consideration for me which he would not feel bound to take out of consideration for himself. If he does not feel himself degraded by any kind of association with Mr. Brothelsbank Flunkivall, it simply proves (in my opinion, & I presume in yours) that he has not the feelings of a gentleman; & that is his own affair. I can only say that I in his place should feel that, if I now allowed the connection to continue for an hour, my name and character were 'tarnished' indeed—as this 'brothel lackey,' the bastard of Thersites, does me the honour—for in his mouth dishonour is honour as

180

MS: Folger. Address: Robert Browning Esq. / 19 Warwick Crescent / W. Postmarks: PUTNEY ZZ X FE 20 81 SW; LONDON EC V FE 21 81 J; LONDON NW X 7 FE 21 81. Black-bordered stationery and envelope. Published: *Swinburne Letters*, IV, 196.

A. C. SWINBURNE TO J. O. HALLIWELL-PHILLIPPS 20 FEBRUARY 1881

THE PINES, / PUTNEY HILL, / S.W. / Feb. 20. 81.

My dear Sir

Enclosed is the fourth copy[1] I have written this morning of a letter which I need not say is in no sense private, but which, in case you should think it worth while, you are more than welcome to show or send to any persons whom you may think it might interest.

Yours sincerely, / A. C. Swinburne

To J. O. Halliwell-Phillipps Esq.

MS: University of Edinburgh Library. Published: *Swinburne Letters*, IV, 195.
1 Of the following letter to RB.

A. C. SWINBURNE TO RB, 21 FEBRUARY 1881

THE PINES, / PUTNEY HILL, / S. W.* / Feb. 21. 81.

My dear Mr. Browning

You will permit me to be as brief and straightforward as yourself in relation to a matter of which I am at least as thoroughly sick, & with at least as good reason, as you possibly can be.

I have of course nothing to do, and no wish and no right to interfere, with any past or present relations between yourself, Mr. Halliwell-Phillipps, & Mr. F. J. Furnivall. The matter, as far as it regards me, lies in a nutshell. I have never, directly or indirectly, in any controversy public or private, disgraced myself by the use of personal insult or allusion to any matter concerning or supposed to concern the private life or character of my opponent. I feel no surprise, & I make no complaint, when I find men of a certain order acting in a contrary fashion. But I do most assuredly feel that I should deserve to be considered a person not of 'damaged' but of ruined character if I were to allow myself to overlook the impossibility of associating with any man, however distinguished, who associates with any person who has written a tenth part of what has been written of me by the Founder & Director of the "New Shakspere" Society. It is not a matter of literary controversy any longer.

You labour under an entire and I must be allowed to say a most unaccountable misapprehension if you imagine for one instant that I at all events—as you say—'call upon you to take my part.' I have never in any case called upon any man to do anything of the kind. Having been publicly & personally insulted in a manner too infamous & blackguardly for description, I did call upon you —as any man with any sense of honour or self-respect would in my place be bound to call upon you, or upon any other acquaintance—to let me know whether or not, after this, your name is to remain in any way publicly associated with one which in my humble opinion it is degrading if necessary, and disgraceful if unnecessary, for a gentleman to pronounce, to transcribe, or to remember.

I am well aware that mine is not a damaged character, & that the man who says otherwise is an infamous and impudent liar. All men, I venture to flatter myself, know that much, who know anything whatever about me.

It appears that you are simply—so to speak—the figure-head of a ship of which the captain is such a person as I have just defined. I am sorry to add to your annoyances in that capacity, but I must call your attention to the unquestionable fact that it is no fault of mine. I have no such impertinent and preposterous pretensions —need I say so?—as would be that of prescribing or suggesting to you any course of conduct. But it is obvious that in addressing the President of the "New Shakspere" Society I could no longer without degradation subscribe myself as yours very sincerely,

A. C. Swinburne

MS: Folger. Address: Robert Browning Esq / 19 Warwick Crescent / W. Postmarks: PUTNEY SW C3 FE 22 81; LONDON [. . .] FE 22 81; LONDON W C4 FE 22 81; PADDINGTON [. . .] FE 22 81 4. Black-bordered stationery and envelope: Published: *Swinburne Letters*, IV, 196-97.

A. B. GROSART TO A. C. SWINBURNE
21 FEBRUARY 1881

My dear Mr S.

I never for a moment thought of your taking such a little [illegible word] as Furnivall into the Law-courts. I agree with Halliwell-Phillipps that he really deserves it; but it would only feed his egregious vanity. Stick to your *before-announced* resolve of—contemptuous silence.

I feel sure that Browning had *not* seen F's [illegible word] tractate. The sneaking creature is careful enough of itself to see to that. It would shatter an ideal of mine to hold B. capable of such a *wrong* to you as silence under such WRONG would mean.

Yours Sincerely / Alex. B Grosart

21 Feby / 81

MS: Folger.

A. B. GROSART TO A. C. SWINBURNE
21 FEBRUARY 1881

Brooklyn House / Blackburn, Lanc[a]shire /
21st Feby / '81

My dear Mr S.

Our letters have crossed. I must add that I also wrote Mr Browning on the matter. I shall be indeed disappointed if I or you do not hear satisfactorily from him. Meantime, many hearty thanks for copy of your own letter to Mr B. I only miss one thing in it—an emphatic re-statement that in no manner of way could *you* have aught to say to Furnivall himself. I expect a collapse on *his* part very rapidly.

Ever cordially ABG

MS: Folger.

RB TO C. M. INGLEBY, 25 FEBRUARY 1881

19, Warwick Crescent, / W.* / Feb. 25. '81.

Dear Sir,

I cannot wonder at your decision in this wretched state of things. I have only to remind you that I know nothing whatever of any function belonging to the figurehead of the ship except to face the salt-water, and any passenger wishing to disembark must speak to the Captain. The proper course will be to formally signify to the "Director," in the fewest words possible, that he should take your name off the list of Vice-Presidents.[1]

Believe me—with every acknowledgement of your great considerateness to myself.

Dear Sir, / Yours very faithfully / Robert Browning.

MS: Folger.

1 Shortly thereafter FJF wrote to Ingleby (Folger): "I write to say . . . that as Browning told me he had, as a matter of course, said to you that he was not the proper officer of the Society to receive resignations, I ask you, not officially, but as the man who put you on the Committee & then proposed you as a V.P., to send your resignation in to [Arthur G.] Snelgrove [Honorary Secretary of the New Shakspere Society] or me. . . . Browning's declaration has put an end to your letter to him." Ingleby officially resigned as a Vice-President and member of the Society on 17 Apr. (see FJF's broadside of 25 Apr., note, below).

A. B. GROSART TO A. C. SWINBURNE
[c. 2 MARCH 1881]

My dear Mr S.

Very unexpectedly I've another letter from B. I enclose it & a copy of my answer. I'm now done with *him*. And mind, don't you by a solitary public word gratify F. with [the] slightest note of even your knowledge of the thing. I feel satisfied F. has taken such length of rope by which [to] hang him speedily. As for B. I'm sore at heart over it. I believe the Committee *will* interfere now.[1]

Ever ABG

MS: Folger.

Date: see date of following letter.

1 On 25 Mar. 1881, at a special meeting of the Committee of the New Shakspere Society, it was resolved that "while regretting [that] the language used, under provocation, by the Director and Founder of the New Shakspere Society has given pain to

valued Members of Society, and while carefully dissociating themselves from the language employed, the Committee cannot consent to interfere in a private and personal quarrel, or to undertake any responsibility for books over which they have no jurisdiction" (Folger W.a.73).

A. B. GROSART TO RB, 2 MARCH 1881

Brooklyn House / Blackburn Lanc[a]shire / 2d March 1881
Dear Mr Browning,

I know not that it would serve any good end to prolong our correspondence on this unhappy violation of all the decencies of literary warfare by Mr Furnivall. But I feel it due to you, and due to myself, to accentuate that I am not aware of having asked you, much less used "a kind of solicitation that even had you been otherwise minded previously should have led you to decline" to withdraw from the Presidency of the New Shakspere Society. That was a thing for yourself alone as a gentleman to determine. Accordingly, if you will take the trouble to re-read my letters you will find that the *maximum* of my respectful request is, that as President and as a gracious thing on behalf of a fellow-great poet, you should state [?] to Mr F. that you for one did not choose to have any Society with which you are associated, so defended. You had a right to decline this; but pardon me, none, to transmute it into a taunt that I not satisfied with myself withdrawing from the New Sh. Socy, insist on your following my example. Then again—you refer to Mr Halliwell-Phillipps acceptance of the dedication of Mr Swinburne's book on Shakespeare & actually accuse me as one of his (Mr Halliwell-Phillipps) supporters, as being "discreetly silent" about it. "Discreetly silent"! I am astounded that any man could read the tractate of Mr F. with its audacity of impertinent demanding from one who might be his godfather, that he should decline the dedication, or forsooth, stand the consequences, be "cut" by him, &c. &c. &c. The man isn't living to whom it would not be a crown of glory to have any book dedicated to him by a genius of the stamp of Mr Swinburne—and especially such a glorious book as his "Study of Shakspere".[1] And yet you actually approve of Mr F's attempt to [illegible word] Mr Halliwell-Phillipps with declinature! More than that—practically place the blackguard-

187

ism of a literary skunk on a level with Mr Swinburne's criticism! This is indeed a 'lower deep or lowest deep'.[2] As for addressing Prince Leopold and the tag-rag of Vice-Presidents, I never dreamed of such a thing. As for the poor prince, who cares a rush [?] for his opinion on anything? But that, as I held and hold, one of the supremest Singers and Thinkers of England in the person of Robert Browning should refuse to speak an arresting word (a protesting word at least) on such language as F's in relation to his young compeer is such pain and humiliation as words are poor to utter.

I sorrowfully close this correspondence, with a conviction that the 'Founder' of the N.S. Socy won't be long of 'foundering' if he goes on much longer in this infamous course—[the remainder of the sentence is illegible].

I am / Dear Mr Browning / Yours Faithfully /
Alex. B. Grosart

Robert Browning Esq

Copy (in the hand of Grosart): Folger.
RB offered the following comment on this letter to George Smith, 5 Mar. 1881 (Murray): "I got, a few days ago, a couple of applications from the Rev. A. Grosart to order Furnivall to behave himself; Mr. G. feeling 'pain and humiliation beyond what words could express' that I did not interefere against 'a blackguardly skunk'!—such is the appropriate reproof of bad language when a parson gets up to preach against it."
1 Swinburne's monograph on Shakespeare was published in 1880.
2 Milton, *Paradise Lost*, IV.76, slightly misquoted.

RB TO CHARLES MacKAY,[1] 2 MARCH 1881

19, Warwick Crescent, / W.* / March 2. '81.

Dear Sir,

My few shelves groan already under the dead weight of books about Shakespeare, mostly unexamined. I cannot think of adding yours to the number. Besides the very name of Shakespeare is made a terror to me by the people who, just now, are pelting each other under my nose, and calling themselves his disciples all the while.

I am, dear Sir,

Yours faithfully / Robert Browning.

Dr. Charles MacKay.

MS: Folger.

1 Charles MacKay (1814-89; *DNB*), poet and journalist. It is not clear what book he was offering to give to RB: in 1884 he published a pamphlet entitled *New Light on Some Obscure Phrases in Shakespeare's Works*, which in 1887 was expanded into a book, *Glossary of Obscure Words and Phrases in the Writings of Shakespeare and His Contemporaries*.

JOHN NICHOL[1] *TO A. C. SWINBURNE*
11 MARCH 1881

14 Montgomerie Crescent, / Kelvinside, / Glasgow.* /
March 11 81.

My dear Swinburne,

This morning, by help of a west wind at length melting & laying the skies full of snow, I have obtained light enough to read the most exasperating characters ever laid before me—I mean of course Grosarts,[2] herein gladly returned. I tried before & failed; now I have succeeded and find the matter excellent, save the expression *"supremest singer"* most absurdly applied to Mr Browning. As to the conduct of the latter I feel no doubt, he is a spoilt conceited jealous man, & much of his recent work is damnable. It is queer to me—I do not condescend to say humiliating—to remember the days when I made him a hero, and felt it a compliment to be thought like him *physically*! I have no doubt either that Grosart was quite right in addressing him as he has done, & as I should have done had I had the honour of his acquaintance which I have not. The only time I met him at Oxford he was evidently angry at not getting all the talk to himself. I have no doubt about this, because I hold that true friends *ought* to make each others quarrels their own, though they seldom do, & it is not the common view. *Ergo* I have—in polite language—told Mr F I think him such a blackguard that I cannot allow even my students to touch a book that has passed through his hands.

When we come to the question of your writing directly to Mr B. there is to use a mean phrase—"something to be said on both sides". I should almost have left it to G & others to make the demand, and on its being refused practically cut Mr B. But I don't see that your writing has done any harm; it has brought matters to a quick point, & what you say is very good though (I will venture to say) in too many words—a mistake most of us are apt to make. I return the whole correspondence, which I suppose I may detail to Ward of Manchester, to whom four months ago I wrote remonstrating against the defilement of the preface to the Chaucer by Mr F's name.[3] [. . .]

Yours Ever / J Nichol.

MS: Folger.

1   John Nichol (1833-94; *DNB*), Professor of English Language and Literature, University of Glasgow, 1862-89.
2   Grosart's letter to RB, 2 Mar. 1881, printed above.
3   Sir Adolphus William Ward (1837-1924; *DNB*), in an introductory Note to his *Chaucer* (English Men of Letters series, 1878; reissued 1881), had declared that his book "could not have been written at all without the aid of the Publications of the Chaucer Society, and more especially of the labours of its director, Mr. Furnivall."

EDMUND GOSSE TO THEODORE WATTS[1]
13 MARCH 1881

29, DELAMERE TERRACE, / WESTBOURNE
SQUARE. W.* / 13.3.87.

My dear Watts

By a strange chance Mr. Browning has chosen, entirely of his own accord, to confide to me the whole story of the Furnivall row, and the correspondence. I confess I never saw anything so disgracefully discourteous & at the same time so stupid as Swinburne's second letter. But perhaps it will be news to you that until Swinburne wrote in this style Browning was quietly acting entirely in his interests, that he had written to Furnivall expressing his extreme displeasure at the language F. had used, and was only anxious to put a stop to the whole affair. But he says himself that his pride won't allow him to be dictated to in this furious style by Swinburne, with whom he considers himself, however, as much friends as ever. He said to me, with a great deal of pathos, that it was not for him, in the close of his life, to embroil himself in a vulgar literary quarrel with which he had nothing whatever to do, and that though it was extremely unlikely he should ever see S. again, if ever he did, he should go up to him and shake him by the hand.[2]

Browning is a man of the world and what is more a man. I feel the greatest respect and sympathy for his annoyance in this matter, and as for Swinburne, I tell you plainly that the best thing for him would be to be put across somebody's leg, and soundly birched.

On the heels of the letter in which S. remarked that he should consider it a *disgrace* even to speak to Browning again, there followed a letter of the most vulgar abuse from Grosart, and the whole pack of hounds have been baying in the ears of this one old gentleman,[3] who very justly says he is no more responsible than Prince Leopold, or Shakespeare himself.

Can Swinburne not be made to apologise? I on my part am gravely beginning to doubt if he, Swinburne, is a proper person for a gentleman to call his friend.

My dear Watts / This is quite confidential / from / Yours always / Edmund W. Gosse

MS: Folger.
1 Walter Theodore Watts, afterwards Watts-Dunton (1832-1914; *DNB*), was Swinburne's unofficial protector and guardian from 1879 onward. Edmund Gosse (1849-1928; *DNB*) was a friend of both RB and Swinburne but disliked FJF intensely.
2 There is no evidence that Swinburne and RB ever met again, and Swinburne declined an invitation to RB's funeral (*Swinburne Letters*, V, 280).
3 C. M. Ingleby—and perhaps others as well—had sent his resignation from the New Shakspere Society directly to RB (see RB to Ingleby, 25 Feb. 1881, above).

FJF TO SOME MEMBERS OF THE NEW SHAKSPERE SOCIETY, 25 APRIL 1881

To the Trinity and other Withdrawers
from
The New Shakspere Society.

Gentlemen,

I have received your note, and have struck your names out of the Society's List.[1]

On the point taken by you, opinions differ. My opinion is that "the duty" of the New Shakspere Society is to mind its own business,—that is, to study Shakspere, and do the work it has set itself in its Prospectus;—not to gad about interfering in its Members' quarrels.

I regard as an impertinence your intrusion of yourselves into a dispute declared by me to be private between Mr. Hl.-Phillipps and myself, and I am now glad to be rid of you, whose return for the faithful work I have given you (and others), is this present censorious caballing against me.

F. J. FURNIVALL

3, St. George's Square, N.W. / *25th April*, 1881.

Text: printed broadside issued by FJF. Note in FJF's hand on Folger copy: "A parting shot at em."

1 On 17 Apr. 1881 a group of fifteen vice-presidents and members of the New Shakspere Society—many of them associated with Trinity College, Cambridge—had announced their resignation from the Society in a broadside.

Articles on Browning by Furnivall

1

Late in the fifties, Ruskin scolded me for not coming in to see him as usual one Saturday when I walkt out to Denmark Hill, because the "visitors" whom I was told he had with him—and from whom I turned homeward—were Robert Browning and his wife, to whom he would have liked to introduce me.[1] It was with no little pleasure then that in the May (I fancy) of 1874 I found Lord Tennyson (before he was lorded) making me known, in his drawing-room in Seamore-place, Hyde Park, to Mr. Robert Browning.[2] Greater pleasure was it to me to tell that poet how I reverenced the memory of his dead wife, and what a revelation of a glorious woman's nature her poetry had been to me in my early ignorant college-days. There was no quicker way to Browning's heart; and when, after a time, in his little library at Warwick-crescent, he showed me his loved wife's little volumes of the Greek poets and her tiny Hebrew Bible, all with notes in her clear small hand, her low table at which she worked, some relics of her childhood, and then told me instances of the beautiful unselfishness of her nature, it was easy to see that his love for her was as fresh as when she was with him in body here, and that the few expressions of it which his reserve allowed him to put into his poems did but proclaim the deepest and most abiding feeling of his heart. Often and often would our talk in after years touch on his "Lyric love, half-angel and half-bird;"[3] the voice would take a tenderer tone as fond memories came back to him; and then we passed to other themes. Every day of her life did she write to him, and every letter is kept, and descends to her son.[4] Next to Browning's love for his wife was that for his son. What "Pen" was doing, had done, and meant to do, he was always glad to tell any friend who knew his boy. Anecdotes of Pen's boyhood, his college-life, his art-work, his foreign experiences, his brave acts, his successes, showed the father's pride in and love for his son,—a pride and love fully reciprocated by that son. How happy Browning was when his son, after leaving College, settled down to hard work in Art; and how happier still when that son married the lady of his love, and gave the poet a daughter to add joy to his old age! Their presence with him at his death, and that of his true kind friend and housemate, his sister, must have sweetened and brightened his last days.

The next qualities that struck me in Browning were his generosity of nature, and his fidelity to his friends. No mean thought did he ever entertain; no unworthy words did he ever speak. Petty gossip and scandal, he would none of; he took every one at his best, and had a kindly word for many whom I unhesitatingly condemned. When once he gave his friendship, he was firm; the vain and mean, the misled and the hasty might say what they liked; of them Browning took no heed. If he were shown that greater profit and popularity would accrue to him by giving up a man who had acted fairly by him, he would say, Never mind them, I stick to — —.[5] His manliness was apparent in every word and act. As to the charm of his frank ways, are there not thousands in Europe and America who can testify to it? It had not the womanly delicacy of Ruskin's early manner—how delightful that was!—but, as an instance of it, take this: this spring when I told him that in no place was he so abused as at the Browning Society, and that I in particular had called him all the bad names I could think of, he leant forward with a cheery smile on his face, gave me one of his frequent pats on the knee, and said, "Ah well, I don't mind. I'm not afraid of you"—as if he'd fight the lot of us, "one down, t'other come on":—how could one help loving him? It was a real pleasure to be with him, and hear his hearty "Goodbye, and mind it isn't so long before you come again! There's always lunch at one." Another characteristic was his wonderful tact, which long experience in Society had given him. His skill in fence was very great; you couldn't get under his guard.

In March 1879, Browning, on my offer, accepted the Presidency of the New Shakspere Society, but on condition that he shouldn't be called on to do any work in connection with it. He promised, during one vacation, to read through Shakspere again in the chronological order that I had assigned to his plays, and to tell me if anything special occurred to him. The reading he did, but said that he had also had other work, and the only general impression he got from Shakspere was, the lordly ease with which he swung up to the Throne whose lowest steps "the rest of us" only reacht with infinite struggle. The hardest of all things, Shakspere did just naturally, as if they were no trouble to him. As to the Sonnets we differed entirely. I tried to show him what a heretic he was, but he didn't care to discuss the point in detail.[6]

In 1881 the Browning Society was founded. One main motive with me for taking this step was some talk and writing of a certain cymbal-tinkler being a greater poet—that is, maker, creator of men and women—than Browning. I couldn't stand that.[7] The lady who acted with me wouldn't take any part in the Society unless Browning approved of it. So I took her across to him one Sunday morning, and said, "We're going to have this Society, but as Miss ——[8] won't work in it unless you approve, here she is to see you. I tell her I don't care twopence whether you approve or not. We want the Society for ourselves; but here we are. We can't expect you to say 'go on;' but we hope you won't say 'stop.' " So far as I recollect, Browning either began talking about something else at once, or did so after saying "Do as you like." And the Society was started. It has been followed by some twenty others, and has greatly stimulated the study of Browning's works. No doubt infinite objections have been made to the Society and the societies; but then the number of fools in this world is infinite too: one needn't bother oneself about them. Browning kept clear of our Society, and we kept it clear of him. But when we couldn't understand a passage or a poem, I either walkt over or wrote to him, and got his explanation of it. At first I didn't take the volume with me, and he amused me very much by saying: " 'Pon my word I don't know what I *did* mean by the poem. I gave away my last copy six years ago, and haven't seen a line of it since. But I'll borrow a copy to-morrow and look at it again. If I don't write before Sunday, come to lunch and I'll tell you about it." So I got up a subscription and on his seventieth birthday, May 7, 1872,[9] sent him a handsomely-bound set of his own Works in an oak case carved with Bells and Pomegranates, and with this inscription in the volumes:

"To Robert Browning on His Seventieth Birthday, May 7, 1882, from some Members of the Browning Societies of London, Oxford, Cambridge, Bradford, Cheltenham, Cornell and Philadelphia, with heart-felt wishes for a long life and happiness.

"These Members, having ascertained that the Works of a great modern Poet are never in Robert Browning's house when need is to refer to them, beg him to accept a set of these Works, which they assure him will be found worthy of his most serious attention."

This tickled him; and whenever afterwards a passage was in question, he walkt me up to his carven case, and settled the difficulty there and then. It is needless to say that when any one has talked to me about the uselessness of the Browning Society, and I've set him one of the puzzles, he has known no more about it than the man in the moon, and has lookt rather foolish. More than once have I talked over the effect of the Society's work with Browning, and he has said, "I know the difference in the pace of publishers' cheques coming to me since the Society started. And when people have asked me why I don't stop the Society, I tell them that to do so would be just like putting a policeman at Smith and Elder's door to say to every one coming in, 'If you want to buy one of Mr. Browning's books, please don't.' Surely I am not such a fool as that."

On two points I often used to attack him. 1. That he wouldn't order his publishers to bring out a shilling Selection from his Works, and get him the wide popularity I knew was his due. But he wouldn't interfere: his publishers were to judge. 2. That he wouldn't put an "Argument" before each of his poems, like Shakspere, Spenser and Milton did. He said No, he wouldn't.[10] He didn't make us buy his poems, we could let 'em alone if we liked; he didn't care; but if we did buy 'em, we must take 'em as he chose to print 'em; and if he'd taken the trouble to write 'em— "Cristina and Monaldeschi," for instance—we surely might take the trouble to look up the historical facts he alluded to. He didn't believe in feeding his readers with spoon-meat. And budge he

196

wouldn't, whatever one might say. Some were content to take him as he was. We scolded him with our tongues, but we honoured him in our hearts: and we *know* that we have brought many men and women to honour and love him too.

His early manhood was happy in the society of the keenest wits and most cultured men in London: his married life was blessed with the love of one of the most beautiful souls that ever dwelt on earth: his later years were cheered by sister, son, and daughter, and an even wider circle of admiring friends, many the choicest spirits of the world. Among those dearest to him he passed from the life he had so enjoyed and adorned, to live again, he trusted, with her whom here he never forgot:

> O thou soul of my soul! I shall clasp thee again
> And with God be the rest!—*Prospice*.

The manliest man of Victorian poesy has left us, with his constant message "Work and Hope!"

I have seen the Dean and Archdeacon of Westminster to-day, and I trust that they will soon announce that a Memorial Service will be held next week at the Abbey in Robert Browning's memory; that a Meeting in the Jerusalem Chamber will follow this, to raise funds to place a bust of him—by his son, I hope—in Poets' Corner, and to establish Browning Medals in English and Greek.[11]

Text: "Recollections of Robert Browning. By Dr. F. J. Furnivall, Founder of the Browning Society," *Pall Mall Gazette*, 14 Dec. 1889, pp. 1-2.

1 This episode occurred in July 1855. See *Letters from John Ruskin to Frederick J. Furnivall . . .* , ed. T. J. Wise (1897), pp. 55-56.

2 This date is evidently wrong, for FJF's letters to RB of 13 Dec. and 17 Dec. 1873 indicate that FJF was visiting RB as early as that time.

3 *The Ring and the Book*, I.1391.

4 Not true, of course. The Brownings exchanged letters only during their courtship.

5 George Smith, RB's publisher.

6 FJF believed that Shakespeare's sonnets were written at about the same time as *Hamlet*.

7 "Some people . . . actually put Swinburne above Browning as a poet. That made me very savage, because I hold that a poet must be a creator, a maker, a shaper. Now Browning is a great creative poet, but Swinburne's gift is a musical gift. He has more sound than sense! Much of his verses is musical jingle; and there is no reason why he should stop when once he begins. He goes right on in good sounding language; but to put him above Browning is like putting a park-hack above the best steeplechaser in England. The latter may have ragged hips and a big head, but he will go over any timber you can put him at." ("The Shelley Centenary: A Chat with Dr. Furnivall, M.A.," *Oracle*, 16 Jan. 1892, p. 12.)

8 Emily Hickey.
9 Error for 1882.
10 While preparing a new edition of his collected poems, RB wrote to George Smith on 12 Nov. 1887 (Murray): "I have changed my mind about the *notes* I thought of adding to the poems in my own case. I am so out of sympathy with all this 'biographical matter' connected with works which ought to stand or fall by their own merits quite independently of the writer's life and habits, that I prefer leaving my poems to speak for themselves as they best can—and to end as I began long ago."
11 At this date it still had not been decided whether RB would be buried in the Abbey.

2

A FEW MORE WORDS ON ROBERT BROWNING

Jotting down hurriedly in the small hours of Friday morning a few recollections of my dead friend, with no time for revision or addition, I left out a few points that should have been noted. Many years before I knew Browning, the Eyebright of his *Sordello*, Miss Haworth, had shown me some letters of his wife's, signed with her pet-name "Ba," and bubbling over with fun, a quality that never appeared in her so earnest poems, which, as she said, she wrote with her whole heart. I often prest him to give us a Life of his wife, and print us some of her letters, that we might know more of her; but he always refused: it would be impossible for him to speak what he felt on the cruelty to her of her Father, who, only because she had married, rejected all her appeals for reconciliation, who answered never a word to her tender yearly missives on his successive birthdays, or to that "most pathetic and beautiful letter that ever woman wrote" which she sent him just before the birth of her child, an event which neither she nor any of her friends thought that her frail frame could survive. No death-bed softening came to the hard father's heart, and the longing love of the devoted daughter was left unsatisfied.[1] What is or is not to be said of his wife, Browning left to his son's discretion. Some little of what he felt for her, his own poems show. Cannot the opportunity be taken now, to put some memorial of her with him in Westminster Abbey? She is confessedly the greatest poetess of modern times; in my belief, of all time. In Italy, Florence has done her due honour. In America the Vassar College[2] for Women has its Mrs. Browning's room sacred to her memory. England alone has nothing, has made no sign. Cannot a memorial of the poet-wife be joined with that to the poet-husband in our Makers' sacred shrine? Cannot her son there record his Mother's as well as his Father's face? Surprise has sometimes been expressed at Browning's long sojourn in Italy after his marriage, away from their native land. It was due solely to his wish to save his wife's life. He took her from what she believed to be her death-bed, to the love and life of which she has told us in her glorious Sonnets, to the joys of wifehood and motherhood, instead of letting her dwindle to the grave. But the possibility of this depended only on her residence abroad, out of the fog and cold of England. That Florence which they both so loved, Browning never entered after his wife's death, not even to see the beautiful tomb over her body which his friend Sir Frederick Leighton designed.

Browning was an admirable reader of his poems. At the request of his son, he read me two or three of his *Jocoseria* poems from his proofs early in 1883. One Sunday soon after I took over to lunch with him my young friend since dead, Miss Teena Rochfort-Smith, a girl with extraordinary intuition into Browning's poetry. He consented to read her some poems; and to my delight—urged by her whispers unheard by me—went on with nearly half the volume. As he read *Ixion*, his voice became impassioned, his proof shook in his hands, and he was almost like one inspired as he proclaimed the triumph of the suffering tortured Man over the tyrant God:

"Out of the Wreck I rise—past Zeus to the Potency o'er him! . . .
Thither I rise, whilst thou—Zeus—keep the godship and sink."

This was the highest point at which I ever saw Browning; and, whenever I've thought of him since, I see him on his green velvet sofa in Warwick Crescent, reading, proof in hand, with the pale eager face of my dead young friend by his side. This is the first image that always rises to my mind. Next comes that of him with the cheery smile on his face and the friendly pat on my knee, which I mentioned in my last letter. And oddly enough comes third, one whose descriptions may sound like bathos after what I have said. I had often been bored by having to stoop to a low coal-scuttle when putting coals on the fire. The first time I saw Browning put them on his fire, he dropt on his left knee, and did it quite happily. I've always followed his example since, and hardly ever do it without thinking of him.

He was very sore about the way in which Macready had treated his plays when first written, and was greatly pleased at the successful production of them in America two or three years ago, and even in the quasi-amateur performances that we Browning-Society folk gave. He much admired Miss Alma Murray's playing of his heroines; so much, that he told me he would write a tragedy for her if she could suggest to him a story that he could treat. Several times he said he should like to write one more tragedy before he died; but it was not to be. With Miss Murray's (Mrs. Alfred Forman's) performance of Beatrice Cenci he was greatly impressed, and wrote her a letter about it which she reckons among her most precious possessions, as she does the bit of Shelley's hair and his portrait which Sir Percy and Lady Shelley gave her after her triumph in Shelley's play. But, to my great disappointment, Browning would not take the Presidency of the Shelley Society when I started it. Much as, from his youth, he had loved Shelley, he, so devoted to his own wife, could not forgive Shelley the abandonment of Harriet, whatever her faults may have been. Hookham had shown him pathetic appealing letters of hers which had gone to his heart; and the Society in honour of Shelley as poet and man must go its own way without him.

To what was said in the *Pall Mall* on Saturday on Browning's appreciation of the honour Balliol did him, I can add emphatic testimony.[3] He seemed to me to value his yearly visit to 'Jowett' and Balliol above every pleasure except seeing his son. He would allow nothing to interfere with it; and when it was near, he always said, "Don't come on so-and-so, because I'm going to Balliol." Mr. Jowett no doubt knows well with what affection Browning regarded him, and what a cruel disappointment it was to him when Miss Nightingale, who was nursing the sick Master, practically forbade the poet's seeing the friend who had askt him to cheer his ailing days.[4] She thought the risk too great. I hope that one tribute of Balliol to Browning will be the printing of the documents on which the poet founded his *Ring and the Book*, and that Lord

Coleridge will contribute to the print his judgment as Lord Chief Justice on the evidence, as he kindly promist me to do for us if Browning let the Browning Society print the Book.

He had a generous admiration of Lord Tennyson's perfect art, and lookt back with fond regret to their earlier closer ties which distance and other causes had severed, the days when he held Tennyson's baby Hallam at the font, and when the father read his *Maud* to a choice set of men in Browning's house. If Lord Tennyson should be moved to write some of his consummate lines to the memory of his old friend, I am sure that no sight will be more grateful to Browning's eye, if where he is, he is conscious of what goes on here. Some of our Browning-Society folk, specially the female ones, would insist on discussing his religious opinions at our Meetings. When I reported this to him, and askt him if he cared to state his belief more definitely, he answered, "No. I've said what I want to say, in my works. You must take them and make what you can of them; you get no more out of me." But Mr. Churton Collins did once get him to say something.[5] After Mr. Disraeli's death, I was very anxious that Browning should vivisect him in a Blowgram [*sic*] poem. He admitted that the subject would suit him; but he had kept aloof from English politics; and how could he treat such a character without offending almost all his Tory friends, many of whom he valued? When my friend Professor Seeley was working at Napoleon, he much wanted Browning to turn the man inside out, and display his astounding duplicity; but the poet was not to be tempted. The subject didn't "come" to him. When I argued against his caring so much more for the Greek writers than the English, he fetcht me his travelling library, all the Greek tragedians in flexible blue morocco buckled together with a broad leather strap: they were his companions, and no Shakspere was allowed among them, intimate as Browning's knowledge of our great dramatist and all our poets was.

As an illustration of the youthfulness of Browning's spirit, and the love-poems which are found in many of his latest works, I mention—in the confidence that it will not be misunderstood—the last sentence of what he said to me early this year when I talkt to him of the charm of English women and girls, and the delight that their admiration of him must be to him: "And as to the girls, God bless them, one would like to throw one's arms round them and kiss them, if one dared." In my champion son's cycling successes, and in my small wins in sculling eights and fours and funnies, he took interest. He saw at once the superiority of sculls over oars, and helped our poor club to buy its sculling eights and fours; and although he wouldn't scull or cycle with us, he sympathised in all we did. Fêted as he was by the highest in the land, he had a working-man[6] and his wife to dinner with him, and treated them just like his grandest friends: and after our Shelley-Society performance of *The Cenci*, it was to this printer's-reader's house that he took his son and sister to tea. To the memory of the dead he was very tender. He said his father burnt some very valuable letters of Nelson and Byron (I think) for fear they should be used to the writers' discredit; and he himself always did the same: let the good of men only live.

A noble and generous spirit, a manly man, was Robert Browning, an honour to this Victorian time. Let there be no weak moaning over his death; but let every one who honoured him be sure, that the truest tribute to him, that which he would soonest have paid, is for each to do more strenuously than before, the work for the world that lies nearest to his hand.

P.S.—Mr. Grove mistakes in thinking that I twitted Browning about his abstemiousness.[7] I am a teetotaller, and have been one for fifty years.

Text: "A Few More Words on Robert Browning. By F. J. Furnivall." *Pall Mall Gazette*, 18 Dec. 1889, p. 3.

1   This paragraph inspired the following comment from Alfred Moulton-Barrett (1820-1904), EBB's brother, in a letter (owned by Edward R. Moulton-Barrett)—dated 23 Dec. 1889—to another brother, Octavius ("Occy") Moulton-Barrett (1824-1910):

   That Dr. Furnival is an insolent hound. He was or boasts himself to have been the chief Dervish in the Browning Culte. The Pall Mall Gazette of 18 Decr has an article "a few more words on Robt Browning by Dr Furnivall"—"I often prest him to give us a life of his wife[']—F says—"but he always refused: it wd be impossible for him to speak what he felt on the cruelty to her of her Father, who, only because she had married, rejected all her appeals for reconciliation, who answered never a word to her tender yearly missives on his successive birthdays, or to that "most pathetic & beautiful letter that ever woman wrote"—(presumption is that these words are Brownings as they carry marks of quotations) "which she sent him just before the birth of her child, an event which neither she nor any of her friends thought that her frail frame could survive. No death bed softening came to the hard father's heart & the longing love of the devoted daughter was left unsatisfied."

APPENDIX B

Surely Pen should be requested to gag this insolent. Many a son would do more & disable the fellow from sitting down for a month. Fancy any one; loving *her* memory; so writing to the public of her Father!!

2 Probably an error for Wellesley College.

3 In the "To-Day's Tittle Tattle" column of the *Pall Mall Gazette*, 14 Dec. 1889, p. 5, a paragraph described RB's association with Balliol College.

4 Benjamin Jowett (1817-93; *DNB*), Master of Balliol (1870-93), was on very intimate terms with Florence Nightingale (1820-1910; *DNB*).

5 For an account of RB's frank talk about Christianity with John Churton Collins (1848-1908; *DNB*) in 1886, see L. C. Collins, *Life and Memoirs of John Churton Collins* (1912), pp. 78-84.

6 William G. Kingsland.

7 In a newspaper interview RB's former valet, William Grove, had declared: "When Dr. Furnivall twitted him [RB] about his abstemiousness he replied, 'If you drink little wine you need not fear about your health breaking down' " ("Robert Browning at Home," *Pall Mall Gazette*, 16 Dec. 1889, p. 3).

Index

Abano, Pietro di, 36-38
Abbott, Edwin A., 65, 166
Abel, Johann Leopold, 147-48
Academy, ix, xxxi, xxxv, 7, 11, 19, 25, 26, 51, 55-57, 60, 64, 66-67, 70, 85, 87, 91, 98, 103-05, 117, 120, 135, 138, 156-57
Accademia delle Belle Arti (Florence), 64
Achurch, Janet, 106
Aeschylus, 127
Aesop, 135
Aiken, W. Main H., 105
Albemarle, William C. K., 119
Alciphron, 48
Alençon, Jean Duc d', 132-33
Alexander, William J., 162
Allingham, H., 37
Allingham, William, 37
Altick, Richard D., 109
Andrea del Sarto, 40-41, 51, 63-64
Appleton, Charles, 7
Appleton, D. F., xii
Arbuthnot, John, 150-51
Aristophanes, 69
Armstrong Browning Library, ix, xi, xiv, 21, 25, 28
Army and Volunteer Gazette (London), 128
Arnold, Matthew, 4, 23, 27
Ashburton, Louisa, Lady, 95
Athenaeum, 1, 10, 15, 103, 143, 162, 178-80
Athenaeum Club, 5, 19, 61, 101-02, 151
Athenaeus, 48
Atlantic Monthly, 28, 30, 42
Austin, Alfred, 130
Austin, James C., 30
Avery, Robert, 109
Avison, Charles, 143

Bacon, Sir Francis, 32-33

Baker, Mrs. Eric, 68
Baldinucci, Filippo, 150-51
Ball, John, 30
Ballad Society, xxvi
Balliol College, Oxford, 30, 90-91, 143, 200, 203
Barker, Mary Anne, Lady, 89
Barnett, Percy A., 151-52
Barrett, Arabella, 49
Barrett, Lawrence, 106-07, 111
Bartoli, Daniel, 143
Baynes, Norman H., 30
Beale, Dorothea, 59-60, 77
Beethoven, Ludwig van, 42
Bell, Clara, 68-69
Bell, Edward, 60, 99
Bell, George, 60
Bending, Edwin, 96-97
Benedict, Sir Julius, 94-95
Benjamin, Walter R., xi
Bentinck, Cavendish, 94
Bentzon, Th., 23
Berdoe, Dr. Edward, 151, 160
Berlin, University of, 109-10
Bey, Arabi, 58
Bible, xxiii, xxv, 31, 82, 122, 160-61, 172, 193
Blackwood's Magazine, 25-26, 65
Blagden, Isa, 36-38, 79
Bloomfield-Moore, Mrs. Clara, 99-100
Boas, Louise S., 79
Bodleian Library, Oxford, xv, 98
Boswell, James, 68
Bowdler, Thomas, 180
Boyle, Robert, 107-08
Brace, Charles L., 53-54
Brace, Emma, 54
Braddon, Mary Elizabeth, 16-17
Brandl, Alois, xxii
Bright, John, 155-56
British Institution, 25, 35

205

206

INDEX

Innocent XII, Pope, 69-70
Ireland, Mrs. Alexander, 162
Irving, Henry, 15-16
Irving, Lawrence, 16
Irving Dramatic Club, 107

Jackson, Carl N., 49
Jaggard, William and Isaac, 15
James, Charles, 89
James, Henry, xxx, 119
Jansenists, 70
Jeanne d'Arc, 132-33
Jeffreys, C. (publisher), 95
John Murray (publisher), xii
Johns Hopkins University, 66-67
Johnson, Edgar, 82
Johnson, Samuel, xxix, 67-68
Jones, Henry Arthur, 158
Jones, Jenkin Lloyd, 91
Jowett, Benjamin, 200, 203

Kant, Immanuel, 51
Kean, Edmund, 131
Keats, John, xxiii, 161-62
Kelley, Philip, xiv, 3, 163
Kennedy, Benjamin H., 113
Kent, Christopher, xxxv
Kenyon, Frederic G., 21, 71
Kenyon, John, 40-41
Ker, Bellenden, xxiii
King's College (London) Library, xi, xii, xv
Kingsland, William G., 128-29, 202-03
Kingsley, Charles, xxiii
Kintner, Elvan, 38, 82
Kirkman, Rev. Joshua, 42
Knight, Charles, 108
Knight, John P., 33-35

Laffan, William M., 92
Lairesse, Gerard de, 143
Lamarck, Jean, Chevalier de, 36
Lamb, Charles, 8-9, 101
Landis, Paul, 124
Landor, Walter Savage, 43
Lang, Andrew, 54-56
Lawson, Malcolm, 94-95
Le Parlement, 57-58
Leicester, Robert Sidney, 1st Earl of, 6-7
Leighton, Sir Frederic, 20, 33-34, 124, 199
Leipzig, University of, 102
Leopold, Prince, 173-74, 188, 191
Lever, Charles, 36-37
Lewis, Sir George Cornewall, 27

Lewis, Mary A., 25, 27, 43, 48-49
Lhombreaud, Roger, 61
Library of Congress, xv, 92
Lind, Jenny, xxiii
Lippi, Fra Lippo, 63-64
Litchfield, R. B., xxv
Literary World (Boston), 66, 69-70
Lloyd, Captain, 70-71
London Browning Society, ix, xi, xxi, xxvi, xxxi-xxxiii, 18-19, 21, 23, 27-28, 30-31, 39, 41-42, 44-45, 47, 50-52, 55-57, 60-62, 66, 71, 77, 90-91, 94-97, 104-07, 124, 128, 130, 133-34, 136, 138, 140, 144, 146, 151-54, 156-57, 160, 162, 194-95, 201
London Browning Society (reconstituted), 88-89, 200
Longfellow, Edith, 62
Longfellow, Henry W., 2, 62
Lounsbury, T. R., xxxv
Lucas, E. V., 101
Ludlow, John Malcolm, xxiii
Lushington, Vernon, xxv
Lyceum Theatre, 15-16
Lytton, Edward Robert Bulwer, 1st Earl of Lytton, 147-48

McCabe, Joseph, 109
Machann, Clinton, 88
MacColl, Norman, 178-80
MacKay, Charles, 188-89
Maclise, Daniel, 24-26, 33, 35
Macmillan, Alexander, xxv
Macmillan, Daniel, xxiii
Macmillan's Magazine, 27, 156
MacNaughten, Miss, 149
Macready, William C., 25, 27, 107, 112, 140-41, 200
Macready, William C., Jr., 27-28, 43

Mahaffy, John P., 28
Mahoney, Rev. Francis S. (pseud. "Father Prout"), 22-23, 36-38
Mandeville, Bernard de, 143
Manzoni Palace, 121-22, 125-26
Markus, Julia, 23, 41
Martin, Sir Theodore, 33
Massey, Gerald, 2-3
Massinger, Philip, 108-09
Masson, Rosaline, 96
Maurer, Oscar, 165
Maurice, C. Edmund, xxxv
Maurice, Rev. F. D., xxiii, xxv, 3, 139
Maurice Rowing Club, 110, 133

210

INDEX

INDEX

xxxi, 17, 89, 166-92 *passim*, 197
Symonds, John Addington, 70
Symons, Arthur, 60-61, 124, 132-33, 138-39

Tait's Edinburgh Magazine, 23
Taylor, Sir Henry, 131
Temple, Frederick, 145
Tennyson, Alfred, xxii-xxiii, xxxv, 3-4, 16, 35, 37, 65, 86-87, 126, 136, 145, 193, 201
Tennyson, Alfred Stanley Browning, 37
Tennyson, Hallam, 3-36-37, 201
Terry, Ellen, 16
Thackereray, W. M., 37, 81
Thompson, Francis, 156-57
Times, The (London), xxix-xxx, 49, 69-70, 93-94, 127, 137-38, 156
Timmins, Samuel, 176-77
Todhunter, Dr. John, 132, 141
Toynbee, William, 43, 141
Trinity College, Cambridge, 167-68, 191-92
Trinity Hall, Cambridge, xxiii
Turner, J. W. M., xxiv

University College, Bristol, xxvii
University College, London, xxii-xxiii, 5

Vane, Sir Henry, 135
Vassar College, 198
Vernon, Rev. John R., 136
Vezin, Hermann, 131
Victoria, Queen, 174
Victoria and Albert Museum, 23, 26
Virgil, 55-56
Vogler, Abbé Georg Joseph, 153

Wade, Rev. Nugent, 58
Wagner Society (London Branch), 114, 131
Walker, Mary Grace, 109
Wanley, Nathaniel, 28
Ward, Sir Adolphus William, 190
Ward, Maisie, 31, 99
Watts-Dunton, Theodore, xxxi, 190-91
Webster, Miss, 141
Webster, John, 154
Wedmore, Frederick, 105
Weld, M. R., 97
Wellesley College, 203
West, Elizabeth D. (Mrs. Edward Dowden), 40
White, Richard Grant, 75-76, 78-79
White, William Hale, 33
Whitehall Review, 69
Whittington Club, xxiii
Wilkes, John, xxxi
Williams, Rev. John D., 102-04, 113
Willis, William G., 16
Wise, Thomas J., xi-xii, xxxv, 26, 62, 82, 87, 89, 91, 134-35, 148, 179, 197
Wiseman, Nicholas, Cardinal, 22-23
Woolner, Thomas, 20-21
Wordsworth, William, 1-2, 83, 156
Working Men's College, xxi, xxiv-xxvi, xxviii, xxxv, 2-3, 139
World, The (London), 132-33
Wrenn, John Henry, xii
Wright, W. Aldis, 162, 168, 176-77
Wyclif Society, xxvi

Yates, Edmund, xxxi

Zago, Emilio, 120
Zeller, Edward, 153

213